D0266383

WITHDRAWN FROM
THE LIBRARY
UNIVERSITY OF
WINCHESTER

C

KA 0084898 0

THE PASSING OF BARCHESTER

RECTORY-GATE HADLEIGH, SUFFOLK.

Dedicated by permission to the Very Rev.ᵈ J H Rose B D. Rector of Hadleigh,

to his obliged, & Humble Servant,

Wᵐ Ruffell.

The brick tower of the Deanery at Hadleigh (Suffolk), the gatehouse of a vanished palace built by Archdeacon Pykeham in 1495. William Rowe Lyall, later Rector of Hadleigh and Dean of Canterbury, attended the meeting here in July 1833 that sparked off the Oxford Movement, which he did not join.

THE PASSING
OF BARCHESTER

CLIVE DEWEY

THE HAMBLEDON PRESS
LONDON AND RIO GRANDE

283. 42
DEW   00848980

Published by The Hambledon Press, 1991

102 Gloucester Avenue, London NW1 8HX (U.K.)

P.O. Box 162, Rio Grande, Ohio 45672 (U.S.A.)

ISBN 1 85285 039 6

© Clive Dewey 1991

British Library Cataloguing in Publication Data

Dewey, Clive
   The passing of Barchester
   1. Church of England. Clergy. Remuneration, history
   I. Title
   331.281262143

Library of Congress Cataloging-in-Publication Data

Dewey, Clive
   The passing of Barchester/Clive Dewey
   Includes bibliographical references and index
   1. Lyall, William Rowe, 1788-1857 – Friends and associates
   2. Patronage, Ecclesiastical – England – History – 19th century
   3. Church of England – Parties and movements – History – 19th century
   4. Anglican Communion – England – History – 19th century
   I. Title
BX5199.L88D48   1991   90-28648 CIP
283'.42 – dc20

Printed on acid-free paper and bound in Great Britain
by Biddles Ltd., Guildford

Contents

Preface

For every member of the public who reads a history of the Victorian clergy, a hundred read one of Trollope's Barsetshire novels. A century after his death, the received impression of the Church of England in the era of reform is dominated by Trollope's power to create stereotypes brimming with vitality in wonderfully-convincing settings. His cast of characters places every sort and condition of clergyman in his natural habitat, from the grandee in his palace to the poverty-stricken incumbent in his isolated hamlet. There are scholarly high churchmen with influential connections, uncouth low churchmen desperate for preferment, and opportunist broad churchmen busily commending themselves to politicians; all gravitating towards the definitive cathedral close.

Trollope must have been tempted to write a polemic against a soft target – the lethargy and nepotism of the unreformed clergy: something on the lines of Dickens' hatchet-job on the Barnacles and the Circumlocution Office in *Little Dorrit*. In his early years in the Post Office, he knew what it was to see less deserving rivals with the right patrons promoted over his head. He knew, too, that 'informed opinion' was moving in favour of meritocracy: that the civil service was about to be thrown open to competitive examination. He desperately wanted his novels to *sell*, and an imaginative *exposé* of clerical abuses would have caught the mood of the moment. Yet his sympathies were on the side of the old order. The most attractive priests in Barsetshire – the self-denying Harding, the model Arabin, the much-loved Bishop Grantly – were old high churchmen. They were well-born and well-educated, so they had the instincts of scholar-gentlemen. They combined piety with dignity, so they hit the happy medium between worldliness and cant. Their opponents, the self-made reformers who disrupted the peace of the close – the intriguer Slope, the radical Bold, the trimmer Proudie – were devious, fanatical or weak.

The Passing of Barchester is a study of Trollope's heroes, the old high churchmen. It follows the fortunes of a single clerical connection – a small group of nine related clergymen, revolving round their patron, a mid-

Victorian dean of Canterbury – through each phase in the connection's life-cycle – formation, operation, dissolution – in as much detail as a rich set of family papers allows. It shows how an ambitious young cleric, William Rowe Lyall (1788-1857), commended himself to a particularly influential patron, a future Archbishop of Canterbury; clambered slowly up the ecclesiastical hierarchy, with his benefactor's assistance; and persuaded his kinsman to accept his offers of preferment, despite the low financial returns of a clerical career. It appraises the performance of Dean Lyall's clients – from a royal chaplain with a fashionable congregation on the fringes of Mayfair, via conscientious parish priests, to an indolent and absent-minded recluse. It analyses the declining economic, social and ideological attractions of the clerical profession, which doomed Lyall's happy band of brothers to extinction, as their sons refused to take holy orders and their daughters refused to marry clergymen. Above all, it spells out the implications of the connection for nineteenth-century religious reform. The leitmotiv of *The Passing of Barchester* is the insistence that a reactionary instrument, in the hands of instinctive conservatives, could be a great engine of reform: that patronage – patronage controlled by the old high churchmen – helped save the Church of England from disestablish-ment and disendowment, during the greatest onslaught on the Anglicans' privileges and property since the Civil War.

Lyall and his clients belonged to a 'party' stretching out into every episcopal palace, cathedral close, Oxbridge college and ancient public school; a party with a faltering monopoly of the more desirable ecclesiastical offices, and a small army of sympathisers in fat parsonages in the shires. From the 1800s onwards the leaders of this party used their control over preferment in an increasingly meritocratic way, to reward gifted protégés: able theologians, effective propagandists, efficient administrators, gifted 'statesmen'. Of course they also rewarded their friends and relations; Lyall distributed preferment to his younger brother, four nephews and three nephews-in-law. But their nepotism had un-expected advantages. It kept the clergy's status up by keeping poor ordinands down: an important consideration in a highly hierarchical society. The families of successful professionals and rich businessmen – the dominant class in 1850 – could easily have sealed the Church of England's fate by going over to the non-conformists. Instead, they sent their sons into a poorly-paid occupation: sons whose expensive educations and private means extorted deference from their congregations. The social standing of the clergy was the great attraction, as long as patronage stopped pauper literates swamping the upper reaches of the profession.

Trollope published his first foray into Barsetshire in 1855, two years before Lyall died at Canterbury. It is unlikely that the dean ever read *The Warden*. The book was a failure: only a few hundred copies were sold. But the other members of his connection almost certainly devoured the saga of Hiram's Hospital, once the success of *Barchester Towers* turned it into a best-seller. The dispute over Mr Harding's emoluments raised a moral dilemma close to their hearts. By what title could the beneficiaries of a system of patronage defend their perquisites? Lyall's charges to the clergy of his archdeaconry were widely regarded as one of the most effective replies to contemporary attacks on the property of the clergy. *The Passing of Barchester* asks whether Lyall's practice lived up to his precepts: whether his connection proves Trollope's instincts right or wrong.

Burton Overy
March 1990

At the end of the first quarter of the century, say about 1825-30, two characteristic forms of Church of England Christianity were popularly recognised. One inherited the traditions of a learned and sober Anglicanism, claiming as the authorities for its theology the great line of English divines from Hooker [onwards] . . . preaching, without passion or excitement, scholarlike, careful, wise, often vigorously reasoned discourses on the capital points of faith and morals . . . There was nothing effeminate about it, as there was nothing fanatical; there was nothing extreme or foolish about it; it was a manly school, distrustful of high-wrought feeling and professions, cultivating self-command and shy of display, and setting up as its mark, in contrast to what seemed to it sentimental weakness, a reasonable and serious idea of duty. The divinity which it propounded, though it rested on learning, was rather that of strong commonsense than of the schools of erudition. Its better members were highly cultivated, benevolent men, intolerant of irregularities both of doctrine and life, whose lives were governed by an unostentatious but solid and unfaltering piety, ready to burst forth on occasion into fervid devotion. Its worst members were . . . hunters after preferment . . . Its average was what naturally in England would be the average, in a state of things in which great religious institutions have been for a long time settled and unmolested – kindly, helpful, respectable, sociable persons of good sense and character, workers rather in a fashion of routine which no one thought of breaking, sometimes keeping up their University learning, and apt to employ it in odd and not very profitable inquiries; apt, too, to value themselves on their cheerfulness and wit; but often dull and dogmatic and quarrelsome, often insufferably pompous.

R.W. Church, *The Oxford Movement* (1891)

Acknowledgements

The popular conception of a historian is of a solitary hermit: a St Jerome in his study. Yet every author of an original monograph knows how completely he depends on the assistance of large numbers of people – many of whom have no incentive to help him, except their innate public spirit. I am particularly grateful to the owners of the private papers on which this book is based. Without their cooperation – without their trust – it could never have been written. The late Avril van Biervliet, General Sir Kenneth Darling, Miss Sarah Darling, Mrs Ann Holland, Miss Jennifer Lyall, Mr John Lyall and Lt.-Col Godfrey Robertson all put valuable family records at my disposal.

I am also indebted to the guides who showed me round the Lyall connection's habitat and the correspondents who gave me the benefit of their specialist knowledge: Mrs Barbara Brinton (the Lyall family); Mr D.J. Brown (Weeley); Mr J. Carlin (Godmersham); Mrs Finetta Chamberlain (the Brandreth family); the Rev. L. Cox (Thanington); Canon J.S. Fowler (St Dionis, Parson's Green); Canon D. Ingram Hill (Canterbury); Mr David Holland (the Holland family); Ann Hoffman (Bocking); Miss Judith Jackson (the Lyall family); Commander Ian Johnston (the Lyall family); Mr C. Morgan (Godmersham); Dr P.B. Nockles (The Old High Churchmen); Mary Peter (the Peter family); Mr G. Pike (Canterbury Buildings Survey); Mrs Margaret Sparks (co-editor, History of Canterbury Cathedral); Mr T. Tatton-Brown (Godmersham); the Rev J.S. Tunbridge (Harbledown); and Mrs Margot Walker (the Lyall family).

The archivists, librarians and curators who patiently answered my queries and gave me access to their collections saved me days of work. By the end, there were so many of them that I practically lost count: Mr E.G.W. Bill (Lambeth Palace Library); Dr R. Bingle (India Office Library); Mr R. Blow (Royal Commission on the Historic Monuments of England); Mr R.A. Bowden (Marylebone Library); Angela Broome (Royal Institution of Cornwall); Dr L. Carter (Centre for South Asian

Studies, University of Cambridge); Mr C. Cooper (Guildhall Library); Mrs Kathleen Court (Simon Langton School, Canterbury); Mr D.S. Cousins (Canterbury Central Library); Jane Dansie (Colchester Central Library); Mr G. Davenport (Royal College of Physicians); Mrs M.P.G. Draper (Bedford Estates); Mr C. Driver (Greater London Record Office); Rosemary Evison (National Portrait Gallery); Mr J. Fisher (Guildhall Library); Patricia Gill (West Sussex Record Office); Mr M. Hayes (South-Eastern Divisional Library, Worthing); Joanne Hillman (County Studies Library, Redruth); Mrs Charlotte Hodgson (Canterbury Cathedral Library); Mr M. Holme (Swiss Cottage Library); Mr J. Hyde (St Augustine's Foundation); Miss A.M. Oakley (Canterbury Cathedral Library); Karen Reader (Surrey Record Office); Mr K. Reedie (Royal Museum, Canterbury); Miss J.T. Smith (Essex Record Office); Susan Snell (Suffolk Record Office); and Mr C. Thom (Survey of London).

A text without illustrations would be a poor thing. A large number of people helped me track rare images down or gave me permission to reproduce paintings, sketches, engravings and photographs in their possession. Most of them have been mentioned already, but six have not: the Very Rev G.W. Arrand; Mrs Dorothy Brandreth; Mrs Irene Hand; Mr Paul Jackson; the Very Rev J.A. Simpson; and Mr Ronald Suckling. Mrs Brandreth and Mr Simpson were the sources of the only known portraits of Dean Lyall.

Mrs Gillian Austen and Mrs Margaret Christie word-processed the text with more patience and greater accuracy than an author with illegible handwriting and a penchant for innumerable revisions has any right to expect. The Research Board of the University of Leicester gave me a grant towards the cost of collecting the illustrations, and the Central Photographic Unit produced the prints from which most of them are taken. Peter Boulton photographed the engravings of Hugh Rose and the deanery at Hadleigh by permission of St Mary's parish church.

Lastly, I should like to thank my publisher, Martin Sheppard. He accepted a manuscript on a highly unusual subject – a manuscript which might not sell – at a time when publishers generally were terrified of taking any kind of risk. His criticisms of the original draft were so sensible and so shrewd that I had no hesitation in accepting them *en bloc*; and university presses, which charge inordinate prices, would do well to match his tolerance of tables and illustrations.

Illustrations

Tables

Chapter 1

The Church

All sensible men were alive to the fact that the miserable, slavish Erastianism on which the Church was resting was not the rock which could withstand the breakers that were driving in upon her. If the Government which brought in the great reform Bill had at that time proposed the disestablishment of the church, the measure would probably have been carried with very little opposition. Among the foremost of these [far-sighted men] was the Archbishop of Canterbury, Dr Howley, who set a noble example of impartiality and public spirit in the distribution of the vast patronage that then belonged to his see, and surrounded himself with the ablest and most highly reputed divines and theologians of his day.

W.N. Molesworth, History of the Church of England from 1660 (1882)

The history of the Church of England in the nineteenth century was the history of a struggle for survival against daunting odds. The onslaught on the privileges and property of the clergy gathered momentum in the 1820s and the 1830s. A formidable coalition – English dissenters, Irish Catholics and middle-class radicals, under the leadership of worldly Whigs – launched a wide-ranging attack on the Anglican monopoly of public life. One by one the citadels fell: parliament; the corporations; the universities; the Irish executive. The Church of Ireland narrowly escaped expropriation; the Ecclesiastical Commissioners laid sacrilegious hands on the cathedrals' historic endowments; tithes were commuted and church rates were abolished. The social changes which underlay these political developments were more ominous still: the mass desertions to nonconformist sects, which made a mockery of the Anglicans' claims to constitute a national church; the readiness of the Irish cottiers to resort to violence, whenever the Catholic priesthood felt their spiritual interests were at stake; the rejection of aristocratic dominance by a newly-assertive middle class. As the political climacteric passed, the crisis of faith took its place. The advent of biblical criticism and the popularity of scientific method – reinforcing the agnosticism of the eighteenth-century *philosophes* – made doubt respectable in intellectual circles; and the secularisation of the European mind subjected religious institutions to utilitarian criteria. When fellows of Oxbridge colleges, the sons of clergymen, started renouncing their orders, the *trahison des clercs* was complete; and the first religious censuses showed how far their reservations spread down the social pyramid. The national church had lost the allegiance of the majority of the nation. On every side the foundations of the existing religious order were shifting, and no one knew how far the process of 'reform' would go. The threat of disestablishment and disendowment was real.

Yet the Church survived. In a modest way, it prospered. A theological renaissance restored the credibility of the Anglican *via media*; a parochial revival spread the gospel into every hamlet and every slum. In the 1880s more communicants attended services, more priests were ordained and more churches were built than in any previous decade. Explanations of this remarkable recovery have always attributed it to two incessantly canvassed causes: the zeal of the new brand of religious militants, and the institutional reforms which were pushed through parliament. The enthusiasm of the evangelicals and Tractarians brought about a spiritual revival; legislation put the Church's material resources – its property and manpower – to more efficient uses. But it may be that posterity has been the victim of contemporary propaganda. History is on the victors' side, because historians take successful movements at their own evaluation; it saves them the trouble of working out new interpretations for themselves. If the religious militants did nothing else, they worked out wonderful statements of their own claims to fame. Then their successors wrote their hagiographies. Anglo-Catholics beatified the martyrs of the Oxford movement; evangelicals eulogised the members of the Clapham Sect; Newman counterbalanced Wilberforce. The one point on which they all agreed was the unworthiness of their mutual opponents, the old high churchmen: the self-perpetuating oligarchy which came close to monopolising the upper reaches of the ecclesiastical hierarchy. The zealots denounced the dignitaries of the Church of England, in countless diatribes, as apathetic, temporising and corrupt. The politicians who debated legislative reforms were little better. Many MPs – all the Irish nationalists and most of the northern radicals – represented the Catholic or non-conformist lobbies: they had no reason to pull their punches when they attacked the official hierarchy. Even well-meaning Anglicans, working in collaboration with the bishops, concentrated on abuses, to justify the bills they promoted and highlight their own achievements.[1]

The Passing of Barchester advances an alternative explanation of the Church of England's survival. It maintains that the Anglican recovery originated in the least likely quarter: in the very heart of 'Old Corruption'. Like most reforms in England, it was a defensive reaction on the part of a conservative establishment. The old high church party – the villains of the conventional historiography – saw what needed to be done and did it. Moreover, they used traditional means. The great instrument of reform was neither the printed word nor the law. It was the bogey of progressives; it was patronage. The crux of the old high churchmen's power was their cohesion – they were bound together by a dense web of personal contacts – and the mass of preferment they controlled. Acting as a block, they could determine their successors and make or break hundreds of careers.

The bulk of their patronage was derived from the benefices they held. The bishops were far more important patrons than the grandest landed magnates. A magnate might own a dozen advowsons; the best-endowed bishoprics presented candidates to ten times as many livings. Besides the bishops, there were the ancient corporations. The cathedral chapters and Oxbridge colleges were in exactly the same hands: they were strongholds of the old high churchmen to an even greater extent than the bench. Then there was vicarious patronage: the patronage derived from the high churchmen's influence over others. The bishops' only rivals, as patrons, were the ministers with crown patronage at their disposal; and the ministers' natural advisers, on clerical appointments, were the dignitaries they had just appointed. Pious laymen followed the politicians' example. When they filled vacant livings, they looked to the leading clerical patrons for guidance.

In the 1820s and the 1830s and perhaps also the 1840s the fate of the Church of England depended on this self-perpetuating oligarchy. The old high churchmen had the potential to retard a religious revival, perhaps even smother it, by promoting the indolent and incompetent; or they could galvanise the clergy as a whole, by bringing ability to the fore. The French Revolution and its aftermath – the emergence of an irresistible demand for changes in *ancien régimes* all over Europe – persuaded them that the meritocratic option was essential to their survival. They needed competent lieutenants and successors, capable of defending the religious establishment against its enemies, so they started head-hunting talented and energetic acolytes. The new recruits raised the respect in which the priesthood was held, by raising the general level of scholarship. They made plausible propagandists – defending the Anglicans' privileges and formularies in eloquent sermons and widely-read tracts. As parish priests, they threw themselves into good works; and as archdeacons and heads of colleges, they made efficient administrators. At the highest levels of the hierarchy, they acted as 'statesmen in disguise', consolidating the clergy's alliance with conservative politicians.

The Lyall connection is evidence of these contentions. At first sight, the little band of nine related clergymen revolving round William Rowe Lyall looks like an obsolescent anachronism. Patronage-hunting collectives based on kinship riddled the eighteenth-century clergy. They reek of aristocratic influence, not bourgeois meritocracy. Zealous Victorian reformers attributed all the abuses of the Georgian clergy to the sloth induced by nepotism. But the more closely one examines the connection, the less convincing this sterotype appears. If anything, Dean Lyall and his dependents become living proof that patronage was compatible with merit: that everything depended on how patronage was used. The fact is that the Lyall connection was a transitional form, midway between the Georgian Church, with its entrenched legal monopolies, where an individual's prospects depended on influence, and the career open to the talents, which developed in the late nineteenth century, in a much freer market for religious services.

Lyall epitomised this ambivalence. He was a broker in a hierarchy of patronage. He obtained preferment from patrons above him and distributed preferment to his relatives below. At the same time, he rose by merit. When he took orders, his family had no influence in clerical circles whatsoever. His father was a Scotch immigrant, the son of a small farmer in Berwickshire, and a practising Presbyterian to boot. He got his deanery from Sir Robert Peel by doing all the things a modern ecclesiastical dignitary was supposed to do, and doing them exceptionally well. He was a profound theologian, an accomplished publicist, an organiser who 'made things happen' and a practical politician. His clients were men in his own image. They were the recipients of his favours, the beneficiaries of a corrupt system. They were also men with genuine vocations. They made significant financial sacrifices when they took holy orders – they had tempting offers from rival patrons who would have given them a start in more lucrative professions; and with two exceptions, they made conscientious and effective priests. The most outstanding became a chaplain to Queen Victoria and a highly respected canon of Canterbury.

The social origins of Lyall's clients are the key to the importance of these ambiguities. His connection acted as a social melting-pot. His clients-by-birth were the sons of successful, mainly Presbyterian, businessmen and professionals. His clients-by-marriage, the three clergymen who married his nieces, were younger sons from old-established landed families in decline. His promises of preferment lured the natural enemies of the religious establishment – the *nouveaux riches* from other denominations – into a working alliance with the establishment's natural supporters, the squires. This alliance – repeated over and over again, in a thousand similar microcosms – rejuvenated the Church of England. Despite pathetic stipends, the new men lavished their energy and their wealth on the Church by Law Established for the sake of social acceptance and job satisfaction. At the same time, their co-option weakened dissent. A constant haemorrhage of talent and capital decapitated the anti-clerical lobby. A clergy recruited by competitive examination would not have achieved the same result. Patronage was the Trojan Horse through which the arrivistes entered the Church, because patronage was so much more selective; it preserved the clergy's social cachet – the great attraction of a clerical career for the upwardly-mobile.

The emergence of the transitional connection and the consolidation of the new alliance were promoted by high church ginger groups like the Hackney Phalanx. The importance of the Phalanx has been consistently underestimated by historians, because it was on the losing side. In its heyday, it was the high church counterpart of the Clapham Sect. The Phalangists acted as a theological think-tank, defending the Laudian doctrines and rituals beloved by the great seventeenth-century divines, against Protestants and sceptics alike. They ran some of the most successful voluntary societies in British history. The National Society (for the Education of the Poor in the Principles of the Established Church) educated *millions* of children in its schools; the Church Building Society grant-aided thousands of restorations and new churches; the Society for the Propagation of the Gospel and the Society for the Promotion of Christian Knowledge are still household acronyms. Above all, the Phalanx operated a clerical employment agency. A network of sympa-thisers was constantly on the watch for strategic vacancies and promising young clergymen to fill them.[2]

The Phalanx's dense web of personal contacts – stretching out into all the strongholds of the old high churchmen: episcopal palaces, cathedral closes, rich rectories, public schools, Oxbridge common rooms – made it possible for them to pool information in a way no individual could hope to do. Their talent-scouts spotted prospective protégés, generally high-flying undergraduates or particularly impressive curates. Then middle-ranking brokers tried them out in temporary jobs, as preachers and writers and organisers. If they passed the appropriate tests, senior members of the

Phalanx placed them with sympathetic bishops, as chaplains. Once they cut their teeth as members of the bishops' kitchen cabinets, they moved onto archdeaconries and canonries; posts in the bishops' gift which gave them the prominence they needed to catch the politicians' eyes. If they 'danced before Herod' with sufficient dexterity, deaneries and sees were waiting in the wings. Then, as deans and bishops, they were in a position to act as patrons in their own right – distributing the preferment which was needed to begin the cycle again. The Lyall connection evolved out of this milieu. The Phalanx took Lyall up, tested him out, and drew his virtues to his patrons' attention. If Archbishop Howley and Sir Robert Peel had failed to rise to the bait, the Phalangists would have found him other protectors. Remove their solicitude, and Lyall would never have become a dean. His connection would never have come into existence.

It is difficult to say exactly when the revolution in the use of patronage began, or when it was completed. It seems clear that Manners-Sutton (as Archbishop of Canterbury from 1805-28) and Howley (as Bishop of London from 1813-28) made conscious decisions to distribute the preferment at their disposal on new principles. But very few laymen, in the 1820s, had much confidence in the bishops' ability to reform the Church of England. As a class, their reputation was compromised by scandal. The eighteenth-century bench was notorious for its nepotism; some of the most blatant pluralists were bishops' sons. Even if they turned into committed reformers, informed commentators were conscious of their weakness. Lay patrons controlled six times as many livings; prime ministers awarded the glittering prizes to the nominees of magnates with electoral influence; and every section of society, from Tory grandees to radical agitators, would have united in opposition to the transfer of patronage to the bishops. Yet within a generation, the popular perception of the episcopate was transformed. The proud prelates lived down their self-interested past, with the Phalanx's sympathisers in the van. Between 1835 and 1878 the number of livings at the bishops' disposal doubled, and the purity of their presentations gave them the moral authority to impose higher standards on others. The official inquiries of the 1870s regarded the inexorable increase in episcopal patronage with equanimity. In fact, the only danger contemporaries perceived was the risk of partisan dignitaries victimising members of other schools of churchmanship – a danger which Queen Victoria's well-advertised preference for broad churchmen kept in check.

Chapter 2

The Dean

From all I . . . heard of the relative merits of the canons, I was disposed, after consulting you, to submit the name of Archdeacon Lyall [for the deanery of Canterbury]. He is wholly unknown to me, and I should have made the selection solely from the persuasion that . . . looking to his professional character and services, he was entitled to a preference.

Sir Robert Peel to Archbishop Howley, 1845

By the standards of the day, William Rowe Lyall was self-made. His father gave him a good education. In fact, he gave him the best education money could buy. But that was all he had to offer – and Eton and Trinity were not enough. When it came to obtaining preferment, it was the family that counted, not the school or the college; and Lyall's father was an incompletely assimilated Scots shipowner with no contacts outside the City circles. His elder brother George had the potential to do more. As Chairman of the East India Company and MP for the City of London, George Lyall stood at the pinnacle of the commercial establishment. He had contacts among the political elite; but none of his connections had any say in the patronage William received, until the very end – until Peel appointed him to his deanery; and all the evidence suggests that Peel made the appointment without anyone having 'moved' him to do so. At most, George's eminence showed that William came from the right stock.

Nine out of ten curates starting out with the same advantages got no further than a good living. Lyall overtook his peers in the race for preferment because he was the perfect all-rounder. He possessed, in an oustanding degree, all the qualities an Anglican dignitary required. As his books and articles showed, he was an accomplished scholar and a talented publicist. His *magnum opus* (on the religion of the Jews) was a well-researched and cogently-written antidote to the corrosive rationalism of the biblical critics, which showed that he could hold his own with the most intelligent infidel. Churchmen acclaimed the charges he delivered as an archdeacon, as the most plausible apologies for the property of the church; laymen welcomed his accessible yet authoritative restatements of their traditional faith. His achievements as an administratior were equally creditable. He initiated the parochial revival in two dissent-ridden counties and helped found a theological college to improve the professional training of the clergy. As an ecclesiastical statesman he did even more: he charmed local landowners, cultivated rich philanthropists, cooperated with the Peelites over church reform and tried to guide the Oxford Movement into safe channels.

The presence of such a *Wunderkind* in a deanery strengthened the Church of England against its enemies, and the old high churchmen were shrewd enough to make use of his talents. Two individuals – a primate and a premier – recognised Lyall's merits. As sources of preferment, William Howley and Sir Robert Peel were the ideal combination: the dream ticket of any aspiring clergyman. Howley's bishoprics (London 1813-28, Canterbury 1828-48) made him the greatest clerical patron of the age; Peel's twenty-odd years in office made him the most important lay patron. Howley plucked Lyall out of relative obscurity and gave him a chance to distinguish himself; Peel recognised his distinction and set the capstone on his career.

Between 1820 and 1827 Howley asked Lyall to edit the *Encyclopaedia Metropolitana* (the Anglican riposte to the Godless *Britannica*); drew him into Fulham Palace as his examining chaplain (all the candidates for ordination in London had to pass Lyall's tests); made him archdeacon of Colchester (the effective ruler of the rural part of his diocese); and persuaded the Benchers of Lincoln's Inn to let him deliver the prestigious Warburton Lectures (on Jewish Prophecy as proof of Christianity). After his translation to Canterbury, Howley persuaded his old lieutenant to help him run his new diocese. In 1841 he offered Lyall a stall in Canterbury cathedral, if he exchanged Colchester for the newly-created archdeaconry of Maidstone. Four years later, Peel made Lyall dean, 'looking [solely] to his professional character and services'. If only his health had held out, the next Tory premier might easily have made him a bishop. Every dean of Canterbury was *papabile*, and most of them were promoted to the bench. Lyall had just started doing the kind of little jobs for the government which led inexorably to a palace of one's own, when his first stroke left him partially paralysed.[1]

Lyall's intellectual ability was the first thing that impressed his peers. He had a mind combining 'great readiness of apprehension [with power] of analysis, justness of observation and accuracy of thought'. It came out in his conversation. Whether the topic was some abstruse metaphysical proposition or the Whigs' latest atrocity, he inspired 'warm esteem and regard'. The virtual head of the high church party

> once said of him that he had known some as fair in argument, and others possessed of as good judgment, but none who so united both qualities. It was curious to see how he would pause in the middle of an animated discussion, if a reason on the other side struck him as correct, and frankly yield the point at once.[2]

The same qualities were apparent in Lyall's writings. At this distance in time, it is difficult to see why his articles on Dugald Stewart created such a stir. They constituted a cogent commentary on the leading Scottish philosopher of the day and showed that Lyall was an authoritative metaphysician. But no one now supposes that Stewart was a particularly deserving target. He had a flair for popularising his predecessors' ideas, but he made no breakthroughs of his own; and as soon as the need for vulgarisation passed, he fell out of the 'great tradition'. Moreover, Lyall's articles were distinctly heavy-going. The issues he addressed, mainly problems of perception, were remorselessly abstract. His subtle distinctions and long chains of reasoning made painful demands on his readers' stamina. Yet his rejoinders to Stewart underpinned the whole of his subsequent career. More than forty years after they first appeared in print, his obituaries agreed on their importance.[3]

One reason for the favourable reception of Lyall's articles was Stewart's symbolic importance. He personified the Scottish enlightenment. He was the chief ornament of the University of Edinburgh and the most famous professor in Scotland; his very existence was supposed to be a standing reproach to the ossification of Oxbridge. For fifty years luminaries like Smith and Hume had contrasted their own creativity with the somnolence of their southern counterparts – and the enemies of the Church of England were quick to identify the torpor of the English universities with the Anglican monopoly of higher education. The Scottish universities were open to all denominations and their most illustrious teachers tended to be laymen; *therefore* they were in the forefront of knowledge. Oxford and Cambridge only admitted members of the Church of England and the fellows of Oxbridge colleges were obliged to take holy orders; *therefore* they were backward. The solution? Liberate the colleges from the dead hand of the church and all would be light. Lyall's critique was an implicit refutation of these contentions. The quality of his dialectic showed that a product of the Oxbridge system – an obscure curate with an unremarkable degree – could trounce the most famous representative of the Scottish system on his chosen ground. When the Cambridge David drubbed the Edinburgh Goliath, a thousand parsons cheered.[4]

The fact that Lyall's articles appeared in the *Quarterly Review* ensured that they were read in the right quarters. The *Quarterly* was the house journal of the high churchmen. It was founded out of sheer revulsion, when the *Edinburgh Review* degenerated into a Whig rag. Once the *Edinburgh* began treating every subject from a savagely partisan point of view, thinking conservatives realised that they needed an organ of their own, and the *Quarterly* was the result. By the time Lyall's first article appeared it was a runaway success. Conservative ministers made regular appearances in its pages: Canning, Wellington, Peel and Stanley all sent contributions. But the backbone of the subscription lists was the Oxbridge-educated incumbent. Parsons liked the *Quarterly*, because it told them what they wanted to know in the manner they instinctively preferred. They were not, by and large, apopletic reactionaries. The clergy as a whole were aware of the deficiencies of existing institutions, and never denied the possibility of progress. But they were strongly attached by sentiment and self-interest to the existing order of things; and they were suspicious of reforms, especially reforms advocated by their hereditary enemies. As far as they were concerned, the onus of proof was heavily on the innovator, and innovators easily put themselves out of court. If the advocates of change were at all intemperate, high churchmen dismissed them as unbalanced. The High and Dry school consisted of men of measured dignity. They were creatures of the Augustan age, proud of their judiciousness – men whose love of solemn ceremonial, free from subjective excesses, permeated their whole cast of mind. In their eyes, violence was self-defeating. A single issue of the *Edinburgh Review*, full of 'sneers and sarcasm', inspired instant distrust. Who could rely on men like Brougham or Macaulay to be fair? No one supposed they knew the meaning of the word; they were natural polemicists.[5]

Lyall's remonstrance was all the more effective because it damned the metaphysical heresies of the Scottish school with faint praise. If he had repaid the *Edinburgh Review* in kind – if he had adopted the 'slashing style' pioneered by Stewart's pupil, Jeffrey – it would have been his turn to discredit himself. As things were, his willingness to weigh the value of opposing ideas won him admirers in strategic places. In fact, the only positions Lyall conceded were those which could be safely surrendered without compromising the vital interests of the Church. Stewart's theory of aesthetics was a case in point. It held no terrors for the religious establishment. His assertion that taste – 'so often represented as a gift of nature' – was actually 'a power of rapid judgment gradually acquired by habitual attention to the particulars which produce or obstruct the emotions of beauty and sublimity' stated the case for a class of well-educated and well-endowed aesthetes as clearly as any Tory apologist. In effect, it validated the lifestyle of the cultured parson. The best-known connoisseurs were members of the gentry, but the clergy constituted a reserve army of the dilettanti; and in some spheres, such as the recovery of classic antiquity, they were supreme. The moral was obvious: take away the scholar-clergyman, and English cultural life would be immeasurably impoverished.[6]

The rest of Stewart's 'science of mind' was a different matter. He presented his theories of perception as alternatives to the 'scholastic prejudices' currently masquerading as philosophy at Oxbridge. Neither the Oxford Platonists nor the Cambridge Aristotelians were prepared to let this challenge pass. They believed that their Hellenic tradition – the common heritage of western Europe – was at least the equal of their northern neighbour's home-made offerings. The problem was one of containment, and Lyall approached it in two ways. He took each of Stewart's theories separately and subjected it to a more minute and rigorous dissection than it had ever received before. Lyall's negative criticism, for those with the acuity to appreciate it, could be devastating; his logic-chopping was so obviously superior to his victim's. Then he launched a general attack on the whole quality of Stewart's thought, as methodologically unsound. Lyall seized on the 'seductive charm' of Stewart's prose – the chief source of his popularity – and pilloried the slipshod self-indulgence it disguised:

> He often contents himself with hints and loose general remarks, when the subject requires full and continuous elucidation; and ... he rarely condescends to assist his reader by concisely stating the sum of what he proposes to prove, and the grounds and limits of his argument. His style is remarkable for its purity and elegance; for its harmonious flow and uniform majesty; but it is somewhat too diffuse and oratorical for pure metaphysical discussion.[7]

In short, the greatest living luminary of the Scottish universities was an appealing vulgariser, not an irresistible authority. Stewart's indictment of the classical tradition was not proven, because he had no revelation to offer, only a limited arsenal of poorly worked-out instincts.

Despite the *succès d'estime* of his strictures on Stewart, Lyall never went back to metaphysics. As he reluctantly conceded, the market for philosophic speculation was too small. Young men regarded the 'science of mind' as a waste of time. The controversies went round in circles, without definitely establishing anything; and the language in which the combatants expressed their uncertainties became more impenetrable with each turn of the screw. Stewart's fate was a warning: the chances of writing a treatise on metaphysics which was both popular and original seemed slim. In many ways, history was a better bet. History had claims to being the discipline of the century – it even invaded natural science in the guise of evolution – and Lyall was nothing if not a creature of his times. He needed an audience; and if his readers wanted to absorb their doses of theology in the form of history-coated pills, he was willing to supply them. At first he tackled ancient Greece. The classics were the common culture of the entire educated class; the classical revival in the arts was still at its height; and philhellenes regarded the ancient world as the source of all wisdom.[8] But Greek history did nothing for Christianity. If anything, the Socratic philosophers seduced men from their proper religious allegiance; they were too free-thinking by far.

Lyall realised that his duty lay elsewhere, and devoted the rest of his scholarly life to refuting the 'annihilating scepticism' of the German biblical critics. Theologians of the Tübingen School began with the rationalist premise which was also their conclusion: the supernatural elements in the Bible were mistakes – innocent mistakes, but mistakes nonetheless – on the part of ignorant and prejudiced observers. There were no miracles, and Christ was as other men. Lyall used the same methodology – the detailed study of Jewish history – to prove the converse, to reassert the possibility of revelation and the divinity of Jesus. His 'big book', *Propaedia Prophetica*, posed a simple question: Why did so many Jews accept Christ as the Son of God, when all they had to go on was the Old Testament? The solution, Lyall suggested, lay in prophecy. It was the fulfilment of the Jewish chroniclers' predictions that made the Second Coming credible; and the fact that God kept his promise to mankind was still a powerful 'ground of belief' two millenia later.

The intellectual qualities of *Propaedia Prophetica* were probably as reassuring as the book's arguments. It was a learned tome: Lyall's researches on Jewish religion and Jewish society were profound. And it was learning brilliantly analysed. Everything Lyall wrote displayed the same flair for elegant exposition. The sequences in which he laid out his material had an irresistible internal logic of their own; his prose was succinct and precise; there were no longueurs or diversions. It was all proof that a man of transparently high intellectual ability could still believe in the Thirty-Nine Articles. Yet Lyall on prophecy made no new converts. *Propaedia Prophetica* stiffened the waverers; it 'drew forth from Archbishop Howley, and from many other competent judges of its merits, the warmest and strongest testimonies of admiration and approval'. But it represented the final, and in some senses the finest, flowering of a theological tradition which was about to be rendered obsolescent. Within a few years of the dean's death, history and science – biblical criticism and Darwinism – destroyed the atmosphere of acceptance in which his approach to the evidences of Christianity flourished. By the time the third edition of *Propaedia Prophetica* appeared, forty-five years after the first edition, Lyall's original reading public was dead and his book must have seemed like a survivor from a past age: an age in which 'the excellent works of Paley were in almost complete possession of the field, while . . . an influential philosophic school . . . spoke with some slight scorn of [submitting] the Gospel to the procedure of our criminal courts'. In 1885 a different kind of Jewish history held sway: the school of Stanley's *Jewish Church*. Stanley sanitised the scripture story by substituting local colour for the supernatural. He reassured 'thoughtful people' that 'scripture may be made as interesting and instructive as Herodotus'. There was no nonsense about treating the Bible as the sole repository of divine revelations.[9]

Lyall's work as a publicist complemented his activities as a scholar. The charges which nineteenth-century archdeacons addressed to the clergy of their archdeaconries at the end of their visitations must be among the least-read pamphlets ever published. Lyall's disquisitions were different. They dealt with the most controversial issues of the day – issues such as church rates and church courts – 'with a firmness of principle, depth of understanding and moderation of language that were very rare in combination at that critical time'. One charge, in particular, ran through three editions: a defence of the clergy's property. Lyall's address opened with the usual cliché: if the rights of the church were overriden, no one else's property would be safe. But the possibility of a general confiscation was only his minor premise. He was perfectly prepared to defend the Anglican establishment on utilitarian grounds, by subjecting the Church of England to a crude cost-benefit analysis. On the benefit side of the equation, there was the bedrock of the church: the parochial system. As long as the Church of England maintained a clergyman in every parish in the country, there was no danger of 'dreary tracts' emerging 'in which the sound of the sabbath-bell is never heard'. Lyall claimed that there was no period since the Reformation when the clergy were more zealous. Take away the tithes and the glebes and the system would collapse. Urban congregations could afford to maintain their own priests, but villages could never meet the cost of a full-time incumbent out of collections or subscriptions. Without their parsons the rural population would suffer from spiritual destitution. Their immortal souls, deprived of the sacraments, would be in danger of damnation; while their all too feeble flesh gave way to the vices of the countryside, from drunkenness to incest.[10] Above all, the clergy would cease to reconcile the rural poor to their wretched lot, and the Pandora's box of class conflict would be opened, never to be shut:

> The rich and affluent – those who live at ease . . . with no business except what the pursuit of pleasure affords – may, as far as this world is concerned, do well enough without religion. But take away the restraints of religion from [the minds of the labouring classes] – teach them to believe that their only portion in this life [is drudgery and deprivation] – and immediately all the arrangements of society become changed in their eyes. By taking away the reason of those arrangements, you alter their very nature. It makes all the difference in the view of a man who can with difficulty earn his bread, whether the subordination of ranks and the inequalities of condition in society be founded upon God's will or merely upon the will of his fellow man. Bid him understand that these things are of human contrivance – and rulers and superiors become so many task-masters [and] the conditions under which he lives merely the instruments of that oppression, by which his labour is exacted.[11]

When it came to calculating the cost of all these services, Lyall insisted that England got its priesthood cheap. He produced statistics showing that the fabulous wealth of the Church was just that: fabulous. The average benefice was only worth £181 a year – a pittance, considering the calibre of the normal clergyman – and the aggregate income of all the clergy came to just two million pounds: a small price to pay for social stability in a period of persistent unrest. The great prizes of the church, the bishoprics, were worth far more than the representative living: £4,000 each, on average. But there was no point in cutting them down to size. If their revenues had been redistributed among the parochial clergy, they would only have added a few pounds to each stipend, and 'young men of rank and talents' would have ceased to enter the church. The 'shining prizes' won by a handful of clergymen were the 'pious frauds that induce and decoy . . . parents to risk their child's fortune' in a clerical career. The gentry's willingness to invest large sums of money educating their younger sons for the church 'raised the whole body of the clergy in the estimation of the community and . . . daily imparted dignity and splendour to religion itself'. At the same time, the existence of a ladder of preferment gave ambitious meritocrats a powerful incentive to exert themselves:

> [How many of] the highest dignities of the church . . . are held by men who had no other claim except that of merit . . . by persons whose fathers were in very humble stations in life . . . The dignities of the church are so many paths between the lower and upper classes of society, by means of which the sons of the humblest man may rise to take his seat among the nobility of the land . . . Some fixed portion of the rental of the soil is set apart to be disposed of, not as all other property is, according to a rule which shuts out all except the children of the present possessor; but according to a rule, which admits the claims of learning, and talents, and character.[12]

Lyall's achievements as an editor of other men's writings were at least as valuable as anything he wrote himself. Howley asked him to take over the *British Critic* soon after his arrival in London. The *Critic* was the forerunner of the *Quarterly*. It was aimed at the same readership – the Tory churchman – but it was edited on completely different lines. Instead of a small number of long articles discussing selected topics at great length, it tried to cover everything. It published short notices of 'all worthwhile publications in all fields of knowledge'; notices which were classified after the fashion of an encyclopaedia, with elaborate indices and 'valuable prefaces' highlighting the most important works. It was an ambitious format: a format worthy of the *philosophes*. But it suffered from competition with the *Edinburgh Review*. A few issues of the *Review* relieved its readers of the need to read anything else; it supplied all the opinions they could possibly require on the most controversial issues of the day. The *Edinburgh* was also more entertaining. No one trusted its contributors, but their polemics were amusing. As a result the Whig propaganda machine set the agendas discussed over 'serious' dinner tables; the *Critic* never exercised a tithe of its influence over educated opinion. Lyall's solution was to drop the comprehensive format and steal his competitor's. The remodelled *Critic* looked like a regular review, but the contents were different. There was a distinct theological bias, catering for the tastes of the predominantly clerical readership, and a readiness to defend the religious establishment which commended the *Critic* to the Tractarians, when they started looking round for a mouthpiece in the 1830s.[13]

Howley was so impressed by Lyall's revival of the *Critic* that he asked him to take over another ailing enterprise; the *Encyclopaedia Metropolitana*. The encyclopaedia was the loyal Anglican's alternative to the agnostic

Britannica: a huge historical conspectus, reconciling the past with the formularies of the Church of England. It had 'fallen through in the hands of its first projector, Mr Coleridge', and it was Lyall's job to 'put it on a sound footing'. He revised the contents, wrote one of the most important articles, and enlisted some distinguished contributors. The most accomplished high church theologian at Cambridge (Rose) and the most notorious broad church theologian at Oxford (Hampden) both contributed chapters on religious history: a remarkable meeting of incompatible minds. Lyall also brought younger talent to the fore. Newman – currently an unknown fellow of Oriel – published his first articles (on Cicero and Apollonius Tyranneus) in Lyall's *Encyclopaedia*; and if one went through the entire cast list, it would probably be possible to find some leading evangelicals. It was perhaps the last time in English history when members of such mutually-hostile schools of churchmanship could be persuaded to collaborate in a common literary endeavour, and the fact that they were willing to do so says something for Lyall's diplomacy and breadth of mind. A few years later, Newman was leading the agitation against Hampden's appointment as Regius Professor of Divinity. Lyall's third and last project was less inclusive, because the battle-lines were being drawn up. The *Theological Library* provided middle-brow Anglicans with a suitable set of paragons. The first volumes, including a *Life of Wiclif*, fixed the ecumenical tone of the series. Wyclif (1324-84) 'brought down upon himself the bitter emnity of the Roman Catholic leaders' because his principles anticipated the Reformation. Yet the life of this distinctly low church hero was written by a prominent Tractarian: Charles Le Bas, a professor at Haileybury.

An editor capable of marshalling obstreperous and idiosyncratic contributors into an effective team had the makings of a good administrator. Six years after Lyall started trouble-shooting at the *British Critic*, he became Howley's chaplain. His remit was to examine all the candidates for ordination in the diocese of London, eliminating those who were unfit to become clergymen. In the eighteenth century the examination of ordinands frequently degenerated into a mere formality, bishops ordaining anyone with an offer of a curacy. Charles Blomfield, Lyall's immediate predecessor, set a new standard and Lyall kept it up. He took up references, conducted interviews, set written question papers. He did everything he could to stop the incompetent and the immoral slipping through the net; and judging by his subsequent promotion, he succeeded. When the archdeaconry of Colchester fell vacant in 1824 – as a result of Blomfield's elevation to the see of Chester – Howley made Lyall the head of the church in Essex.[14]

As an archdeacon, Lyall faced two recurrent problems: the negligence of the clergy and the condition of their churches. He started out, in the approved Victorian way, by setting his subordinates an example. He left London, the centre of all his literary interests, and buried himself in his rural livings. Unfortunately Fairstead and Weeley were too small to have much demonstration value. The combined population of the two hamlets was tiny and the villagers were untouched by dissent. So in 1833 Lyall exchanged his pocket parishes for one of the most difficult livings in East Anglia: the market town of Hadleigh. Hadleigh was 'populous and impoverished' and dominated by noncomformists. It had over 3,000 inhabitants; its traditional handicrafts were in decline; and the majority of the leading citizens (including the largest landowner in the parish) were dissenters. It needed vigorous rectors deploying teams of carefully chosen curates; it got a succession of placemen culminating in Lyall's immediate predecessor: a distinguished academic theologian suffering from acute asthma, who had neither the energy nor the inclination to do much for his parishioners. Hugh Rose published *A Letter to the Inhabitants of Hadleigh* protesting that the living was worth far less than they supposed, and claiming that he had to earn extra money by writing and teaching if he was to subsist at all; but his pleas fell on deaf ears. During his brief ministry, the Baptists put up a Tuscan chapel within sight of the dilapidated parish church and the Congregationalists built a magnificent Grecian temple (with a thousand seats) on a prominent site immediately opposite the Town Hall. The Church of England was visibly in retreat. It took Lyall eight years to turn Hadleigh round: to revive the religious life of his parish. He made no startling innovations; he simply did everything a good parish priest was supposed to do. He held more services, including a daily evensong; he delivered 'eminently practical' sermons in 'terse and manly English'; he charmed the leading members of his congregation with the 'peculiar amiability and sweetness of his disposition'; and he 'applied himself. . . to improving the conditions of the poor'. The Religious Census of 1851 showed the measure of his success. On the Sunday of the census, almost two-fifths of the total attendance (1,930 in all) was at the parish church.[15]

The only drawback with this kind of miniature revival was the difficulty of disseminating it. Lyall trained a number of curates, but there were no theological colleges to improve the professional training of the clergy as a whole. In 1840 Lyall got his chance to found one. He was one of the instigators of the St Augustine's College, Canterbury. St Augustine's raised the professional standards of Anglican missionaries throughout the

British empire, and it may well have raised the standard of the English priesthood, as missionaries drifted home. Lyall collected funds, by cultivating individual donors and promoting a public appeal; he sat on the original committee of management; and he may well have been the effective head of the college during the long interregnum which followed the illness and death of the first warden, an elderly colonial bishop. The sub-warden nominally in charge of day-to-day administration was Lyall's nephew and client; he must have reported back to deanery and accepted the dean's lead on matters of policy. As the senior clergyman and the only 'manager' resident in Canterbury, Lyall would have been the obvious source of authoritative advice even if the sub-warden had been a complete stranger.[16]

Lyall's church restoration campaign was the rural counterpart of Blomfield's crusade for church extension in London. His triennial visitations disclosed the full extent of the problem: both his archdeaconries contained hundreds of medieval churches in varying states of neglect. He gave churchwardens eminently practical instructions as to repairs, but everything depended on their willingness to carry out his directives. What if the churchwardens refused to cooperate, or the vestries refused to levy a church rate to pay the bills? Before Lyall's appointment, the culprits generally got away with their dereliction. The new archdeacon changed all that: he took defaulters to court. Lyall put a stop to vestries refusing to elect churchwardens by getting a writ of *mandamus*, forcing the electors of Wix 'to make an unqualified submission . . . after an expenditure of many hundreds of pounds [falling] principally upon individuals'. Another vestry agreed to levy a rate as soon as Lyall offered to pay the churchwardens' legal costs, if they took the matter to court. Only the dissenters of Bocking and Braintree held out against him, and their resistance developed into a national *cause célèbre*: a test case of the non-conformists' political muscle. Under the leadership of Samuel Courtauld, the mill-owner whose silk works dominated both towns, the Anti-Church Rates Committee fought the churchwardens through the Consistory Court of Canterbury (twice), the Court of Arches (once), Queen's Bench (twice), the Court of Exchequer (twice) and the House of Lords (once). Four of the eight verdicts came down on the churchwardens' side, three found for the dissenters and one was ambiguous. When Chief Justice Tindell ruled that parishioners had an absolute obligation to maintain their parish church, which could not be evaded, it must have seemed that the Anglicans had won a decisive victory. Lyall's directions were obeyed so completely that he 'had no duty to perform, except thanking the churchwardens'. Then, in 1853, disaster struck. The dispute finally reached the House of Lords, and the law Lords decided that church rates could only be levied with the approval of a majority of the vestry. Their judgement stopped the collection of church rates in every parish in which a majority of the ratepayers were nonconformist. Gladstone's first administration abolished the resultant anomaly by abolishing church rates altogether. It is difficult to say whether Lyall's tactics accelerated or delayed this *dénouement*. They certainly added to his reputation as a doughty champion of the Church.[17]

There were three tests of Lyall's statesmanship: three groups which called for careful handling, if the interests of the Church were to be served. The battle over church rates was only one front in a wide-ranging assault on the Anglicans' legal privileges. Nothing short of complete disestablishment and partial disendowment would have satisfied the more extreme nonconformists. Their assault had to be faced down with the appropriate mixture of firmness and conciliation. Then there were the Church's most ardent supporters. In many ways the Tractarians and Ecclesiologists posed a more difficult problem than the avowed enemies of the religious establishment. The new breed of militant had the zeal to galvanise the priesthood; but there was always the danger that their Romanising innovations would alienate the more conservative laity. The activists had to be used *and* restrained. Between these extremes, there were the traditional patrons of true religion. The members of the ruling class who used their power to protect the clergy's interests were faltering; it was vital to revive their commitment. In a hierarchic society, the Church of England needed lay protectors: landlords with enough influence to suppress dissent on their estates; philanthropists with enough cash to build new churches or endow new livings; and politicians with enough conviction to defend the establishment in parliament.

Lyall's archdeaconries brought him face to face with dissent in its most belligerent form. Colchester and Maidstone were full of chapels. Every sect was represented – Baptist, Methodist, Congregational: and every sect was steadily extending its tentacles into the surrounding countryside. Their scurrilous attacks on the Anglican clergy tapped a well of popular resentment and suspicion which has never run dry, and they had the wit to concentrate their attack on the church's weakest spot: its finances. Disestablishment appealed to everyone who had ever paid a church rate or a tithe. It united self-interest with self-righteousness: a spurious demand for equality with successful tax evasion. A better recipe for a broad-based coalition has yet to be invented:

One person seeks to benefit his estate – and he proposes to do away with tithes; another seeks to strengthen his party – and he proposes to turn bishops out of the House of Lords; a third looks to the advantage of his sect – and his plan is to abolish Church rates and obtain a share in marriage and burial fees. But what has all this to do with the interests of God's kingdom? How is the glory of God and the salvation of mankind concerned in schemes of this kind? A fine controversy this for Christians to be engaged in.[18]

Lyall would have been perfectly justified in whipping up a hate campaign against the schismatics; their own lapses were sufficiently flagrant. But his rejoinders struck a note more of sorrow than anger. They were full of carefully-reasoned arguments expressed in carefully-rounded periods which could always be reduced to a single proposition; non-conformists had nothing to complain about. As far as Lyall was concerned, the negligence which justified earlier schisms was a thing of the past:

I do not believe that, since the Reformation, there was ever a period . . . when the Church of England . . . possessed stronger claims upon the regard and affections of her members. Never was there a period when there was more learning and talent, more activity and propriety of conduct among her ministers; nor when the great truths of the Gospel were laid more fully before the people, or more zealously enforced.[19]

Sometimes it seemed as if the harder the clergy tried, the more they were abused:

They hated me before they hated you, said Christ to his apostles. It is not because a church Establishment is useless to religion, that it has now so many active enemies, but because it is the main support of religion in this country; it is not the indolence, or ignorance, or vicious lives of churchmen, which excites that malevolence by which our order is assailed; that which is disliked is the activity, the learning, the zeal and piety . . . of the . . . clergy, [whose influence] stands between a certain class of politicians . . . and the designs at which they evidently aim. But the persecution of those who think and feel in this manner is an evil which we must be content to bear with, until it shall please God to change their hearts. The present state of the public mind is not one which can be permanent: all excesses of opinion, arising out of temporary excitement, must necessarily be short-lived.[20]

Lyall's dealings with the non-conformists' most intemperate opponents were more intimate and more ambivalent than his running battle with dissent. His literary projects brought him into touch with the Tractarians. They made ideal contributors; they were powerful and prolific writers on the religious issues of the day. Lyall commissioned Newman's first book for the *Theological Library* and accepted four volumes written by another tractarian, Charles Le Bas. Eight months before Keble's celebrated assize sermon marked the official opening of the tractarian campaign, he invited Newman to a conference at his rectory at Fairstead; and for a time it seemed possible that his associate, Hugh Rose, would 'place himself at the head of the Oxford Movement'. When the conclave finally took place, at the deanery in Hadleigh, Lyall impressed the deputies from Oxford with his zeal. Froude reported back to Newman that the archdeacon was 'most agreeable and clever and . . . not . . . a mere conservative'. Lyall's links with the Ecclesiologists were closer still. He was a Cambridge man, well-known in university circles; he mediated between Beresford Hope and Howley, while St Augustine's was in the making; and at least three of his client-nephews were in touch with the founders of the Camden Society. George Pearson was the first sub-warden of St Augustine's; Thomas Darling employed Butterfield, the Ecclesiologists' favourite architect, to restore his own churches; and William Hearle Lyall corresponded with the titular leader of the Cambridge Movement, John Mason Neale.[21]

The conference at Hadleigh and the seminary at Canterbury proved to be the high water-marks of Lyall's association with the Oxbridge activists. Once they came out of the closet – once the stream of polemics started pouring from the press – he distanced himself from his erstwhile protégés, along with the rest of the old high church party. Up to 1833 Lyall's name appears in all the indices of Newman's correspondence; thereafter it disappears. The fate of Newman's *The Arians of the Fourth Century* illustrated the process of disengagement. Lyall asked Newman to write the volume on the Thirty-Nine Articles for the *Theological Library*. He wanted a treatment which was both popular and orthodox; a book which would provide middle-brow clergymen and serious-minded communicants with a historic justification of their traditional creed. What he got was a scholarly monograph sustaining a distinctly partisan interpretation of the past. The technical deficiences of *The Arians* could have been eliminated by rewriting. It presupposed too much knowledge; the necessary explanations could have been inserted. Lyall never gave Newman a chance to revise his manuscript. He arranged for his printers to publish *The Arians* separately, because he knew that the Newman's 'Romanist' views on the relative authority of scripture and tradition would offend the *Theological Library's* predominantly Protestant readership. A similar chill overtook Lyall's collaboration with the Ecclesiologists. At first, the Cambridge Camden Society seemed innocuous enough. What could be more innocent than a group of antiquarians visiting country churches and drawing up reports on their architecture? Unfortunately it was only one step from determining the ideal form of a medieval church to determining the ideal rituals which the church was designed to house. The emergence of a hard core of ritualists determined to revive the liturgy in use at the Reformation – if not at some earlier point – produced the inevitable low church backlash. The society split from top to bottom, as the evangelicals staged a mass exodus; and Lyall let the *provocateurs* build All Saints, Margaret Street without his help.[22]

Lyall's *Realpolitik* exposed him to the usual accusations of trimming. He deferred to Protestant susceptibilities, pulled his punches with dissenters and bent the knee to politicians guilty of 'national apostasy'. As the old high churchmen took the measure of the Oxford Movement and reacted against its divisive zeal, his erstwhile allies must have wondered whether he had compromised his spiritual integrity as comprehensively as the servile Howley. In fact, he was innocent of equivocation. If he made concessions, he was conciliatory out of conviction. It was the nature of his vision that distanced him from the militants. His first loyalty was to the Church as an organisation, rather than a package of dogmas or a set of rituals. Years of grappling with metaphysics taught him the impossibility of ascertaining abstruse theological truths with any degree of precision or finality; and he was not prepared to jeopardise the church's historic mission – the leading of men to God – for the sake of the Young Turks' educated guesses. Of course, doctrines and rituals mattered; it was important to get them right. But almost all of the Tractarians' innovations had been anticipated by the old high church party, and none of them were incompatible with the existing religious order. On Lyall's view, the interdependence of church and state represented the accumulated wisdom of generations, struggling to create an environment conducive to salvation. If the high churchmen taught their flocks to render 'the most ready and cheerful submission to the rulers whom it has pleased God to place over them', the rulers gave the clergy enough leverage over their parishioners to maintain a creditable level of church attendance and a semblance of popular morality. Disputes over the validity of doctrines and rituals deprived Anglicans of their sense of spiritual security, by undermining the clergy's authority. What use was a priesthood incapable of giving pious laymen authoritative guidance on religious matters? What were men supposed to believe, and what were they supposed to do, to avoid hell-fire? Lyall and Blomfield were at one in their aversion to the kind of public controversies which disturbed the peace of the church:

I concur with you in thinking that whatever improvements might be suggested in the formularies of our church . . . are not . . . of such a kind as to render it [a] positive duty . . . to insist upon them . . . at the risk of the Church's peace and safety. I have, therefore, uniformly deprecated the agitation of this question in times of unsettledness and danger . . . I have never yet expressed in public any opinion on the subject, and I would gladly be spared the necessity of doing so . . . The question might have been suffered to rest for the next few years at least and there was . . . a pretty general understanding to that effect when the [Oxford] Association stood forward and broke the truce. The public mind is not in a proper state for the consideration of the subject.[23]

As far as Lyall was concerned, the onus of proof lay on the innovator: radicals must show, 'plainly and incontrovertibly', that the reforms they advocated were real improvements. But once a new order emerged, it was just as entitled to support as the old. Lyall saw no virtue in lost causes; it did the Church more good if conservatives regrouped around more defensible positions. He opposed the Reform Bill because he thought it went too far. It would have been enough to remove some of the more blatant anomalies; there was no need for such sweeping change. He urged the clergy of his archdeaconry to oppose the bill; they could not remain 'passive spectators of a great constitutional revolution which might lead to the disestablishment of the Church of England'. But once the bill was passed – once it became part of the law of the land – Lyall not only told the clergy to accept it; he urged them to persuade their parishioners to accept it also. Lyall's attitude to nonconformists ran on much the same lines. Dissent was an historic fact; there was no getting rid of the dissenters. The most that sensible men could hope for was some *modus vivendi* which minimised the damage. For more than a century, Anglicans had lived in harmony with sectarians of every kind. As long as there was any possibility of restoring that historic equilibrium, Lyall refused to slam the door on peaceful coexistence. Despite evidence to the contrary, he persisted in believing that a valid distinction could be drawn between the minority of vociferous fanatics, who slandered the Anglican clergy, and the mass of moderate non-conformists who were embarrassed by the violence of their self-appointed spokesmen.[24]

When it came to stroking the Church of England's allies in the right direction – the third test of Lyall's statesmanship – he proved the perfect ambassador. His gaiters gave him the *entrée* to the county set; in fact he was a notable in his own right. Towards the end of his life, his income from all sources put him on a financial par with the gentry; and his disposable income, since he had no children and no debts, may well have equalled the purchasing power of some of the more heavily encumbered magnates. As

Dean of Canterbury, he occupied a historic mansion in a spectacular
situation in the centre of a sacred city; and in the absence of the
archbishops, who lived at Lambeth and Addington, he was the natural
leader of clerical society. No one refused his invitations, and his
acceptance of hospitality was a mark of condescension to his hosts.

Lyall's contacts in the great metropolis supplemented his contacts in
Kent. He kept up with the men of letters and the high churchman he met
during the ten years he spent in London (1815-24), and he added a
sprinkling of Canningite statesmen to his 'acquaintance'. His elder
brother – the Chairman of the East India Company and MP for the City of
London – was a crucial intermediary. George Lyall lived in the middle of a
flux of financiers and politicians, and the dean stayed with him when he was
in town. He moved easily in such circles. Evangelicals and Tractarians could
be embarrassments on social occasions. They had their stock of pious
catchphrases which they interjected into ordinary conversation; the more
histrionic were forever striking sanctimonious attitudes; and underlying it
all, there was the intensity of monomania. Lyall never embarrassed
anyone: he had too much savoir faire. His father's investment in his
education – his decade at Eton and Trinity – gave him the manners of a
gentleman. If the panegyric printed in *The Gentleman's Magazine* is
anything to go by, his piety was under strict control. It was possible to
forget that he was a clergyman: the highest accolade the ruling class could
confer. His religion contained 'no taint of asceticism or pride'; it was too
'humble' to be 'paraded for a moment in public view'. In fact, his most
prominent characteristics were his infectious optimism ('his temper was
cheerful and buoyant'), his sense of humour ('a keen sense of the
ridiculous') and his exquisite politeness ('no word of discourtesy ever
passed his lips').[25]

One can see Lyall's social virtues coming into operation whenever he
needed to raise large sums of money. The great wave of church-building in
Essex sent him scurrying to his plutocratic friends. Local landlords were
reminded of their obligations; philanthropists known to be interested in
church extension were carefully targetted; the Society in London for
Enlarging and Rebuilding Churches gave thousands of pounds to the
parishes in his archdeaconry. The restoration of Canterbury Cathedral
made even greater demands on Lyall's diplomacy. It took all his powers of
persuasion to get a particularly fractious chapter, threatened with the
confiscation of its estates, to unite behind a long-term programme which
aimed at a complete overhaul of the entire fabric. His handling of St
Augustine's greatest benefactor – A.J. Beresford Hope – was another
example of his talent for tickling human trout. Hope was a generous

patron of high church causes: so generous that he permanently impaired his estate. Sadly, he was also an impossible man to do business with. His manner was dictatorial; his whims were arbitrary; he was quick to take offence. In the end, he quarrelled with all his associates; and he pursued his *quondam* allies with spectacular vindictiveness. He puffed William Butterfield to the skies in the *Ecclesiologist* (which he controlled) until they fell out over the decoration of All Saints, Margaret Street. Then he tried to blast Butterfield's reputation by publishing a series of anonymous attacks on his professional competence. Hope's relationship with Archbishop Howley could easily have developed into a similar feud, jeopardising St Augustine's prospects before it opened. Howley was loathe to lend his name to an aggressively ritualist project which was bound to provoke Protestant opposition, and he only supported the appeal for funds on the strict understanding that he, as Visitor, would draft the college's statutes, appoint its officers and monitor its activities. As soon as sufficient money had been raised, Hope tried to renege on this agreement. He refused to convey the site to the trustees unless the statutes were submitted for his approval; and when Howley demurred, he asked for an interview in the hope that he could bear the old man down. He grossly underestimated the archbishop's determination; and if the interview had ever taken place, 'it might have pushed matters to a very undesirable crisis'. It took all Lyall's diplomacy – all his approved mixture of firmness and conciliation – to reconcile the parties to the dispute.[26]

Lyall's dealings with the politicians were equally effective. His reputation as an administrator made him an obvious adviser on church affairs, and his elder brother gave him access to Peel's back-benchers. Whenever ministers looked round for clerics who could represent the working clergy on the various inquiries busily reforming the Church of England, his name must have sprung to mind. He did his first little job for the government in 1849, as a member of the Episcopal and Capitular Revenue Commission. The commission was set up to help the government decide how the estates of the bishops and the cathedrals should be run. There were two issues at stake: the terms on which the church lands were to be let; and the bodies to be entrusted wth their management. Under the old system of fines on renewal, the lessees of church estates got them dirt cheap. They paid a third or a quarter of the sums which they would have paid under a system of rack-rents. A Tractarian commissioner would probably have seen systematic enhancement as a wonderful opportunity to solve half the Church of England's financial problems. Practical men looked at the problem in a different light. They saw the lessees as a powerful political lobby with a vested interest sanctified by custom: a lobby which it might be dangerous to provoke. The commission eventually recommended a compromise. In effect, they split the difference: the lessees paid more, but nowhere near the market rate; and they got a right of perpetual renewal, which ratified their customary interest in the land. Lyall and his colleagues also fudged the question of management. Deans and chapters wished to retain control of their lands, because landownership was a source of status and authority; but they were inefficient managers, and there was a strong case for transferring their estates to the Ecclesiastical Commissioners. In the event the deans and chapters remained in control of their estates, but all their surplus income – over and above their fixed stipends and the sums allowed them for the maintenance of their cathedrals – was paid to the Ecclesiastical Commission, which gave that body a powerful incentive to insist on new standards of management. These pragmatic arrangements were exactly what the cabinet was looking for, and they were grateful to Lyall for his acquiescence. As the only representative of the cathedral clergy on the inquiry, he could easily have sabotaged its findings by raising the cry of spoliation. As things were, he helped bring in a unanimous report. If only he had kept his health, he might well have become the first clergyman below the rank of bishop to sit on the Ecclesiastical Commission; he was so useful.[27]

Chapter 3

Patrons

Singularly conscientious in the exercise of his patronage, Archbishop Howley was besides a great discerner and rewarder of merit: he instinctively attracted to himself good and learned men.

J.W. Burgon, *Lives of Twelve Good Men* (1884)

Peel realised an important truth of the new political world. The national movement towards duty and responsibility demanded an end to aristocratic patronage and called for ecclesiastics chosen for merit and capacity. Peel saw that there came a point where a government would suffer more damage from a blatant political appointment than by the loss of a secure vote or a single influence however eminent. He saw that to elevate the patronage of the church beyond politics would in the long run promote the interests of his party.

Owen Chadwick, *The Victorian Church* (1966)

In 1812-13 Howley's appointment as Bishop of London and Peel's appointment as Chief Secretary for Ireland put a mass of preferment at the disposal of Lyall's future patrons, while they were still comparatively young. Nothing in their characters or careers suggested that they would use this patronage in new ways, concentrating appointments and promotions on deserving meritocrats. By temperament and habit they were cautious conservatives. They collaborated with an aristocratic establishment, and the establishment propelled them to the peaks of their professions. Why should they change a system which had served them so well? If they ever harboured subversive thoughts, they quickly suppressed them. It was only in middle age – when Howley was in his fifties and Peel was in his forties – that they slowly and reluctantly went over to reform.

Between the end of the Napoleonic wars and the passage of the first Reform Act, the emergence of a radical political culture overwhelmed a system which revolved around patron-client relationships. The demand for the elimination of abuses – sinecures and pluralism in the church, pocket boroughs and bribery in politics – became irresistible. With their instinctive pragmatism and their disdain for ideologues, the primate and the premier reacted to the new challenge in similar ways; and in the course of the 1830s, they devised a common strategy: a strategy of containing the enemies of the church through discriminating reform. Howley accepted that the Church of England must mend its ways or risk the loss of its privileges and property. Peel realised that the Conservative Party stood to gain more votes from a priesthood held in high regard – a powerful ally capable of influencing public opinion – than it could hope to win by rewarding its supporters. The first moves towards the conclusion of a working alliance between the high churchmen and the high Tories foundered on the reefs of Catholic Emancipation. Then, in 1835, the Ecclesiastical Commission put the old partnership on a permanent footing. Peel's masterstroke – a royal commission packed with realistic bishops and sympathetic politicians – began the complicated and time-consuming process of redistributing the Church of England's endowments. Changes of personnel were an essential corollary of the institutional changes which the commission devised. If the clergy were to become more efficient suppliers of spiritual services, able administrators had to be inserted at key points in the ecclesiastical hierarchy and outstanding parish priests had to be rewarded. The only way to attain these goals was to distribute patronage on new principles. Instead of letting the occasional meritocrat slip through the sieve of connection, patrons like Howley and Peel had to *search* for candidates whose professional services qualified them for promotion. Lyall was one of their joint discoveries.

As Bishop of London (1813-28), Howley had over a hundred livings in his gift; and as Archbishop of Canterbury (1828-48), he controlled half as many again – not counting sinecure stalls and a grab-bag of miscellaneous appointments. The largest landed magnate was lucky to own a dozen advowsons. Howley spent thirty-five years on the episcopal bench; the only laymen with a comparable number of livings at their disposal – the Prime Ministers and Lord Chancellors – were birds of passage in comparison. With the possible exception of long-serving premiers like Pitt and Liverpool, Howley must have presented more clergymen to livings than

Table 1
The Sources of the Lyall Connection's Patronage

Patrons	Value	Per Cent
THE BISHOPS[1]	£120,700	52
Bishop of London and Archbishop of Canterbury (William Howley)		
THE CROWN	£38,400	16
Prime Ministers (Peel and Gladstone)		
THE CATHEDRALS	£33,200	14
Dean and Chapter of Canterbury (William Lyall)		
OXBRIDGE COLLEGES	£28,700	12
Jesus College, Cambridge (Robert Peter)		
PRIVATE PATRONS	£11,000	5
The Quebec Chapel (Trustees of the Rev. J.K. Gurney)		
HOSPITALS AND INNS OF COURT	£1,700	1
St Thomas's Hospital; Lincoln's Inn; Gray's Inn		
TOTAL	£233,800	

[1] Includes two presentations obtained through exchanges with other patrons and £2,500 (1 per cent) from Howley's successors.

any other individual in modern English history; he certainly ranks among the greatest patrons the Church of England has known. Of course, part of his patronage was pre-empted by traditional obligations. The powerful allies who helped a bishop clamber up the ecclesiastical hierarchy expected some *quid pro quo*; a prelate's relatives were entitled to suitable provision; and the indigent clergymen belonging to his diocese had ill-defined rights to relief. But none of these prior claims was particularly onerous in Howley's case. He had no aristocratic patrons to repay. He rose by royal favour, and the House of Hanover wanted personal services from their archbishop, not billets for their hangers-on. Again, he had no sons to enrich. They all died young, before he could promote them. One of his sons-in-law and a couple of nephews-by-marriage were in holy orders, but that was all. There were more than enough poor clergymen to absorb everything he had to give away, but public opinion was satisfied if he gave a certain proportion of his poorest livings to curates who had laboured for the better part of a lifetime without ever getting a parish of their own. The residuum – hundreds of pieces of preferment – was free-floating, and an archbishop could do what he liked with his own.

When Howley was first elevated to the episcopal bench, there was no reason to suppose that he would initiate a revolution in episcopal patronage by putting this residuum to new ends. Rather the contrary: his highly-rewarded career as a royal sycophant and his all too justified awareness of his own limitations as a communicator filled him with cautious trepidation. Howley became 'the last Archbishop of Canterbury to live like a prince of the Church' in the only way open to the son of an obscure Hampshire parson, by propitiating his superiors. First he pleased his teachers at Winchester and Oxford: that financed his education (through scholarships) and brought him into contact with the sons of prospective patrons (as a fellow of New College). Ambitious tutors, at Oxbridge, normally cultivated undergraduates from landed families. Howley went one better: he taught the heir to the Dutch throne. His association with the Prince of Orange drew him to the attention of the royal family – and the House of Hanover gradually discovered that he made the perfect chaplain. He was pious and learned; he conducted court ceremonies, from baptisms to burials, with becoming solemnity; above all, he never obtruded religion into private life. However scandalous the conduct of the sons of George III, it never occurred to him to reproach them; he was too humble. As a result, preferment poured upon him: a rich living in the gift of the Lord Chancellor; a canonry at Christ Church; a regius chair; one of the most valuable bishoprics. Then, in 1820, he plumbed the depths of self-abasement. As the bill divorcing George IV from Queen Caroline scraped through the House of Lords, Howley assured the assembled peers that the king could do no wrong. George IV never forgot the moral support which Howley had given him at one of the most embarrassing junctures in a reign full of petty indignities, and he made his faithful courtier primate as soon as the see of Canterbury fell vacant.

Howley's drawbacks as a publicist would have prevented him giving the rest of the clergy a decisive lead over reform, even if he had been a committed radical. His speeches and sermons were disasters. His delivery was appalling: he mumbled and hesitated; and when he lost his way, he lost his audience also. In print he was urbane but anodyne. His charges – 'printed by request' – were full of unctuous platitudes expressed in rotund periods. It was impossible to attack them; there was so little to attack. He was almost as ineffectual as an administrator. The head of the Hackney Phalanx, one of his closest collaborators, accused him of 'hiding from business'. He only agreed to accept a seat on Peel's Ecclesiastical Commission after much misgiving; his manner in business meetings was 'cringeing'; and when it came to taking hard decisions, he was hopelessly overshadowed by Blomfield, his successor as Bishop of London. In any conflict, his talent for procrastination came to the fore. After the Oxford Movement provoked a Protestant backlash and both sides appealed to the primate for authoritative guidance, he instinctively appealed to the combatants to observe a ten-year moratorium on further discussion: he probably counted on dying before the next round of hostilities broke out.

Yet even Howley's bred-in-the-bone conservatism gave way to the pressure for reform. His conversion can be dated: it took place in the mid 1830s. In 1832 he was praying for a counter-revolution, huddled together with the rest of the bishops at Lambeth; four years later, he was the 'inexorable supporter of quasi-revolutionary measures' in the Lords. His change of heart seems to have been sincere. 'It is inconceivable', Best writes, 'that he did not believe in the Commissioners and their work, that he was only assuming a politic pose'. One reason for his accommodation with the spirit of the times may have been a change in his advisers. The mild archbishop was easily influenced by the strong personalities around him, and two of his more intransigent counsellors – Hugh Rose (his most assertive domestic chaplain) and William van Mildert (the most forceful bishop) – were in the grip of terminal illnesses. Their place was filled by reformers like Blomfield (Howley's first choice as Archdeacon of Colchester) and Lyall (Blomfield's successor). Yet underlying this switch in Howley's counsellors was the realisation, as the onslaught on the church gathered momentum, that reform from within would preserve far more of the clergy's privileges and property than reform from without. As the reaction against reform put Peel in power, a preemptive strike became possible. Peel offered to protect the church, provided the clergy put their house in order; the fact that Howley agreed to work with him shows how irresistible the demand for change had become.[1]

Peel's access to clerical patronage was broadly comparable with Howley's. The preferment he controlled at the peak of his career was far more valuable than the 150-odd livings in the archbishop's gift, because it included bishoprics and deaneries; but the first call on any minister's favours – the need to mobilise a majority in the House of Commons – soaked up so much patronage that the freely disposable surplus was a very small, if not a negative sum. Under the *ancien régime*, patronage was the decisive factor in general elections. Well-entrenched governments were virtually certain of victory. But getting the right candidates elected and keeping MPs walking into the right lobbies absorbed all the good things an administration had to offer – and could have absorbed many more. The influence-peddlers' appetite for patronage was insatiable. For every client Peel satisfied, ten claimants went disappointed away. Clerical meritocrats, with no political influence worth mentioning, came well down his list of priorities; and until his last path-breaking ministry, there were no signs that he wanted things any other way. He accepted the system he inherited and threw all his energies into making it work.

Like Howley, Peel was a product of the old corruption. He represented three pocket boroughs – two of them spectacularly corrupt affairs. His father bought him his first seat when he was just turned twenty-one. It was a wonderfully straightforward transaction. Sir Arthur Wellesley (as he then was, six years before Waterloo) wrote to the honest and independent electors of Cashel – there were about two dozen of them – telling them to return a Mr Peel by such and such a date and promising to let them know his Christian name. Peel was elected *in absentia*. He may never have visited his constituency: there would have been very little point. Twenty years later, after he lost a self-inflicted by-election at Oxford, the government bribed Sir Manasseh Lopes to resign his seat at Westbury in Peel's favour. Given the increased public sensitivity to corruption and Peel's prominence as Home Secretary, Westbury had to be handled more discreetly than Cashel. Instead of paying Lopes a lump sum, the Foreign Office made his nephew consul at Pernambuco, a post worth £1,000 a year. On the one occasion on which Peel could have had a popular constituency for the asking – the City of London, in 1847 – he stuck to Tamworth, the town at his park gates. He inherited Tamworth from his father, and passed it on to his son. For ninety years, three generations of the Peel family represented the town. It was only in 1880 – forty-seven years after the first Reform Act – that their 'interest' finally lost its grip.

Peel's policies complemented his constituencies. He devoted his mastery of the Commons – his grasp of detail, his recourse in argument, his ready eloquence – to defending every bulwark of the old regime, until each cause was thoroughly lost: Catholic disabilities; the Corn Laws; the Church of Ireland; boroughs like Cashel and Westbury. He applied his clerical patronage to the same ends. As Chief Secretary for Ireland (1812-18), he co-ordinated the distribution of the twenty-two bishoprics, thirty deaneries and 280 livings in the Lord Lieutenant's gift. Because private patrons were comparatively insignificant in Ireland (only one advowson in six was privately owned) and two-thirds of the livings were controlled by the bench, the choice of bishops was far more important in Ireland than England. Yet Peel made no serious or sustained attempt to promote deserving candidates. He continued Pitt's policy of letting the most influential and rapacious Anglo-Irish landlords bring the Church of Ireland into total discredit, by dividing it up amongst themselves. In his next incarnation – as Home Secretary (1822-27) – he had very little clerical patronage in his own hands; but he had the right to ask his cabinet colleagues for a share of theirs. Successive chancellors and premiers conferred livings and stalls on his brother and brother-in-law, en route to their deaneries; Liverpool made his old tutor Bishop of Oxford at his insistence. It was very much business as usual.

Then the underswell of unrest finally caught the Tories out. Wellington's ministry collapsed in 1830 and Peel failed to get a majority in 1835 because traditional techniques of political management were breaking down. From 1830 onwards jobbery *lost* elections. After the first Reform Act, a party needed a popular programme backed by good organisation *as well as local influence*, if it was to stand a chance of success. Peel bent with the prevailing wind. He announced his conversion to Catholic Emancipation in 1829, as the only solution for unrest in Ireland; he accepted the Reform Act as an irreversible settlement of a great constitutional question; he embraced free trade in 1841-46, as the only policy appropriate to a great commercial power. Above all, he saw the need to regenerate the Church of England by promoting merit. He made Samuel Wilberforce Bishop of Oxford, despite reservations about his Romanising tendencies; and Wilberforce became the most energetic diocesan of his generation. He made William Whewell Master of Trinity College, Cambridge, despite reservations about his piety ('too much the scientist, too little the divine'); and Whewell became the most prominent university reformer. His nominations to deaneries were equally 'pure'. He used the cathedrals to reward distinguished scholars and teachers. Dr Buckland became Dean of Westminster, in recognition of his eminence as a geologist; Dr Butler became Dean of Peterborough, after twenty years as headmaster of Harrow; and Dr Jenkyns became Dean of Wells, because he turned Balliol into the leading college at Oxford. Lyall fell into this category: the emerging bourgeoisie of intellect. After going into the relative merits of the canons at Canterbury, Peel decided that Lyall 'was entitled to a preference', looking solely to his 'professional character and services'. In a letter to Howley explaining his choice, Peel claimed that Lyall was 'wholly unknown to him'; and it is perfectly possible that they never met. But Lyall's brother, the Chairman of the East India Company was certainly known to Peel's brother Laurence; in fact, George Lyall had just presented one of Peel's nephews with a cadetship in the Indian army.[2]

Lyall's merits were brought to his patrons' attention by members of the old high church party. The Hackney Phalanx noted his potential while he was still a scholar of Trinity. The college was the most important single source of their recruits: more important than their citadel at Oxford, Christ Church. When Lyall first went into residence, around 1807, Charles Blomfield – the phenomenally-energetic Bishop of Chester and London (1824-56) – was a scholar two years ahead of him and the senior common room was stuffed with Phalangists. James Monk (Bishop of Gloucester 1830-56), Henry Bayley (Archdeacon of Stow 1826-44) and Charles Le Bas (Principal of Haileybury 1837-44) were all fellows. Their attention must have wavered when Lyall only got a second-class degree, instead of the anticipated first; but he soon wrote his way out of his Hampshire curacy. His critique of Dugald Stewart showed that he had the makings of an outstanding theologian; so the Phalanx tried him out in London, to see what else he had to offer. His performance – as a preacher at Lincoln's Inn, as chaplain at St Thomas's Hospital, and as editor of *The British Critic* – was sufficiently impressive to warrant their commending him to Howley. Blomfield may have been the crucial go-between. He was in constant contact with Howley at the critical juncture (1818-24), as rector of a particularly problematic London parish and archdeacon of Colchester; and he is known to have wanted Lyall to edit the *Encyclopaedia Metropolitana*, the first piece of patronage Howley put Lyall's way. The encyclopaedia led to Lyall's incorporation in Howley's kitchen-cabinet, as his examining chaplain; the chaplaincy led to his archdeaconries; and the archdeaconries drew him to Peel's attention.

It would be interesting to know how Peel came to think so highly of a man he never met. Who told the Prime Minister that the Archdeacon of Maidstone was head and shoulders above the other canons at Canterbury? It may have been Blomfield, second time round. He had every reason to know what Lyall was like: the two men had worked together for half a lifetime. Lyall was Blomfield's archdeacon for twice as long as he was Howley's, and Blomfield confided in him during the great reform crisis of 1833. Moreover, politicians respected Blomfield's judgment. He was the leading reformer on the bench – *facile princeps* in the House of Lords and the Ecclesiastical Commission; Peel was in the habit of consulting him on appointments as well as policies. It is also possible that Peel heard of Lyall from Gladstone. Gladstone first met Lyall in 1829, when he was a twenty-year old undergraduate and Lyall a forty-one year old archdeacon. They dined together at the Bishop of Oxford's – the bishop being Charles Lloyd, Peel's old tutor. Lyall was in Oxford drumming up authors for his *Theological Library*; Gladstone was a potential contributor. They had (and continued to have) a great deal in common: a preoccupation with the theological issues of the day; mutual acquaintances in high church circles; a powerful attachment to the religious establishment; and a practical political acceptance of the need for discriminating reform. Lyall's brother was another link. As MP for the City, George Lyall was a committed free trader. In 1843 he moved a resolution in the Commons, calling for the appointment of a committee of inquiry into the operation of the Navigation Acts. He wanted to be certain that the government would accept his motion, so he drafted the details in consultation with Gladstone, currently President of the Board of Trade. Gladstone is known to have taken a keen interest in ecclesiastical appointments – going to great lengths to obtain reliable information on rival candidates. As a member of Peel's cabinet, he could easily have briefed the premier on the relative merits of the chapter at Canterbury. Of course, the exact identity of Peel's informant may not matter very much. Lyall's reputation was the creation of a group, rather than an individual. In 1845 his name was 'in the air'.[3]

Chapter 4

Clients

Every spare moment of my time was spent in canvassing for votes in favour of my wife's Eldest Brother, then a candidate for the office of a Director to the East India Company . . . As they have much power and many good things to give away there are always a host of candidates for every vacancy.

Dr George Darling to his brother Thomas, 26 May 1830

My son Thomas is at the Charterhouse School. He has declined the opportunity in India – in a worldly point of view a very tempting one – for the Church.

Dr George Darling to his brother Thomas, 9 July 1833

The only thing desirable [in accepting a living in a manufacturing district] is the increase of employment and consequently the promise of increased usefulness and happiness. But that is hardly a sufficient reason for leaving so soon the situation in which your uncle has placed you and depriving yourself of the advantage of his patronage hereafter. Discouraging as the condition of your parish appears, much may be done by affectionate attentions to the people and by simple and earnest teaching. [Eventually, your uncle will help you] obtain a more extensive . . . field of labour.

Dr George Darling to his son, the Rev Thomas Darling, 27 March 1844

The rapid development of the Lyall connection between 1839 and 1855 – the years in which the oldest and the youngest clients first obtained livings – was the outcome of two related tendencies. Lyall's male relatives by birth showed a marked propensity to take up clerical careers, and his female relations showed a pronounced preference for clerical husbands. Working out the exact ratios is an arbitrary exercise, because the pool of

Table 2
Dean Lyall and his Clients: A Family Tree
(Preferments obtained with Lyall's assistance are italicised)

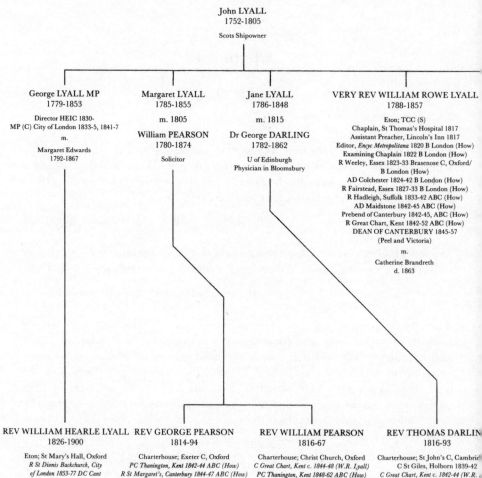

John LYALL
1752-1805

Scots Shipowner

George LYALL MP
1779-1853

Director HEIC 1830-
MP (C) City of London 1833-5, 1841-7
m.

Margaret Edwards
1792-1867

Margaret LYALL
1785-1855

m. 1805

William PEARSON
1780-1874

Solicitor

Jane LYALL
1786-1848

m. 1815

Dr George DARLING
1782-1862

U of Edinburgh
Physician in Bloomsbury

VERY REV WILLIAM ROWE LYALL
1788-1857

Eton; TCC (S)
Chaplain, St Thomas's Hospital 1817
Assistant Preacher, Lincoln's Inn 1817
Editor, *Encyc Metropolitana* 1820 B London (How)
Examining Chaplain 1822 B London (How)
R Weeley, Essex 1823-33 Brasenose C, Oxford/
B London (How)
AD Colchester 1824-42 B London (How)
R Fairstead, Essex 1827-33 B London (How)
R Hadleigh, Suffolk 1833-42 ABC (How)
AD Maidstone 1842-45 ABC (How)
Prebend of Canterbury 1842-45, ABC (How)
R Great Chart, Kent 1842-52 ABC (How)
DEAN OF CANTERBURY 1845-57
(Peel and Victoria)

m.

Catherine Brandreth
d. 1863

REV WILLIAM HEARLE LYALL
1826-1900

Eton; St Mary's Hall, Oxford
*R St Dionis Backchurch, City
of London 1853-77 DC Cant*

REV GEORGE PEARSON
1814-94

Charterhouse; Exeter C, Oxford
PC Thanington, Kent 1842-44 ABC (How)
R St Margaret's, Canterbury 1844-47 ABC (How)
Sub-W St Augustine's C 1848-52 ABC (How)
PC St Gregory's, Canterbury 1852-61 ABC
Preacher, Canterbury Cathedral 1867-74 ABC
Hon Canon of Canterbury 1874-94 ABC

REV WILLIAM PEARSON
1816-67

Charterhouse; Christ Church, Oxford
C Great Chart, Kent c. 1844-48 (W.R. Lyall)
PC Thanington, Kent 1848-62 ABC (How)
V Cranborough, Worcs 1862-67 Mrs Halse/ABC

REV THOMAS DARLIN
1816-93

Charterhouse; St John's C, Cambric
C St Giles, Holborn 1839-42
C Great Chart, Kent c. 1842-44 (W.R. ?
PC Thanington, Kent 1844-48 ABC (?
R St Michael's Paternoster Royal,
City of London 1848-93 DC Cant

ABBREVIATIONS:

ABC	Archbishop of Canterbury	m.	married
AD	Archdeacon	PC	Perpetual Curate
B	Bishop	R	Rector
C	College or Curate	S	Scholar
DC Cant	Dean and Chapter of Canterbury	TCC	Trinity College, Cambridge
F	Fellow	U	University
HEICS	Hon East India Company's Service	V	Vicar
How	William Howley	W	Warden
		†	The Crown

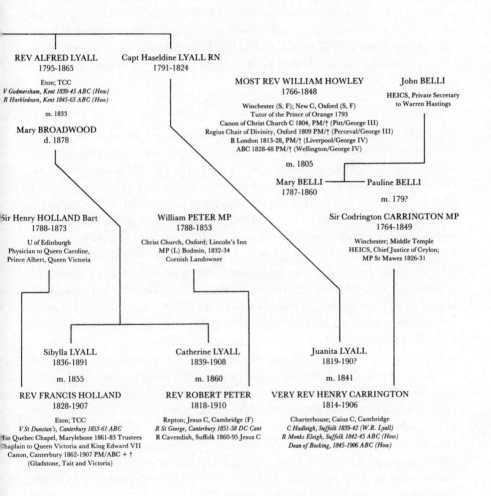

REV ALFRED LYALL
1795-1865

Eton; TCC
V Godmersham, Kent 1839-45 ABC (How)
R Harbledown, Kent 1845-65 ABC (How)

m. 1833

Mary BROADWOOD
d. 1878

Capt Haseldine LYALL RN
1791-1824

MOST REV WILLIAM HOWLEY
1766-1848

Winchester (S, F); New C, Oxford (S, F)
Tutor of the Prince of Orange 1793
Canon of Christ Church C 1804, PM/† (Pitt/George III)
Regius Chair of Divinity, Oxford 1809 PM/† (Perceval/George III)
B London 1813-28, PM/† (Liverpool/George IV)
ABC 1828-48 PM/† (Wellington/George IV)

m. 1805

Mary BELLI ——— Pauline BELLI
1787-1860

m. 179?

John BELLI

HEICS, Private Secretary
to Warren Hastings

Sir Henry HOLLAND Bart
1788-1873

U of Edinburgh
Physician to Queen Caroline,
Prince Albert, Queen Victoria

William PETER MP
1788-1853

Christ Church, Oxford; Lincoln's Inn
MP (L) Bodmin, 1832-34
Cornish Landowner

Sir Codrington CARRINGTON MP
1764-1849

Winchester; Middle Temple
HEICS, Chief Justice of Ceylon;
MP St Mawes 1826-31

Sibylla LYALL
1836-1891

m. 1855

Catherine LYALL
1839-1908

m. 1860

Juanita LYALL
1819-190?

m. 1841

REV FRANCIS HOLLAND
1828-1907

Eton; TCC
V St Dunstan's, Canterbury 1853-61 ABC
Min Quebec Chapel, Marylebone 1861-83 Trustees
Chaplain to Queen Victoria and King Edward VII
Canon, Canterbury 1862-1907 PM/ABC + †
(Gladstone, Tait and Victoria)

REV ROBERT PETER
1818-1910

Repton; Jesus C, Cambridge (F)
R St George, Canterbury 1851-58 DC Cant
R Cavendish, Suffolk 1860-95 Jesus C

VERY REV HENRY CARRINGTON
1814-1906

Charterhouse; Caius C, Cambridge
C Hadleigh, Suffolk 1839-42 (W.R. Lyall)
R Monks Eleigh, Suffolk 1842-45 ABC (How)
Dean of Bocking, 1845-1906 ABC (How)

relations can be demarcated in different ways; but if one takes the most obvious pool of all – the children and grandchildren of John Lyall, William's father, the effective founder of the family fortunes – one arrives at a total of eleven males who chose occupations and five females who chose husbands while the dean was in a position to offer them preferment. Of the eleven males, six opted for ordination; and three out of the five females marrried clergymen. By any standard this is a remarkable concentration on a single profession – and the existence of rival patrons makes it more remarkable still. When the dean's clients embraced the comparative poverty of holy orders, they had an array of well-connected relatives willing to give them a start in more lucrative occupations.[1]

Clients by Birth

John Lyall – the immigrant Scottish shipowner who founded the family firm – pursued a deliberate policy of building up a bank of related patrons to give his descendants a choice of careers. He left his father's farm in Berwickshire, took an interest in the coastal trade and moved to London in search of fame and fortune. As his shipping business grew, he bought a small estate near Brighton and started planning his children's future. He knew that there was only one way of infiltrating his offspring into the English upper-class: by incorporating them into the web of patron-client relationships. Patronage was both a measure of a family's acceptance and a means of perpetuating its pre-eminence. Once a cluster of relations had access to patronage, all the rest followed: secure incomes, assured status, rewarding vocations. So Lyall did what other arrivistes had done before him. He invested his human assets – his seven children – in a wide range of socially acceptable occupations, in the hope that enough of them would make the crucial breakthrough into the patronage-conferring elite to drag the rest of their siblings after them. In the event, two of his sons and two of his sons-in-law made the grade. His eldest son, George, inherited the family shipping business and became Chairman of the East India Company. His second son, William, became Dean of Canterbury. His eldest daughter married George Darling, one of the most successful physicians in London; and his youngest daughter married William Pearson, a moderately successful solicitor. All four men were in a position to help their sons and nephews get a start in life. George Lyall offered them jobs in the City and appointments in India; Dean Lyall to offered them livings; Dr Darling had a prosperous practice to pass on; William Pearson had room in his office for articled clerks and briefs to steer towards fledgling barristers.[2]

With all these options in front of them, more of John Lyall's descendants chose the church than every other occupation combined. It is difficult to explain their preference. The livings which Dean Lyall obtained for his clients were not particularly rich, and there was no guarantee that an ordinand would ever earn more than a pittance – only a vague expectation that 'Uncle William would provide'. The financial returns to a clerical career fluctuated wildly. Some very crude calculations suggest that the dean's best-endowed clients may have made as much as £1,000 a year out of the church at the peak of their earning power, while his poorest retainers earned £60-£80 per annun. The average member of the connection (excluding the dean) enjoyed a gross stipened of just over £400: roughly double the Anglican norm, but still far less than the same men could have hoped to earn, if they had commended themselves to the dean's rivals.

In George Lyall's hands, the family firm proved a positive cornucopia. He diversified out of shipping into docks and insurance just as London became the commercial and financial capital of the world. He made one fortune out of government contracts during the Napoleonic Wars, and another out of the steady expansion of the Port of London. With their grand town house overlooking Regent's Park, their residential estates in Surrey and Sussex, their expensive educations (Eton and Trinity) and their careers in politics (both George Lyall and his son were Tory MPs), the senior branch of the family had all the paraphernalia of gentry without its concomitant obligations. Appointments to the Indian Civil Service – the second string to Chairman George's bow – held out the prospect of salaries equal to the stipends of the most senior ecclesiastics. The governor of a major province (on £6,000 a year plus a government house) was on a par with a bishop (£4,000 a year plus a palace); while commissioners and deputy commissioners earned salaries similar to the stipends of deans and canons (£2,600/£1,200 compared with £2,000/£1,000). These superficial similarities conceal dramatic differences in an individual's chances of reaching these high offices. Every Indian civilian got to be the head of a district, and many – perhaps most – got to be commissioners. The vast majority of the clergy never rose out of the ruck of humble parish priests, and the average living was worth about £180 a year: the pay on which a twenty-year-old civilian started out at the bottom of the lowest salary scale, and less than a fifth of his pension after twenty-five years service. Earnings in medicine and the law are more difficult to calculate, but George Darling and William Pearson both lived in London town-houses in some style, sent their sons to Oxbridge colleges and left small fortunes when they died. They could hardly have done as much on less than £1,000 a year, and Dr Darling's income was almost certainly much higher. The bequests in his will came to over £20,000: enough capital to generate an income of £1,000 a year from investments alone. Sir Henry Holland, the father of one of Dean Lyall's clients-by-marriage, deliberately restricted his income from his practice to £5,000 a year, so as to have time to travel – and still left 'under £140,000' when he died.[3]

The other disadvantage of Dean Lyall's patronage was its uncertainty. A Chairman of the East India Company knew, within limits, how many nominations at Haileybury or Addiscombe would fall to his lot; and his nominees stepped straight into a world of incremental scales and promotion by seniority. Ill-health and inflation could play havoc with the most careful calculations; accelerated promotion and deflation could lead to the overfulfilment of the most optimistic expectations; but the terms on which a civilian served were perfectly clear-cut and the mean returns were generally known. Clerical careers founded on the favours of a single patron were a very different matter. There was a crucial gap between the decision to take holy orders and a client's installation in some terminal benefice: a benefice rich enough to last him for life. It was rarely less than five years; it could easily be fifteen; and it was essential that it should be crossed before the flow of patronage was staunched. The right livings – livings amenable to Lyall's influence – had to fall vacant at the right time; rival candidates and their backers had to be fought off; above all, Lyall's special relationship with Archbishop Howley had to last the course. The septuagenarian archbishop was visibly failing from 1845 on, and the dean's health became a poor risk in 1852, when he suffered the first of a series of paralysing strokes. His death in 1857 left half his clients stuck in the difficult transitional phase, and at least two of them failed to commend themselves to alternative benefactors. The Pearson brothers stagnated in pathetically poor livings (worth about £60 a year) until William died and George opted for premature retirement.

Table 3
Preferments Obtained by Members of the Lyall Connection
(*Lifetime averages and totals are italicised*)

Dates	Age	Preferment	Annual	Gross	Patron
THE DEAN					
William Rowe Lyall (1788-1857)			*£1,850*	*£64,000*	
1817-24	(29-36)	Chaplain, St Thomas's Hospital	£100 E	£700	
1817-24	(29-36)	Assistant Preacher, Lincoln's Inn	£100 E	£700	Benchers
1822-24	(34-36)	Examining Chaplain	£100 E	£200	BL
1823-33	(35-45)	Weeley, Essex	£600	£6,000	Brasenose
1826	(39)	Warburton Lecturer, Gray's Inn	£300 E	£300	Benchers
1827-33	(39-45)	Fairstead, Essex	£540	£3,240	BL
1833-42	(45-54)	Hadleigh, Suffolk	£1,453	£12,105	ABC
1842-52	(54-64)	Great Chart, Kent	£675	£6,750	ABC
1842-52	(54-64)	Prebend of Canterbury	£1,000 E	£10,000	ABC
1845-57	(57-69)	Dean of Canterbury	£2,000	£24,000	Peel
THE DEAN'S BROTHER					
Alfred Lyall (1795-1865)			*£415*	*£10,800*	
1839-45	(44-50)	Godmersham, Kent	£305	£1,830	ABC
1845-65	(50-70)	Harbledown, Kent	£450	£9,000	ABC
THE DEAN'S NEPHEWS					
William Hearle Lyall (1826-1900)			*£445*	*£21,000*[4]	
1853-77	(27-51)	St Dionis', City of London	£491	£11,784	DCC
1877-1900	(51-74)	Pension	£400	£9,200	
Thomas Darling (1816-93)			*£225*	*£11,500*	
1844-48	(28-32)	Thanington, Kent	£61	£244	ABC
1848-93	(32-77)	St Michael's, City of London	£248	£11,160	DCC

Dates	Age	Preferment	Annual	Gross	Patron
George Pearson (1814-94)			*£37*	*£1,900*	
1842-44	(28-30)	Thanington, Kent	£61	£122	ABC
1844-47	(30-33)	St Margaret's, Canterbury	£60	£180	ABC
1848-52	(34-38)	Sub-Warden, St Augustine's	£100 E	£400	ABC
1852-61	(38-47)	St Gregory's, Canterbury	£50	£450	ABC
1867-74	(53-60)	Preacher, Canterbury Cathedral	£100 E	£700	ABC
William Pearson (1816-67)			*£90*	*£1,600*	
1848-62	(34-46)	Thanington, Kent	£61	£854	ABC
1862-66	(46-50)	Granborough, Warwickshire	£178	£712	Mrs Halse[3]

THE DEAN'S NEPHEWS-IN-LAW

Dates	Age	Preferment	Annual	Gross	Patron
Henry Carrington (1814-1906)			*£1,000*	*£64,100*	
1842-45	(28-31)	Monks Eleigh, Suffolk	£590	£1,770	ABC
1845-1906	(31-92)	Braintree, Essex	£1,107/£880	£62,300	ABC
Robert Peter (1818-1910)			*£505*	*£29,800* [4]	
1851-58	(33-40)	St George's, Canterbury	£156	£1,092	DCC
1860-95	(42-77)	Cavendish, Suffolk	£900/£670	£28,740	Jesus
Francis Holland (1828-1907)			*£540*	*£29,100*	
1853-61	(25-33)	St Dunstan's, Canterbury	£180	£1,140	ABC
1859-82	(31-54)	Preacher, Canterbury Cathedral	£100 E	£2,300	ABC
1861-83	(33-55)	Quebec Chapel, Marylebone	£500	£11,000	Trustees
1883-1907	(55-79)	Canon of Canterbury	£1,000/£600	£14,400	Gladstone

GRAND TOTAL   £233,000

ABBREVIATIONS
ABC   Archbishop of Canterbury
BL   Bishop of London
DCC   Dean and Chapter of Canterbury
E   Estimated
Jesus   Jesus College, Cambridge

[1] *Valuations:* Valuations are taken from *Crockford's*, which means that they suffer from at least three defects. *Crockford's* only contains valuations for regular livings. The value of 'fancy' items of preferment (such as chaplaincies and preacherships) has had to be estimated and the estimates are often only rough guesses. Fortunately, these exceptional preferments only represent a tiny fraction of the connection's aggregate income, so the discrepancies are not particularly important. The divergences between the nominal valuations in *Crockford's* and the sums which the members of the connection actually received are much more serious. Sometimes *Crockford's* gives the gross value of a living; sometimes it gives the net value (allowing for the non-payment of tithes, the payment of local taxes, etc.); sometimes it gives a figure without saying whether it is meant to represent the gross or the net income. For the sake of consistency, I have used gross figures wherever I could obtain them, because net values are only available in a minority of cases. This inflates the value of the patronage which the Lyall connection obtained. It is difficult to work out the degree of exaggeration: it could easily be as high as a third. Fluctuations in the value of benefices over time are another serious source of error. The incomes of incumbents dependent on tithes and glebes fell with the onset of the agricultural depression, and the valuations in *Crockford's* lagged behind the decline in agricultural prices. The majority of the members of the connection escaped the worst effects of the depression because they vacated their benefices in time or held urban livings; but the dean's nephews-in-law, who held preferments heavily dependent on tithes and rents, all survived into the twentieth century. I have therefore used valuations taken from the first edition of *Crockford's* in which they occur, except in the case of the three longest-lived members of the connection: Henry Carrington (d. 1906); Francis Holland (d. 1907); and Robert Peter (d. 1910). In those three instances rough downward adjustments have been made to allow for some fairly drastic reductions in income. Given the defects of the data, more sophisticated corrections would involve too much labour for too small a gain in accuracy.

[2] *Longevity:* If Lyall had lived as long as his clients, he would have done much better, financially speaking. Only one member of the connection was younger when he died: William Pearson. Pearson was a mere stripling of fifty when he was called to meet his maker, and he made a paltry £1,600 out of the church. Henry Carrington's £64,100 illustrates the importance of getting hold of a good living young and clinging to it till the very end of an exceptionally long life. Carrington's living at Braintree was the richest the Lyall connection ever annexed, and he died in office at the age of ninety-two. If one excludes William Pearson, the average age at death of Lyall's clients was just over eighty.

[3] *Exchanges:* Weeley (a living belonging to Brasenose College) and Granborough (a living in the gift of a Mrs Halse) were exchanged for benefices controlled by Howley.

[4] *Pensions:* W.H. Lyall was given a pension of £400 p.a. when his church was closed and the site sold for redevelopment. I assume that he went on drawing it until he died, but he may have relinquished or forfeited it when he became a Roman Catholic. The date of his conversion is unknown. Robert Peter may have retained some lien on the living at Cavendish after he resigned, fifteen years before his death.

Table 4
Types of Preferment Obtained by Members of the Lyall Connection

	Annual Value	Population	Patron	Dates Held
Poor Parishes in Canterbury				
St Gregory the Great: George Pearson	£50	1,280	ABC	1852-61
St Nicholas', Thanington:[1] George Pearson, Thomas Darling and William Pearson	£61	380	ABC	1842-62
St Margaret's: George Pearson	£60	700	ABC	1844-47
St George the Martyr: Robert Peter	£156	1,600	DCC	1851-58
St Dunstan's: Francis Holland	£182	1,300	ABC	1853-61
A Poor Country Living				
Granborough, Warwicks:[2] William Pearson	£178	460	Mrs Halse	1862-66
London Churches				
St Michael's Paternoster Royal: Thomas Darling	£248	370	DCC	1848-93
St Dionis' Backchurch: William Hearle Lyall	£468	530	DCC	1855-77
Quebec Chapel, Marylebone: Francis Holland	£500		Trustees	1861-83
Good Country Livings				
Godmersham, Kent: Alfred Lyall	£305	950	ABC	1839-45
Harbledown, Kent: Alfred Lyall	£450	640	ABC	1845-65
Fairstead, Essex: William Lyall	£540	350	BL	1827-33
Monks Eleigh, Suffolk: Henry Carrington	£590	720	ABC	1842-45
Weeley, Essex:[3] William Lyall	£600	630	Brasenose	1823-33
Great Chart, Kent: William Lyall	£675	750	ABC	1842-52

	Annual Value	Population	Patron	Dates Held
The Plums				
Cavendish, Suffolk: Robert Peter	£900/£672	1,300	Jesus	1860-96
Braintree, Essex: Henry Carrington	£1,407/£880	3,850	ABC	1845-1906
Hadleigh, Suffolk: William Lyall	£1,345	3,700	ABC	1833-42
Prebend of Canterbury: William Lyall	£1,000 E		ABC	1842-52
Canon of Canterbury: Francis Holland	£1,000/£600		Gladstone	1883-1907
Dean of Canterbury: William Lyall	£2,000		Peel	1845-57
Chaplaincies, Preacherships				
Chaplain, St Thomas's Hospital: William Lyall	£100 E		Governors	1817-24
Assistant Preacher, Lincoln's Inn: William Lyall	£100 E		Benchers	1817-24
Examining Chaplain: William Lyall	£100 E		BL	1822-24
Warburton Lecturer, Gray's Inn: William Lyall	£100 E		Benchers	1826
Preacher, Canterbury Cathedral: Francis Holland; George Pearson	£100 E		ABC	1859-83; 1867-74
Sub-Warden, St Augustine's College: George Pearson	£100 E		ABC	1846-52

ABBREVIATIONS
ABC   Archbishop of Canterbury
BL   Bishop of London
DCC   Dean and Chapter of Canterbury
E   Estimated
Jesus   Jesus College, Cambridge

NOTES
[1] Thanington was the first hamlet out of Canterbury on the Ashford Road.
[2] An exchange. The ABC presented the incumbent of Granborough to Pearson's old living at Thanington, making the stipend up to the same level as Granborough.
[3] Another exchange. The BL regularly exchanged livings with Brasenose.

Dean Lyall made the best of the little he had to offer by taking all the embarrassment out of supplication. Instead of waiting for his younger relatives to come to him to ask for favours, he took the initiative and approached them. His youngest brother was his first recruit. 'With his love of foreign travel and desultory reading', he would 'have spent his life rather aimlessly, but for the urgent representations of [the future dean]'. The future dean also cajoled his nephews. He invited Thomas Darling to stay at the parsonage at Hadleigh before he went up to St John's. He explained his views on the religious problems of the age – the views of one of the Church of England's more prescient statesmen; he showed Darling how an energetic incumbent could revive the spiritual life of a market town overrun by dissenters; he gave him the free run of the library in which the Oxford Movement had been born; and he drove him over to Cambridge in his carriage to introduce him to some of the leading high churchmen in the university. Hugh Rose, the most famous theologian at Cambridge, monitored Darling's progress and reported back to the dean:

> I saw [Mr Rose] in the Senate House. He spoke very well of you in all the most important points, except one – and that was that you were taking matters much too easy. You were not reading with *vigour and energy*. Now, my dear Tom, this is the whole matter – one hour of *rigorous application – of active and unremitting attention*, is more value than three, aye, or six hours of such reading as is sometimes called study.[4]

Darling was just nineteen at the time – a pious and impressionable youth. He must have felt that he was at the centre of the one thing that really mattered: the defence of the one true church against its enemies. Even nephews who refused the dean's offers of preferment felt the emotional tug of his affection. Long after Sir Alfred Lyall went out to India, he remembered how, of all the farewells that took place, his parting from his uncle was the only one that reduced him to tears: 'I walked home through the cathedral yard in the dark, sobbing and crying [and unable to] leave off. My poor uncle's memory always brings tears into my eyes.' The feeling was reciprocated: the dean's clients were the children he never had.[5]

Lyall's recruitment campaign stressed the non-economic advantages of a clerical career – the assured status and the rewarding vocation – because he knew that his nephews could afford to discount income against social acceptance and job satisfaction. They all stood to inherit enough money to support a reasonably genteel lifestyle, whatever livings they acquired. The status of the clergy, judging by the Lyalls' correspondence, was largely a function of their security of tenure. The dean's clients appreciated the independence and the leisure conferred by the parson's freehold. They knew that subordination robbed the ruling class of its superiority, and they wanted time to pursue their intellectual interests. William and Alfred Lyall grew into heavy-weight theologians in their rural fastnesses; Thomas Darling wrote hymns on extended tours round the continent; Henry Carrington spent his winters in the Mediterranean; George Pearson became an omnivorous reader. 'Easy' livings and cheap curates were the obvious solution. None of the members of the connection was ever presented to a bloated slum parish, with a population running into tens of thousands, all suffering from acute spiritual destitution. A representative client ministered to about 800 parishioners uncorrupted by dissent. Only Lyall at Hadleigh and Carrington at Bocking had parishes which were at all difficult to work.[5]

Job satisfaction was largely a matter of fitting round pegs into round holes. All Lyall's clients had in common was their relationship to the dean. If the church was to make use of their talents, some form of selection was necessary; and Lyall did his best to provide it. He insisted on putting his protégés through a probationary period. First they served as curates in his own or his brother's parish; then he presented them to apprentice livings: livings with such low stipends and such low populations that only curates desperate for an independent charge could be persuaded to serve them. This probationary period had two functions. It constituted a kind of professional training – all the professional training a mid-Victorian clergyman was likely to get; and it gave Lyall a chance to sum up his protégés' strengths and weaknesses, before matching them against the appointments available. Carrington was his curate while he turned Hadleigh round; it is possible that Archbishop Howley sent his nephew to be trained by Lyall before presenting him to a particularly rich and difficult living. George Pearson and Thomas Darling acted as Lyall's curates at Great Chart; they held the fort for him while he was away on business connected with his archdeaconry or his prebend. The next stage – the apprentice parish – gave young priests a chance to learn-by-doing. They could acquire experience in an underpopulated living without making disastrous mistakes. Lyall's favourite proving-ground was the cluster of poor parishes in and around Canterbury, controlled by the archbishop or the dean and chapter. At one point or another all his clients bar two held poor livings in Canterbury; and three of them served as perpetual curates of Thanington – a living worth £61 a year a mile or two outside the city, which virtually became an hereditary possession.[6]

Lyall's terminal appointments – appointments to livings which were good enough to last a man until he died – were based on his clients' performance as probationers. Smooth men were steered towards fashionable congregations; prolific patriarchs got fat rectories rich enough to support their expanding broods; townsmen were dispatched to urban parishes; scholars and invalids were installed in light charges which gave them time to study or convalesce. Francis Holland – the son of the most celebrated physician in London: a baronet with an income to match – spent twenty years ministering to the Top Ten Thousand in a proprietary chapel on the fringe of Mayfair. Alfred Lyall, with five sons and four daughters, needed every penny of his £450 stipend and every bedroom in his sprawling parsonage at Harbledown. Thomas Darling (the son of a doctor who treated London business men) and William Hearle Lyall (the son of a Chairman of the East India Company) were both presented to livings in the City of London. George and William Pearson stuck in pauper parishes in Canterbury because George was a scholarly recluse and William was in the grip of a fatal disease. Of course there were constraints on the dean's ability to fit round pegs into round holes; everything operated on too small a scale. A tiny pool of prospective incumbents (who were only available for presentation during a particular phase of their life-cycle) had to be matched against a tiny pool of benefices (which only became available at irregular intervals). The need to provide for a particularly clamorous client from the limited range of livings falling vacant in the early 1840s led to the connection's most maladroit appointment: Howley's presentation of his nephew to Bocking.[7]

Lyall's clients were conscious of the drawbacks of the alternative occupations which they might have taken up. They accepted – as a kind of basic fact – that businessmen and doctors and lawyers ranked below clergymen in the social scale. Businessmen were in trade; and even if they were in trade on a massive scale, large profits were no compensation for a lifetime tied to an office stool. Doctors were associated in their minds with artisans and shopkeepers – with barber-surgeons (who cut open diseased bodies) and apothecaries (who dispensed the drugs they prescribed: an obvious conflict of interests). The man of law, in the early nineteenth century, was only one step removed from the crooked attorney who betrayed his clients' trust instead of protecting his clients' interests. Underlying these unfavourable stereotypes, there was the brute fact of competition. Businessmen, doctors and lawyers all existed in a free market for their services; and free trade compromised their gentility. As self-employed pieceworkers, they could only maximise their incomes by sacrificing their independence and their leisure. They had to cultivate their customers, and they had to work very hard at cultivating them.[8]

Hungry men – first generation arrivistes with their ways to make in the world – had enough motivation to develop the skills which made for survival in these market-places, but their better-endowed sons shrank from the rat-race. George Lyall I, the dean's eldest brother, succeeded in building up a business empire and set the seal on his career by becoming MP for the City of London and Chairman of the East India Company. But as soon as his branch of the family started sending their sons to Eton and Wellington, the Lyalls' entrepreneurial flair withered on the bough. Before the advent of limited liability and bureaucratic management, a single severe depression or a single incompetent heir could dissipate the patient accumulations of a lifetime in a matter of weeks. It was altogether safer, as well as less effort, to become passive rentiers: part-time army officers with a taste for field sports and magistracies; nothing too demanding. George Darling, the dean's brother-in-law, was another first-generation workaholic. His father, like John Lyall's, was a small farmer on the wrong side of the Scottish border. Dissatisfied with his prospects in the Gala Valley, he worked his way out of the southern highlands via the Edinburgh medical school. The moment he qualified, he set sail for India as a ship's doctor. After two or three voyages round the Cape, he had enough saved to set up a practice in Brunswick Square. Within five years he was earning two or three times the average Anglican stipend. The development of Bloomsbury – the squares and terraces were just rising from the ground as he moved into the area – brought thousands of prospective patients to his door, and he took a puritanical pride in working fourteen hours a day. He responded to emergencies, whenever they occurred; he regularly cancelled his holidays if his favourite invalids begged him to stay; he treated local clergymen free in the hope that they would recommend him to their congregations; he worked up a useful little corner in famous artists, from the indigent and suicidal Hayden to the affluent and complacent Chantrey; he even published a treatise on the reform of the medical profession (on Benthamite lines) which made his name as a radical and earned him his place in the *Dictionary of National Biography*. His dreamy Oxbridge-educated sons were made of softer stuff. The eldest spent his summers wandering round the Continent, comparing cathedrals, composing wishy-washy hymns and communing with nature in a sub-Wordsworthian vein. The younger son, a briefless barrister, 'wanted occupation' and filled the void by writing elegant little pamphlets on what the Bible said about esoteric legal points. William Pearson, the dean's remaining brother-in-law, spent his whole life looking after other people's affairs. His sons, educated in the same way as Darling's, were barely capable of looking after themselves. The eldest, George, was so indolent that he resigned his last living in his forties, rather than face his female parishioners; and so absent-minded that he regularly forgot invitations to dinner. The younger boy, always known as 'poor William', seems to have suffered from ill-health and died in early middle age.[9]

The Indian services were more genteel than medicine or law. Civilians and army officers might be men under discipline, but the fact remained that they were rulers and warriors. In both roles, they exercised authority over their social inferiors, and the exercise of authority was the most conspicuous characteristic of the gentleman. By definition he was a natural leader of men. Writers and cadets were also shielded from the degrading effects of competition by security of tenure. It was almost as difficult to dismiss a civilian or cashier an officer as it was to deprive an incumbent of his living. Only persistent insubordination or flagrant incompetence could justify so extreme a step. Promotion was generally determined by seniority. An outstanding writer or an outstanding cadet might clamber up the ladder of promotion a little faster than a mediocrity, but sheer longevity generally carried a man to a perfectly respectable eminence. With so many advantages, Chairman George Lyall's offers of nominations should have been more popular than they were.

The discomforts and dangers of an Indian exile were the great deterrent. Life expectancy is probably as good an index of contentment as any. Dean Lyall's clients were extraordinarily long-lived. On *average*, they died in their eighties; two of them lived on into their nineties; and one of the nonagenarians was the oldest beneficed clergyman in his county – perhaps in England – when he died. The Lyalls who went out to India before 1850 never came home, because they died in their mid thirties. John Lyall II, one of the dean's brothers, went into the Indian army; and John Edwardes Lyall, one of his nephews, became advocate-general to the Government of Bengal. They both did well; John got his regiment while he was still remarkably young and John Edwardes married the daughter of a director of the East India Company. Then they committed the unpardonable error of dying before they were in a position to distribute patronage to their relations. As a means of obtaining a permanent foothold in the establishment, their careers proved dead-ends, and their failures sank into the Lyalls' collective consciousness. Twenty years after John Edwardes died of cholera (in the governor-general's house at Barrackpore, within twenty-four hours of dining with the governor-general), Alfred Lyall told his brother James that anything was better than crumpling up with cholera one morning 'and being shovelled before evening into a nameless grave'. For some time the only nephew willing to accept one of Uncle George's nominations was the black sheep of the family, and Walter Lyall resigned his commission almost as soon as he took it up, so he could make an injudicious marriage.[10]

The last Lyalls to take advantage of their uncle's patronage made rather better use of their opportunities. Sir Alfred and Sir James Lyall – both sons of the Rev Alfred Lyall – became governors of major provinces, which was as high as any civilian could reasonably hope to go. They exercised power of a peculiarity personal kind over tens of millions of Indians; they ranked immediately below the viceroy and commander-in-chief; and they lived in a style commensurate with their responsibilities. Minor German princes, the heads of sovereign states, would have envied their palaces and their staffs. Yet the Lyall brothers still spent half their lives wondering whether they might not have done better to follow their father into the church. They were conscious of their good fortune in getting accelerated promotion, but they never knew when their luck might run out. They invested a lot of effort in pleasing powerful patrons and they succeeded in commending themselves to three successive viceroys. Lord Northbrook and Lord Lytton liked Alfred, Lord Lytton and Lord Ripon liked James. But what would happen if they fell from favour? The Lyalls were too sensitive and too impatient to defer to uncongenial superiors. At any moment friction might arise; they might take a false step. Promotion was such a gamble that Alfred stopped his eldest son going out to India 'for it is a wretched waste of life if a man does not suceed in rising out of the crowd, and my luck won't last a second generation'.

The most obvious drawback of an Indian career, after the uncertainty over promotion, was the climate. If the Lyalls stayed in the red-hot plains, the wind burnt the skin off their faces; if they fled to a hill station, the 'ceaseless drumming of rain on the wooden roof' lowered their spirits. Debilitating illnesses made the extremes of temperature and humidity all the harder to bear. When his mother sent him a particularly rose-tinted description of tea in the rectory garden at hay-making time, Sir Alfred remembered the perfect health he enjoyed as a child and broke down:

> Just fancy the contrast; I was lying with a swelled and aching face in my bed in a little stifling room, with a native doctor putting on leeches . . . and now it must be about midnight, and I am sitting up because I cannot get a wink of sleep.[11]

Then there were the psychological trials: the loneliness and boredom of the isolated outposts; the inevitable disappointments over postings and promotions; the constant sniping at English officials in the vernacular press; the financial pressures – the need to keep up appearances conflicting with the need to save against retirement; the prospect of being 'put on the shelf' at fifty-five; the low status of the Anglo-Indian pensioners who congregated at Cheltenham or Bath. Was it all worth it? On balance, Sir Alfred thought not:

> I am sorry that John Lee is coming out here as a cadet. I would not be an officer in the Indian Army if I had the slightest chance of subsistence in England. Wretched pay, nothing to do, and no prospect of a retiring competence except after forty years' service.[12]

When they dreamed of alternative careers, the Lyalls-in-exile dreamed of the church. They remembered the parsonages and the cathedral closes of their childhood, the beauty of the Kent countryside and the historic precincts at Canterbury. Sir James told his sister, after reading the memoirs of a country clergyman, that he often thought

> a parson's life would have suited me well, or perhaps would suit me now that I have seen the folly of some others' aspirations – most of us have a considerable insight into other people's character and a liberal way of judging them, which I take to be one grand qualification for the [life] of a clergyman.[13]

Sir Alfred's ideal was a canonry: a canonry would have given him time to write, and it would have brought him into contact with other intellectuals. Besides which, 'a canonry lasts for life'.[14]

Clients by Marriage

The three clergymen who became Dean Lyall's clients by marrying his nieces had one characteristic in common. None of them had any contact with the Lyalls before they took up their first curacies, but they found their way to their social equals with unerring accuracy. Their families (the Peters, the Carringtons and the Hollands) belonged to the same stratum of English society as the Lyalls: the upper middle-class melting-pot, in which income from investments supplemented incomes from the learned professions and the occasional family firm. At this happy level, men were highly eligible propositions; they had a wide choice of prospective wives and could afford to marry for love. But their actual choices were constrained by common prudence and a clear-cut moral obligation. Marrying the nieces of a childless dean not only improved their chances of preferment; it repaid their parents' investment in their upbringing. They owed it to their relations to use their marriages to extend their connection.

Lyall's clients by marriage knew what was required of them, because 'sensible' marriages ran in their families. All their fathers married well. Sir Codrington Carrington went out to India to try to recoup his family's failing fortunes: multiple inheritance was subdividing their plantations in Barbados. He had no influence with any of the directors of the East India Company, so he had no chance of an official appointment. He simply set up in practice as a freelance advocate in Calcutta. After seven years his health broke down and he was forced to come home. It could easily have been the end of his legal career. Fortunately for Carrington, he had taken out an extremely effective insurance policy by marrying the daughter of Warren Hastings' private secretary. In 1800, at the age of thirty-one, he was appointed chief justice of the newly-conquered colony of Ceylon. Six years later, his health broke down again; but by then it hardly mattered. His wife's dowry was so large and his salary as chief justice was so high that he was able to buy an estate in Buckinghamshire and go into parliament – he represented a pocket borough in Cornwall. Robert Peter's father put this modest achievement in the shade. William Peter acquired a small Palladian mansion, financed a brief spell as a Whig MP, and launched ten children into the world, all on the strength of his marriage to the heiress of the Chyverton estate. Francis Holland's father, Sir Henry Holland, would probably have become the most fashionable physician in London if he had never married Saba Smith: he was socially acceptable and he had a wonderfully reassuring bedside manner. But his marriage, *en secondes noces*, to one of Sydney Smith's daughters, consolidated his special relationship with the Whig grandees; and it was the patronage of the Whig grandees – rather than the patronage of Victoria and Albert – which gave his practice its aristocratic cachet. His eldest son actually became a grandee by marriage. Henry Holland II married, in turn, the heiress of a Hertfordshire landowner and a niece of Lord Macaulay. His seat in the cabinet (1885-92) and his viscountcy were the natural culmination of two generations of carefully-calculated alliances.[15]

The Lyalls' attitude to marriage was no different from the attitude of the families they married into. The children of John Lyall, the shipowner from Berwickshire, spread their risks in the approved arriviste way. The eldest son, the Chairman of the East India Company, carried off a City heiress; the second son, Dean Lyall, married into a medical dynasty – a dynasty so affluent that they were rapidly metamorphosing into landed gentry; the youngest son married a member of the most famous family of piano-makers in England: piano makers with a country seat.[16] The daughters allied themselves to a Scots doctor and an English lawyer, as soon as George Darling and William Pearson showed signs of reaching the upper ranks of their professions. The next generation did even better. The dean's nephews and nieces married, inter alia, the sons, daughters or sisters of five baronets, four members of parliament, three knights, two cabinet ministers and a viscount. If they proved at all reluctant to do their duty, pressure was brought to bear on them. Sir Alfred Lyall started worrying about his sister Barbara's prospects when she was in her early twenties:

> Is there any prospect of Barbara becoming settled in life? I have an uneasy fear she will be too long about it, and I particularly like to see my sisters married – it extends connection.[17]

When Barbara finally settled down with an exceptionally eligible catch, after twenty years of travelling and socialising, her married sisters were aggrieved at her reaping the rewards of child-bearing and child-rearing without any of the travail:

> She is serenely content with her lot, and I really think that she has done very well with her life. After much variety, amusement, travel and freedom, she finds herself exactly where other fortunate women of her own age are. I like Mr Webb. He has all the ease of a perfectly unpretending gentleman born in fairly good circumstances. [I also like his] house and grounds . . . Everything very comfortable, and exactly what one expects. Lofty rooms, large high windows, thick walls, polished doors shutting off passages and staircases, an excellent temperature and solid, quiet, ancestral portraits. A great yew hedge and long sunny walls enclosing a garden full of fruit and flowers; plenty of books, new and old. Witley steeple and Black Down visible, so that you know where . . . you are.[18]

It would be interesting to know how Lyall's clients-by-marriage first met his nieces. Education was one link. Eight of the nine members of the connection went to just two schools: four to Charterhouse and four to Eton. Henry Carrington was at Charterhouse with three of the dean's nephews. Judging by their dates of birth, he was sandwiched between George Pearson (who was a few months older) and William Pearson and Thomas Darling (who were two years younger). Francis Holland was at Eton at the same time as another of the dean's nephews, William Hearle Lyall. They must have known one another, even if they were in different houses.[19] Curacies were another point of contact. Henry Carrington was the son of Mrs Howley's sister, as well as an old Carthusian; but he would hardly have had the opportunity to woo and win Juanita Lyall without becoming her uncle's curate at Hadleigh. Robert Peter's first curacy was in Canterbury. He must have moved in the same social circles as Catherine Lyall; he may even have courted her at the deanery. Francis

Holland's first living was a suburb of Canterbury; his future father-in-law's rectory was just a few minutes' drive away. Propinquity seems to have been a precondition of marriage; there were no long-distance courtships.[20]

The wisdom of recruiting husbands with alternative patrons of their own became apparent after Dean Lyall's death. All his clients by birth – his brother and his three nephews – were stranded in the limbo reserved for clergymen who lose their only backer. Not one of them secured a valuable piece of preferment after 1857. If anything, a process of attrition set in. George Pearson resigned his living in 1861 and William Hearle Lyall lost his church in the City when it was demolished in 1877. Only the nephews-in-law went from strength to strength. Peter fell back on his old college. His performance in the classics tripos of 1842 was sufficiently impressive (he got the fourth highest marks in the university) to justify Jesus taking him back as a tutor. After two years as a 'fellow-in-waiting', he moved to the richest college living, Cavendish in Suffolk. Holland got out of his pauper parish by mobilising his father's patients. The trustees of a private proprietary chapel on the edge of Mayfair gave him a chance to display his talents as a preacher in front of exceptionally fashionable congregations – congregations which included a Dean of Windsor and at least one Prime Minister. Queen Victoria had him preach in St George's Chapel on the dean's recommendation, and subsequently made him a chaplain-in-ordinary; Mr Gladstone made him a a canon of Canterbury.

58

PROPÆDIA PROPHETICA.

A

VIEW OF THE USE AND DESIGN

OF THE

OLD TESTAMENT:

FOLLOWED BY

TWO DISSERTATIONS,

I. ON THE CAUSES OF THE RAPID PROPAGATION OF THE GOSPEL AMONG
THE HEATHEN.

II. ON THE CREDIBILITY OF THE FACTS RELATED IN THE
NEW TESTAMENT.

BY

WILLIAM ROWE LYALL, M.A.

ARCHDEACON OF COLCHESTER;
CO-DEAN OF BOCKING; AND RECTOR OF HADLEIGH, SUFFOLK.

LONDON:

PRINTED FOR J. G. F. & J. RIVINGTON,
ST. PAUL'S CHURCH YARD,
AND WATERLOO PLACE, PALL MALL.

1840.

Dean Lyall's most ambitious work, *Propaedia Prophetica* (1840; 2nd edn. 1854; 3rd edn. 1885), which attempted to prove the existence of God by an appeal to Jewish prophecy. Written with great learning within a conservative theological tradition, it was made to look increasingly old-fashioned by the new school of biblical critics. (*Cambridge University Library*)

Chapter 5

Canterbury

You know – many of you – how constantly through [his] last year, daily, at evening prayer, the wheels of his chair, gliding noiselessly in, placed him where he might join in the Service . . . How great a solace [he] found in the services of God's sanctuary, to the very time when his last seizure confined him to his chamber . . . What an interest he took in the sacred fabric which was committed to his keeping; how he promoted the carrying on of its restoration from year to year, and all that tended to its ornament and beauty.

Archdeacon Benjamin Harrison, *Charity Never Failing. A Sermon Preached in Canterbury Cathedral on . . . [the] Occasion of the Death of the Very Reverend William Rowe Lyall, D.D., Dean of Canterbury* (1857)

The livings occupied by members of the Lyall connection were not scattered at random all over England. They were restricted to a fan-shaped wedge stretching out from the City of London (in the west) to Bury St Edmunds (in the north-east) and Canterbury (in the south-east). The obvious reason for this concentration was the location of Howley's patronage. The livings he controlled as Bishop of London were situated in his see, which included Essex. As Archbishop of Canterbury, the great majority of his two hundred advowsons were found in Kent; and the benefices in the gift of the dean and chapter followed the same pattern, on a much smaller scale. But the location of the patronage attached to these offices only gets one so far. It explains the restriction of Lyall's clients to London and the south-east: it is insufficient to explain the clustering of Lyall livings *within* the golden triangle. The extreme concentration of clients in and around Canterbury is clear evidence of design. Between Lyall's appointment as a prebend (in 1842) and the diaspora following his death in 1857, six of his dependents occupied livings in Canterbury and the immediately adjacent villages; and if one includes villages within a radius of a few miles, the number rises to seven. In effect, a clear majority of the connection ended up in parishes within sight of his deanery. They started out in the poor livings in the old city and its immediate environs; they progressed to rather better livings, sometimes in the villages around; and in three cases they penetrated the *sanctum sanctorum* of the cathedral itself. All told, they obtained seventeen pieces of preferment in the Canterbury area: four presentations to urban livings; eight presentations to rural livings; the post of sub-warden at St Augustine's college; two preacherships at the cathedral; two stalls in the chapter; and the greatest prize of all, the deanery. For sixty-five years – from 1842 to 1907 – members of the connection were continuously resident in Canterbury, and with a short gap they were continuously resident in the precincts. Lay Lyalls also felt the city's magnetic pull. At least three members of the Indian Civil Service – two of the dean's nephews and the husband of one of his nieces – spent their leaves and part of their retirement in Canterbury, often in houses in the precincts rented from their clerical relations.[1]

This concentration of the members of a connection in a small area enhanced the normal advantages of a clerical career. In an age of supportive kinship groups and feeble communications, living within easy reach of one's relations had definite advantages. Family members were sympathetic intimates, family friends leavened the lump of kinship, family events were the regularly returning high-spots of the social calendar. Given a choice of parishes, Lyall's relations always took the proximity of their kinsmen into account, and once they succeeded in building up a satisfactory social circle, they were loathe to leave it. Dean Lyall was the only really mobile member of his connection. He moved wherever his career took him – six times between his ordination and his death. His clients tended to move, if they moved at all, towards established bridgeheads. Canterbury was one such bridgehead; London was another. There were as many Lyalls in Middlesex as there were in Kent, but they were dispersed over a wider area and a wider range of occupations. In Canterbury the connection constituted a tightly-knit group. All the members lived within sight of the cathedral, and all the male members belonged to the same locally-dominant profession.[2]

Canterbury's spiritual amenities were another consolation for low stipends. Conservative clergymen were bound to find cathedral cities sympathetic. They were sanctuaries against the rationalism of the secular intelligentsia and the revivalism of the masses. It is difficult to appreciate the power of religious rapture in a profoundly materialist age, but no one can understand the role of Christianity in Victorian society without invoking the evangelical's experience of conversion or the ritualist's delight in mysticism. A holy city – a city sanctified by its historic associations and its historical buildings – sustained religious exaltation through the dull commonplaces of everyday life better than any other ambience. The seat of St Augustine and the shrine of Thomas à Becket pullulated with the kind of religious activity and the kind of religious symbolism which sent Victorian priests into spiritual ecstasies. The city washed away the doubts of men who might otherwise have been tempted to subscribe for Colenso. At the same time, it provided a dignified alternative to the subjective excesses of popular fanaticism. In the 1840s and the 1850s, when Dean Lyall was in his heyday, Canterbury was a bastion of the old high churchmen. The clergy who set the tone of the precincts were high and dry when they arrived, or the cathedral soon dried them out.[3]

As long as the Archbishops of Canterbury lived at Lambeth and Addington, Lyall's deanery occupied the commanding heights of the local clerical pyramid; and his relatives rubbed shoulders with a stream of celebrities making pilgrimages to the cradle of Christianity in southern England. Incumbents from the city centre parishes and the surrounding villages met bishops and cabinet ministers at his little soirées. Lyall's pre-eminence also gave his clients access to the county set. At his dinner parties, his nephews sat next to jewel-encrusted dowagers. Sometimes he summoned his dependents to make up the numbers at a ball at the assembly-rooms. Sadly, all the clergymen in the connection were too few to save a dance from disaster when the brutal and licentious soldiery failed to turn up:

> The Ball on Wednesday was the completest of failures – No Military save one solitary individual from Dover lately quartered here – No Stewards – one of them being in bed and the other not showing himself – almost twenty ladies and seven gentlemen.[4]

In summer the flow of visits was reversed: instead of country cousins flocking into Canterbury, clients with urban livings started driving out of town to visit the rural rectories. If they were too busy to go themselves, their wives took the children on idyllic excursions:

> The garden at Harbledown is beginning to look pretty with crocuses and daffodils, and the beds under the window are blue and white with the sweet violets. Barbara and I sat there on Thursday morning, and were almost too hot in the sun. Your little ones played about so happily with their spades, carts, and wheelbarrow and made a little dirt garden in the bushes, into which they

stuck crocuses . . . We went up to Miss Webb's wood, where we sat on the
sunny bank, while the five children played with the little streams of water. The
children, the lambs, the water, the flowers and the chorus of birds, filled the
picture with pleasant, dreamy, sights and sounds . . . Agnes looked so pretty as
she came down the road on the donkey, her brown curls blown about, and her
little straw hat pushed back from her flushed face and ornamented with a great
bunch of ferns and celandines. Bernard and Mary ran by the side and behind
whipping Jenny with long Palm-branches . . . The carriage took down my
three monkeys who went off singing a hymn at the utmost pitch of their loud
voices, and to the most extraordary tune, the proud Tomlin [their nurse]
smiling with pleasure at this public exhibition of their learning and piety.
We are in the midst of the most perfect September. The banks of the lanes are
gay with mountain ash, and . . . all the children of England are out
blackberrying, and the plump-faced babes with well-smeared faces look
suddenly out from the bushes as one drives past, [their] baskets and satchels
lying at the side of the road.[5]

In later life, the rural rectories came to seem a land of lost content:

I was at Godmersham and walked in the Temple Woods – which brought back
in an instant you and your brothers and sisters and a thousand by-gone scenes.
There were the soft mossy banks – there were the primroses and violets and the
birds. But it seemed [like] a city of the dead, so completely had the past
vanished. I remembered where I had sat and talked with your aunt Darling –
with Margaret Lyall – with my own brother. The Gales had just left (poor Mr
Gale died about Christmas) and the vicarage looked sadly desolate with all the
untidy remains of packing materials lying about. We crossed the garden and
out by the meadow and across the bridge – I seemed to see you all young again
and could remember your figures and voices – and dear little Arthur's call to
his father from the Attick window![6]

You cannot think how lovely the valley was, especially the turn of it after you
pass Chilham. The light lay like silver over the sloping woods, and the river
ran brimming through rich meadows and blooming orchards. The present
vicar, Mr Wilkinson, is a quiet, simple, self-contained bachelor. He longed for
Godmersham for twenty-five years, while he was a curate at Petham, and got
it at last; now he says he is the happiest man in Kent. The churchyard looked
lovely, and the little graves are beautifully kept. The place is solitary. Mr
Wilkinson says that no one comes by for weeks and sometimes for months
together.[7]

The staple form of social intercourse at the level of the ordinary
incumbent was the dinner party. A few snippets describing family dinners
survive among the connection's letters. The changes in perspective as one
shifts from male to female commentators, or from young to old
correspondents, are an amusing commentary on the war between the

sexes and the gap between the generations. When Thomas Darling wrote his account of a dinner at Harbledown, he was still a young and impressionable bachelor. He paid close attention to the eligible belles, and they paid close attention to him:

> A seat fell to me between Miss Duncan and Mary Brandreth – the former having been violently parted from George; the latter is of a sarcastic turn, fond of seeing things from a ridiculous point of view – also like most other young ladies, partial to champagne.[8]

Forty years on, the survivors of the dinner party were confirmed bachelors or mature matrons united by their common interest in theology. This is how one of the matrons described George:

> The Recluse of St Margaret Street comes here to dine tonight – if he does not forget – to meet the Sixth Prebendary. I am looking forward to hearing the talk. I hope Cousin George will speak out plain about Church matters. I don't suppose we shall see them again after we leave the dining-room, for G.C.P. will never remember to come upstairs.[9]

In the event, Cousin George fulfilled all Cousin Sibylla's hopes:

> G.C.P. drove up on Thursday evening with a bag and stayed the night. He fenced cheerfully all the evening with Aunt Emily, betraying some surprising [knowledge], such as the exact derivation of a slang word, the genealogy of some fashionable lady [and] the position of the Jesuits with regard to the Orleanists since Egalité and their quarrel with Charles X's ministry. Everyone's information appeared so haphazard by the side of his. He took some trouble to talk well, and never said 'more or less' or 'wastepaper basket' at all.[10]

The Lyalls' social calendar reached its annual climax at Christmas, with all the resident clients moving around their separate establishments in a straggling throng, encumbered by womenfolk, children and servants. In 1847 Christmas Day revolved round dinner at the rectory at Harbledown – a positively Pickwickian gathering:

> It was as well that my mother did not execute her half-meditated intention of sending them a Turkey – for they had one with which few others could compare – it weighed twenty pounds. The pudding, as might have been expected from the absence of anything like an experienced regular cook, was a failure – all in ruins. At dessert the Punch Bowl appeared and my Aunt did concoct that insinuating beverage – handing over the remaining half bottle of rum to the party in the kitchen to be by them turned to a like account. We

suffered from the supply being a little too bountiful. As the servant attempted to effect an entrance into the Drawing Room with the tray of tea things, a crash was heard as of the smash of [fragile] crockery. Up jumped the children with my Aunt, and as the door was opened and the scene of devastation was brought to view, the former did all with one consent burst forth into a merry peal of laughter – evidently thinking that it was all a capital Xmas joke – while the latter, conscience-stricken as the recollection of the unfinished bottle of spirits did cross her mind, fell upon her knees and began picking up the pieces without uttering one word of censure or rebuke. Meanwhile the Master sat quietly in his chair at the fire, meaning doubtless to have nothing to do with the tasks of giving a rebuke – yet he heard no angry words falling from the lips of his wife, upon whom he was relying for a good round volley. When he had reason to believe that she was almost abetting the culprit by collecting together in silence the fragments that survived, he thought that muteness on his part would no longer do – but that he must boldly proceed and enter his indignant protest against the proceedings. And as he is particularly bad and inexpert in the art of scolding, he made but a sorry business of his attempts. For my part I am inclined to think that my Aunt showed the greater discretion of the two.[11]

There were some critics of the connection's Canterbury idyll. The old worried about so much frivolity; the young found the smooth tenor of clerical society dreadfully dull. When reports of his son's involvement in a giddy social whirl started filtering through to his town house in Russell Square, Dr Darling sent him one of his most censorious rebukes:

You appear to have no lack of amusements. [I rejoice that] you are happily placed and pass your time agreeably. *But what will be the result?* I cannot help regretting that you have so little to do professionally and fear that your clerical habits and character will not be benefited by living in the midst of such excitement of a purely worldly nature. You cannot be too much on your guard against their influence.[12]

The children of the connection disliked Canterbury because there was so little 'excitement of a purely worldy nature'. The teenagers were particularly fractious:

It was the having nothing to do which was at the bottom of all my vagaries at Canterbury. The complete quiet and want of incident and especially the intense respectability of every visitor, always worried me.[13]

Alfred Lyall's children were disgusted when the family moved from a parish deep in the Kent countryside to a rectory on the outskirts of the city. They looked on their old home – Godmersham, a small hamlet in the most beautiful part of the Stour Valley – as a rural demi-paradise. They could paddle in the river, which burst through an opening in the chalk downs and rippled round the vicarage garden on a gravelly bed; or they could roam all over the deer-park of Chilham Castle, with its drifts of beech-woods, rising behind the old flint-built church. An adventure playground full of infinite possibilities was thoughtfully positioned on their doorstep. How could their new home – a virtual suburb – compare? The possibility that there might be fates worse than Harbledown hardly occurred to them, until Francis Holland was called to a chapelry in London:

It has come at last. Yesterday morning when I came downstairs, Frank, with a face a yard long, handed to me a letter and rushed out of the room. I knew what it was and sat down till the sick feeling which came over me went off. In those few moments I seemed to say goodbye to all my past happiness . . . And so, as the days grow long and the primroses begin to bud, I must strip this poor little house and go with my children to live in a London street and their pleasures must be limited to the worn grass and dirty trees of the squares and parks. It does seem so hard upon them, just when they are beginning to understand the delights of the country. How happy they would have been this year in the farm and orchard, and in the dear, dear old garden at home. And what *shall* I do with myself, shut up in a London house, without even a carriage to get about in, and an immense way off from everyone.[14]

The religious life of the cathedral gave the male members of the Lyall connection as much satisfaction as the connection's social life gave their wives. A cathedral city was their natural habitat. They were high churchmen – and the old high church party was the outcome of generations of clergymen adapting themselves to the demands which the cathedrals made upon them. The Lyalls' love of balance and proportion, their most prominent characteristic, grew out of the kind of services which suited the cathedral's size and plan. Ecclesiologists assumed that the architecture of churches was dictated by the requirements of the liturgy, but once the immense fabric of the cathedrals was in being, the architectural setting overwhelmed the worship. The gaping Gothic voids imposed a mood of solemn reverence; the symbolism built into stone and wood and metal suggested many of the details; and the chapters – freed from financial constraints by their endowments – responded to these stimuli by perpetuating or developing forms of worship which were far more complex and impressive than the normal service in a humble parish church. If they were to perform this intricate ceremonial with becoming grace, the cathedral clergy needed a highly-developed sense of the seemly. Decorum was not something they could put on as they walked through the cathedral door; it was an instinct, pervading every aspect of their lives and every corner of their minds.

The high churchmen's aesthetic sensibility – their appreciation of sacred music and attachment to historic buildings – was another by-product of their corporate acts of worship. The music started out as an adjunct to the services; if religious texts were set to music, it enhanced their impact. But no one with an ear to hear could resist the responses of Tallis or the anthems of Purcell, much less the 'solemn and pathetic strains' of the *Messiah*. The cathedral clergy learned to love music for its own sake, and devoted substantial resources to music-making. Until regular schools of music and stable orchestras emerged in the late nineteenth century, cathedral organists and choirs were the only musicians guaranteed expert training and secure salaries. Many of the most eminent English musicians were employees of the chapters, and every English composer made use of the pool of skills which the church placed at his disposal. In an age which regarded the oratorio as the highest musical form, the cathedral establishments were the natural nuclei of the massive forces needed to perform Mendelsohn's *Elijah* or Gounod's *Redemption*. Like the music, the cathedrals' fabric added extra resonance to the services held beneath their roofs. When Lyall's clients began to congregate in Canterbury, the largest churches were still the largest buildings in England, and they were incomparably the loveliest. They were also in poor repair. The dereliction at Canterbury gave the chapter an opportunity to throw themselves into the work of restoration. Under Lyall's leadership they devoted a higher proportion of their income to repairs and a higher proportion of their time to supervising architects and craftsmen. They even undertook research. The definitive architectural history of Canterbury cathedral was published in the year Lyall became dean. More than a century later, it was described as 'in most respects the last word on the subject'.[15]

All the forces acting on the cathedral clergy – the elaborate liturgy, the exultant music, the historic fabric – bonded Lyall's clients to their sacred place:

> They delighted in the constant hearing of the English Psalms and Lessons. None at Canterbury more constantly attended daily services [at the cathedral], or more deeply felt their beauty.[16]

They delighted in the music also. The cathedral was the connection's concert hall:

> Last night they gave Spohr's *Last Judgment*. I listened to the storm of music which represented the cries of the souls bidden to depart. Then, after a pause, came the song of the blessed. It is an exquisite piece of music.[17]

The fabric of the cathedral dominated the Lyall connection's perceptions of Canterbury. Their correspondence contains innumerable descriptions of the great church's changing appearance, as it moved through the cycle of the seasons and the passing of the day. In a burgeoning spring:

> The wind is slowly veering round to the blessed south, and I hope and believe warm days are coming at last. As I sit and write [at an] open window, the rich odour of the lilacs and sweet briars in the neighbouring gardens . . . are almost oppressive. The trees and flowers have burst out [and] the old cathedral is standing in a garland of beeches and limes.[18]

In a summer storm:

> Last night, just as the bell practice began, a sudden storm from the sea, preceded by a thick mist, swept over Canterbury, great claps of thunder and streaming lightning. It was like an assault on Bell Harry, the lightning played all round him.[19]

In a mellow autumn:

> Our weather is mild, a blustering south-west wind whirling the lime leaves into space, and carrying the rooks and jackdaws round Bell Harry in joyous circles.[20]

In deep midwinter:

> Bell Harry rears himself with all his fretwork picked out with snow and his long grey back clad in a white mantle. The red roofs of the houses and the old ivied walls are all covered up. Mysterious humped-up figures flit round the great church; they may be deans and archdeacons, or they may be butchers and bakers, so levelling of outward distinction is the heaped up dazzling snow.[21]

In fog:

> The fog so thick that at a dozen yards one could not perceive anything of the building, only a thick white blurr. Inside all clear and heavenly.[22]

At twilight:

> Yesterday, at evensong, I observed the great west window of the south transept shining like pale amber in the gloom of the great church. As I came out of the cathedral into the clear twilight, the lovely crescent moon was sinking in the due south, where the sunset still lingered.[23]

By moonlight:

> Fog lifted late at night and the moon shone like silver, streaming over Bell
> Harry and the great church from end to end, while the white masses of mist
> lifted themselves and floated over the city wall at the breath of the south-west
> wind.[24]

Sometimes all three elements – liturgy, music, fabric – came together in a
single cathartic experience:

> I went to the cathedral, on Ascension Day [and] coming in very late did not go
> into the choir, but sat in the south transept on a bench which was exactly
> placed so as to catch a view of the Black Prince's tomb and St Anselm's chapel.
> I could follow the whole service perfectly, and drank my fill of the Norman
> arches and mediaeval ironwork gates of the little chapel. In the anthem the
> sweet boys' voices asked over and over again, 'Who is the King of Glory?', and
> the crash of the organ and men's voices replied, 'The Lord God of Hosts; He is
> the King of Glory'. As though one side could never weary of asking the
> question, or the other of giving the joyful answer.[25]

Lyall's clients knew that their proximity to the cathedral changed
them. It was like a drug: they became dependent on the spiritual
assurance it held out. They 'thought about the influence of the building on
people living . . . close to it and often in it' – and were glad to get back to
the 'soft gothic gloom' of the stately old church. Their 'fatigues and
anxieties' dropped off as soon as they re-entered the precincts and saw 'the
ancient places, Beckett's shrine full of splendid old windows . . . the Black
Prince with his fine Plantagenet face carved in bronze and his coat of mail
hanging above him, and the cloister door where the four knights burst in
to murder the Archbishop'. As Sir Alfred Lyall put it, 'the shadow of the
great cathedral will cool our brains'.[26] Even the country cousins, the
clients with livings in the surrounding villages, were soothed by the sight
of St Augustine's seat. They used to walk to the top of the hills round
Canterbury to look down on the low-lying red-roofed city. Their letters
describe these distant prospects, and every description focuses on the
same 'grey glistening mass'. When Alfred Lyall, the dean's brother,
climbed Harbledown Hill and looked east, he saw the great church bathed
in brilliant sunshine. Watling Street seemed to 'throw itself forward in
great steps in haste to reach it'. Nothing else mattered; nothing else had
any independent existence. All the other features of the landscape were
subordinated to the one dominant landmark. The city was the village
which had grown up at the precinct's gates; it was worthy of remark
because it served the servants of the cathedral. The world of nature was a

mere backdrop for the religious drama in the middle distance. The Stour Valley, widening down to the Thanet marshes with the chalk cliff of the North Foreland beyond, filled the gaps between silhouetted towers. The symbolic centre of the connection's universe sucked significance out of its surroundings, just as it drew Lyall's clients towards their sacred place.[27]

A

REVIEW

OF THE

PRINCIPLES

OF

NECESSARY AND CONTINGENT

TRUTH,

IN REFERENCE CHIEFLY TO THE

DOCTRINES

OF

HUME AND REID.

Etenim duo esse hæc maxima in philosophiâ, judicium veri et finem bonorum ; nec sapientem posse esse qui aut cognoscendi initium ignoret, aut extremum expetendi, ut, aut unde proficiscatur, aut quo pervenien- dum sit, nesciat.   CICERO *Acad. Quæst. Lib. IV. Cap.* 29.

LONDON:

PRINTED FOR C. J. G. & F. RIVINGTON,

ST. PAUL'S CHURCH-YARD,

AND WATERLOO-PLACE, PALL-MALL.

MDCCCXXX.

The only volume, of more than one projected, of the only edition of Alfred Lyall's *A Review of the Principles of Necessary and Contingent Truth* (1830). Lyall's metaphysics make considerable demands on his reader's ability to absorb long chains of abstract argument. (*Cambridge University Library*)

Chapter 6

Performance

Would competitive examinations have secured a better class of clergy? The issue was never put to the test, but the performance of Lyall's clients suggests that patronage was capable of producing reasonably satisfactory results. The careers of seven of his eight protégés can be reconstructed in sufficient detail to form fairly reliable judgments on their professional competence. None of them was in the same league as the dean, but a clear majority justified their stipends. Lyall's youngest brother, Alfred, was an able scholar and an influential publicist. He published metaphysical treatises attacking rationalist philosophers and edited the *Annual Register*, one of the most authoritative nineteenth-century reviews. Francis Holland, a nephew-in-law, perpetuated the dean's mission to the upper classes. His ministrations at one of the most fashionable proprietary chapels in the West End helped keep Mayfair drawing-rooms loyal to the Church of England. Three more clients proved conscientious parish priests. Thomas Darling's City parish was too small to keep him fully occupied, so he went slumming and collected hymns. William Hearle Lyall – another incumbent in the City – blotted his copybook by going over to Rome, but he only deserted the Church of England after the Bishop of London broke his heart by closing his church and selling the site for redevelopment. Robert Peter had a brilliant academic record and more than enough zeal; sadly, his ministry in rural Suffolk was marred by his eccentricities. Which leaves two bad bargains and an unknown quantity. Henry Carrington, the titular Dean of Bocking, let his exquisite sensibility and his termagant wife come between him and his parishioners in a town dominated by dissent. George Pearson, an indolent valetudinarian, circulated round a set of very poorly paid appointments before cutting himself from humanity: he retreated into his library and refused to come out. His younger brother William is the most obscure of

Lyall's clients. Did William Pearson represent good value for money, or bad? No one can tell.

Alfred Lyall (1795-1865): The Learned Parson

Alfred Lyall was one of his brother's more successful placings. His livings were ideally suited to his strengths and limitations. He was not a natural parish priest; he was far too remote. But he was a natural scholar and publicist. He needed benefices to provide him with a decent income and the leisure to get on with his writing. A chair in a university or a stall in a cathedral would probably have been the perfect solution; but he forfeited his chances of academic distinction when he refused to compete for a fellowship – he preferred omnivorous reading to the routine grind of the mathematics tripos; and the Ecclesiastical Commissioners imposed an embargo on new appointments to canonries just as he became eligible for one. Fortunately there was a third option: the 'quiet' parish. Godmersham and Harbledown were reasonably lucrative livings – in the £300-£500 range, roughly double the national average. They were also undemanding. None of the factors which dislocated the parochial system elsewhere deranged Lyall's Kentish villages. The population of each parish was small; dissenters were conspicuous by their absence; and poverty was on a scale which could be relieved, if not eliminated, by traditional paternalism.[1]

As a parson, Lyall was conscientious but uninspiring. He conducted as many services as his parishioners were willing to attend; he preached carefully thought-out sermons to unappreciative audiences; he met a large part of the cost of building a church school and restoring the church; and he gave up his greatest pleasure – long tours on the Continent. No one could accuse him of negligence, and after his death the vestry recorded its gratitude for his 'numberless acts of usefulness and kindness'; but he lacked the common touch. In his youth he was reckoned a 'delightful companion, full of kindly wit'; he even had a reputation as a bold rider. With his ordination and marriage, 'the cares of life gathered upon him'. He became 'grave and silent' and his sons started to complain. They resented their father's absorption in books, and they thought that he was 'inclined at times to take rather a stern view of duty'. The recollections of his grandchildren are even more revealing. Bernard Holland remembered a prematurely-aged man 'pacing round the garden walk of Harbledown rectory after breakfast on far-away summer mornings, abstract in thought, his grey and weighty head bowed a little forwards'. Lyall's lively and practical wife did her best to build bridges between her uncommunicative husband and his unintellectual parishioners. She went in for assiduous visiting, and the 'poor people' wept when she finally left Harbledown. But there were obvious limits to a wife's ability to compensate for a rector 'so entirely devoted to literature [as to] consider everything else mere waste of time'.[2]

Alfred Lyall's scholarship ran on exactly the same lines as his brother's. He attacked the same target – the philosophic movement which posed the greatest challenge to conventional high church theology; he employed the same methodology – tautly-argued metaphysics; and he arrived at the same reassuring conclusions. The common enemy was the school of Hume. William Lyall tackled Dugald Stewart as a surrogate for the great infidel; Alfred demolished Hume's more original acolyte, Reid. In both cases the brothers seized on their opponents' theory of knowledge as the soft underbody of their system and concentrated their critique on problems of perception. The common methodology involved hundreds of closely-printed pages packed with precise definitions and *a priori* arguments expressed with consummate clarity and intimidating rigour. The Lyalls' philosophising – as one of their descendants pointed out – was not 'marked by any great charm of style or sense of humour': it was all consistently austere. Writing *Necessary and Contingent Truth* must have taken immense stamina, and one can understand why the second volume was never completed. Just reading the fragment actually published demands a major effort of concentration. The comparable conclusions maintained the impossibility of disproving the existence or ascertainng the nature of God. One of Alfred's arguments can be expressed as a syllogism: only God has created matter and mind; human beings can only conceive of the kind of power they exercise themselves; therefore God cannot be comprehended by the merely mortal. Another can be reduced to a portmanteau quotation:

> Laplace attempts to show mathematically, what Hume had endeavoured on metaphysical grounds, that the proof of a miracle by testimony is impossible. It results, he says, from the mathematically proved doctrine of probabilities, 'that the probability of mistake or falsehood in the witness becomes greater in proportion as the fact attested is extraordinary'. It seems absurd to resort to the evidence of man to prove the being of God. If his own works cannot speak for Him, those of His creatures cannot do so. The allegation that a miracle is proof of the existence of the Deity assumes . . . the thing to be proved . . . Men have from the beginning acknowledged a God: and it is that conviction which prepares them to accept any message, miraculously accredited, as coming from him. Immortality is an aspiration which man naturally is made to cherish. The message of the Gospel does not so much create as it confirms this expectation; and instructs how we may make the eternity we look forward to, a happy one.[3]

So many parallels produced an astonishing family resemblance. Passages from William's articles in the *Quarterly Review* and Alfred's *Principles of Necessary and Contingent Truth* could be cut out and laid end to end without readers realising where one brother stopped and the other began. Only a slight difference of tone makes it possible to distinguish the two hands. William, a smooth man, was consistently urbane; Alfred, a comparatively hairy man, could be captious at times.[4]

Alfred's work as a publicist, like his brother's, took two forms. He wrote short but powerful polemics, collected in *Agonistes*; and he edited the *Annual Register*, a particularly influential review. *Agonistes* attacked the high churchmen's old enemies, the polemicists of the *Edinburgh Review*; then it went on to attack their new opponents, the Tractarians who went over to Rome. Brougham and Macaulay were two of Lyall's more predictable victims. Brougham's defence of Voltaire against the charge of blasphemy got singularly short shrift; Lyall dismissed *Candide* as 'an obscene tale of some fifty pages; the whole philosophy of which is to mock at all philosophy, and the only conclusion is . . . that no conclusion can be come to'. Macaulay came in for drubbings on at least three issues: Jewish disabilities; the relative merits of Pope and Addison; and the gains and losses of the French Revolution. Alfred Lyall's line on the 'recent events in France' was pure Burke:

> All the foundations of institutions which a thousand years of constantly increasing civilisation and wealth had accumulated in the finest and most refined people and society of Christendom, were brutally swept away upon the spot; and this, too, with the cruellest contempt of the claims of whole orders of men; whose entire fortunes and share of life were involved in the downfall.[5]

The savagest strictures in *Agonistes* were reserved for the high churchmen's treacherous allies. 'Newman on Development' brought out all Alfred's residual Protestantism. He defended the crux of the Reformation: a man's right to exercise his private judgement in the interpretation of the Bible, rather than surrendering his intellectual independence to some supposedly infallible authority. 'God,' he argued, 'has left us in every other human affair to be determined by the balance of probabilities – why not in religion?'[6]

The core of the *Annual Register* consisted of a detailed review of the political developments of the preceding year. It was never a mere chronicle of events. The first editor, Edmund Burke, imposed his own political philosophy on the *Register's* record of events and Lyall worked within the same partisan tradition. In many ways, he faced a similar challenge. Burke confronted the French Revolution; Lyall edited the *Register* during the run-up to the great outburst of reforms in the 1830s and the subsequent revulsion. He championed the Church of England against the Whig-Radical coalition; and his hostility to the infidel permeated all his reports of government measures and parliamentary debates. The ostensible subject of his first preface, written in 1823, was the revolution in Spain. In reality, he treated the rising of the Cortes against King Ferdinand as a dress rehearsal for events in England if the opposition ever gained a majority in the House of Commons. The Cortes, Lyall complained, was neither 'a *national* [nor] a *popular* government'; and the proof of its unrepresentative character was the anti-clericals' onslaught on the Church. The Spanish people prided themselves on their piety, yet the liberals concentrated all their efforts on confiscating religious endowments and persecuting religious orders.[7] The British constitution stopped self-interested doctrinaires attaining supreme power, but how could a delicate system of checks and balances survive the extension of the suffrage or the introduction of secret ballots? Electoral reform only played into the hands of plutocrats and demagogues:

> It is contended that in small constituencies the suffrage is certain to be sold; and the remedy proposed is, either by the ballot [to compel the voters to vote according to their consciences] or, by indefinitely extending the suffrage, to deprive it of a marketable value. But the very statement supposes, either that the electors have no political opinion or conviction, or that if they have such, that they are ready to barter them to the best bidder for a sum of money. In either case, what is the public gain in their 'independent exercise of the suffrage'? What meaning is to be attached to the word *conscience* as applied to such persons, and in such a case? A still stranger remedy is 'extending the franchise'. If ten-pound voters have little political opinion, it is clear that five-pounders are likely to have less. The new class will be still more accessible to corruption. It is only supposed that they will be so numerous that no one will be rich enough to corrupt them. Corruption presupposes a certain soundness and probity consisting in its subject. You cannot corrupt a man who has no opinion. Still less can you corrupt a man whose choice is founded on motives of interest or passion. Such motives are already as corrupt as any you can offer in the shape of money.[8]

When the enemies of the church actually won a general election in 1832, the *Register* reported the debate over the Irish Church Bill and the establishment of the Ecclesiastical Commissioners with a kind of horrified fascination. The development of a new working alliance between the bishops and Peel's ministry demanded another editorial shift; from all-out opposition to discriminating approval of moderate reforms meant to dish the Whigs. Unlike his brothers, Alfred had no hand in formulating the Peelites' pre-emptive strike. He was no man of affairs. But as editor of the *Annual Register*, he waged a minor propaganda war on Archbishop

Howley's behalf. His sustained and successful writing of contemporary history strengthened the centre party against the diehards and the radicals, by rallying high churchmen behind constructive compromise.[9]

Alfred also had a certain representative function. The fact that a man so cultivated was a clergyman automatically raised the prestige of the church in the eyes of those who respected culture. *Necessary and Contingent Truth* and *Agonistes* were proof of his high intellectual ability; but neither of them appealed to a wide reading public. Lyall's reputation with the clerisy (and his entry in the *Dictionary of National Biography*) rested on another book: his *Rambles in Madeira and in Portugal*. After the lapse of a century and a half, Lyall's account of an idiosyncratic Grand Tour still makes entrancing reading; and in the 1820s it must have caught the mood of the moment to perfection. Thanks to Eton and Trinity, he had all the right instincts – all the tastes of a scholar-gentleman. He saw everything through 'dreamy and romantic' eyes, until his sense of humour crept up on him; and he could describe anything – a vista, a person, a building, an incident, an atmosphere – in a most evocative way. Some of his set-pieces are unforgettable. Every reader could compile his own check-list of vividly remembered gems: the gradual revelation of Funchal, seen at sunrise from the deck of a ship slowly approaching the harbour; the English colony in their *quintas*, busy replicating society at home, down to the vegetables they ate at dinner; the torchlit procession carrying an image of the Madonna clad in 'all the gorgeousness of jewelled braid and spangled petticoat'; the lanes passing between high garden walls smothered in fuchsias and vines; an expedition over mountain paths to see the blackened crater of an extinct volcano, at once sinister and sublime; the balmy summer nights, when the city shone white in the moonlight, with the rippling sea beyond; a convent of flirtatious nuns, exchanging gallantries with their visitors. Lyall's comments on one of the nuns – a particularly slender and beautiful girl – reflected his comments on women in general. He was fascinated by his first exposure to the Mediterranean type. He compared and contrasted the worshippers kneeling at a *Te Deum* in the cathedral ('remarkably few that one should call good-looking'); the 'dark-eyed tenants' of the roadside summerhouses, who peeped through their lattices at the sound of approaching hooves; and the dancers at a ball, with their raven hair, fine arms and 'eyes so large and black' ('I fancy that their effect would be rather greater in a *tête-à-tête*'). His only regret was the senoritas' premature decay. The 'undertint of carnation showing through [their] dark cheeks' soon disappeared, leaving swarthy complexions behind; and 'from their singular indolence, [they] soon grow fat. I have seen women of five and twenty whom it was difficult to believe under forty'.[10]

2. Lyall's portrait in the Deanery at Canterbury

1. William Rowe Lyall (1788-1857), Dean of Canterbury (by T.H. Maguire after W. Buckler)

3. (*Below*) Lyall's monument in Canterbury Cathedral (detail)

4. Dean Lyall as a young man

5. Lyall's wife: Catherine Brandreth (d.1867)

6. Lyall's father: John Lyall (1752-1805), the Scottish shipowner

7. Lyall's father-in-law: Dr Joseph Brandreth (1748-1815), a physician in Liverpool (by W. Ward)

8. The Deanery at Hadleigh

9. The Deanery at Canterbury (by Dorothy E. Lightfoot)

10. Lyall's patron: William Howley (1766-1848), Bishop of London and Archbishop of Canterbury (by S.W. Reynolds after W. Owen)

11. Lyall's ally: Charles Blomfield (1786-1857), Bishop of Chester and London (by J. Thomson after George Richmond)

12. Lyall's associate: Hugh James Rose (1795-1838), Principal of King's College, London

13. The 'Little Archdeacon': Benjamin Harrison (1808-87), Archdeacon of Maidstone (by Charles Holl after George Richmond)

14. Canterbury Cathedral in Dean Lyall's time (by S. Lacey after T.M. Baynes)

15. Bell Harry

16. St Augustine's College, Canterbury, in 1850

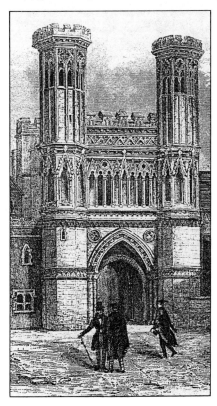

17. George Lyall's seat: Headley Park, Surrey

18. Dean Lyall's elder brother: George Lyall MP (1779-1853), Chairman of the East India Company (by H. Robinson after T. Phillips)

19. George Lyall's wife: Margaret Edwards (1792-1869)

20. Dean Lyall's youngest brother: Alfred Lyall (1796-1865), Vicar of Godmersham and Rector of Harbledown (by Edwin D. Smith)

21. Alfred Lyall's wife: Mary Broadwood (1809-78) (from Sir Mortimer Durand, *Life of Alfred Comyn Lyall*)

22. Alfred Lyall's son: Sir Alfred Comyn Lyall ICS (1835-1911) (by C.W. Sherburn after J.J. Shannon)

23. The Alfred Lyalls' honeymoon: the Bridge of Sighs in 1834 (from Mary Lyall's Sketchbook)

24. The Vicarage at Godmersham in 1839 (from Mary Lyall's Sketchbook)

25. The Hollands' house in the Precincts at Canterbury

26. Dean Lyall's nephew-in-law: Francis Holland (1828-1907), Canon of Canterbury

27. Holland's wife, Dean Lyall's niece: Sibylla Lyall (1836-91)

28. Holland's father: Sir Henry Holland, Bart. (1788-1873), physician to the Royal Family

29. Holland's chapel: the Quebec Chapel, Marylebone

30. Dean Lyall's nephew: Thomas Darling (1816-93), Rector of St Michael's Paternoster Royal (by Frederick Piercy)

31. Darling's wife: Mildred Ford (1844-1912) (by E. U. Eddis)

32. Darling's father: Dr George Darling (1782-1862), a physician in Bloomsbury (by G. Zobel)

33. Darling's mother, Dean Lyall's sister: Jane Lyall (1786-1848) (by Benjamin Haydon)

34. (*Left*) Darling's church: St Michael's Paternoster Royal in 1838 (by I.H. Le Keux after I.B. Thompson; from G. Godwin and J. Britten, *The Churches of London*, 1838-39)

35. (*Above*) St Michael's, Harbledown *c.* 1806-10 (by Henry Petrie)

36. (*Below*) William Hearle Lyall's church: St Dionis' Backchurch, by Wren, demolished 1878

'SIXTY YEARS A DEAN The Very Rev. Henry Carrington is approaching the sixtieth year of his term of office as dean and rector of Bocking, Braintree. The son of Sir Edmund Carrington, first Chief Justice of Ceylon, he was born in the year before Waterloo. Educated at Charterhouse and Caius College he entered the Church in 1838 as curate of Hadleigh in Suffolk, but he has been in Essex since 1839. He has translated Victor Hugo, Thomas à Kempis, and Baudelaire, and has published an anthology of French poetry. He has stated that his recreations are "geology, Greek, chess, landscape gardening, formerly fencing, skating, lawn tennis, and sketching." Probably it is his many occupations which have given him such a long lease of life.' (*The Sphere*, May 1904)

37. Dean Lyall's nephew-in-law, Archbishop Howley's nephew: Henry Carrington (1814-1906), Dean of Bocking

38. Carrington's father: Sir Codring-
ton Carrington MP (1764-1849), Chief
Justice of Ceylon (by Sir Joshua
Reynolds)

39. Carrington's mother: Pauline
Belli, Archbishop Howley's sister-in-
law (by Sir Joshua Reynolds)

40. Carrington's carriage

41. Dean Lyall's nephew-in-law: Robert Peter (1818-1910), Rector of Cavendish

42. Peter's wife, Dean Lyall's niece: Catherine Lyall (1839-1908)

43. Dean Lyall's nephew: George Pearson (1814-94), the recluse

44. Pearson's father, married Dean Lyall's sister: William Pearson (1780-1874)

45. John Broadwood (1732-1812), Scottish piano-maker (by W. Suy after John Harrison)

46. John Broadwood's grandson, Alfred Lyall's brother-in-law: the Rev John Broadwood (1798-1864)

47. The Broadwoods' seat in Surrey: Lyne (from Mary Lyall's Sketchbook)

48. Archbishop Howley's funeral: Dean Lyall was one of the pall-bearers (*Illustrated London News*, 26 February 1848)

49. Lyall's monument in Canterbury Cathedral

One wonders whether Lyall ever regretted committing his roving eye to print. What was entirely acceptable in a young bachelor under the Regency must have seemed sightly improper in a grey and weighty clergyman in the increasingly puritanical 1850s. He was already under pressure to take holy orders (with a view to getting married) when he went out to Madeira, and he gave way after his return. Some of his accounts of his adventures read like a nostalgic farewell to his carefree youth, before the shutters of middle-aged respectability came slamming down. He clearly felt the lure of the south: the escape from the stiffness of English society which attracted so many Victorian travellers to the Mediterranean. He loved the English colony's gaiety: a gaiety expressed in their exuberant masquerades. In England 'nothing [was] more dismal' than a masquerade, because everyone was afraid 'to give way to the frolic of the moment'. In Madeira nothing was more delightful. The atmosphere made all the difference: the *dolce far niente* was

> one of the advantages of being abroad. You are allowed to amuse yourself with trifles like the rest; to forget politics and money-making; and indulge in that light-hearted carelessness which is the charm of boyhood. Foreigners, indeed particularly Frenchmen, seem never to lose their brightness of mind and habit. The severer discipline to which we are subjected in England may give us some advantages in political institution[s], but we purchase it at considerable expense. It might be doubted whether the object be worth the price, were there reason to believe that it was men's business to be happy.[11]

Francis Holland (1828-1907): Chaplain to the Top Ten Thousand

> Frank went down to Windsor and preached in the presence of the whole Royal Family, assembled to celebrate the Prince of Wales' birthday. He [was] commanded to preach extempore [and] it was intimated to him that he might be sent for again. [Frank] and Sybil say it is only a compliment, but I think it is an *augury* of future promotion.
>
> Mary Drummond Lyall, mother of Sibylla Holland, to her son, (Sir) Alfred Lyall, ICS, 29 October and 12 November 1868

Of all the members of the Lyall connection, Francis Holland came closest to emulating the dean's success. He got his first living when he was twenty-five, younger than any other client; and it was a proper living, not a pauper training-ground: a parish with a population of 1,300 and a stipend of £180. After eight years on the outskirts of Canterbury, the trustees of a proprietary chapel on the border between Mayfair and Marylebone summoned him to London. Then, in 1883, Gladstone made him a canon of Canterbury. He was fifty-four at the time: the same age as Dean Lyall when he first joined the chapter. But there was no deanery to come. He lived for another twenty-five years without further preferment.

Holland owed his steady if unspectacular progress up the clerical hierarchy to his family's connections and the exact match beween his sacerdotal style and the religious preferences of his upper-class congregations. His father was the most fashionable physician in London. Sir Henry Holland, the son of a doctor in Knutsford, earned £5,000 a year, the income of a poor peer, from a practice which included six prime ministers, Queen Victoria and Prince Albert. His love of travel brought him scientific acclaim. His journal of a visit to Iceland in 1810 was published by the Hakluyt Society, 177 years after it was first written, for its historic interest. His social success was equally phenomenal. His name-dropping but terribly discreet memoirs show him circulating round an ever-expanding circle of celebrities – his grandson said his *Recollections* read like Kelly's *Directory of the Titled, Landed and Official Classes*. He was *persona grata* in the great Tory households and the grandest Whig salons: he even formed a collection of heads of state. His childen were just as upwardly mobile. His eldest son married an heiress, went into politics, served as secretary of state of the colonies and retired with a viscountcy. His eldest daughter married into the Buxton clan: the great dynasty of millionaire brewers and radical MPs descended from Sir Thomas Fowell Buxton, Wilberforce's ally in the struggle for emancipation. The Trevelyans and the Wedgwoods were relatives of the Hollands, but they were the least of the family's connections; the list of potential patrons was almost endless.[12]

Without these connections, Holland would never have been summoned to the Quebec Chapel. But once he was installed in the heart of the West End, everything depended on his ability and application. In some way proprietary chapels were much closer to non-conformist tabernacles than regular Anglican churches. They had no captive congregations, because they had no parishes; they existed in the religious free market which develops in any great city. It was up to each minister to 'establish such pastoral relations as he could between himself and his . . . eclectic flock'. Holland built up a loyal personal following by giving upper-class communicants what they wanted: dignified services, intelligent but unemotional sermons, and day schools which their daughters could attend. Under his direction, the Quebec Chapel

> became one of the 'high' churches of the West-end. The ritual adopted by him would now be considered moderate, if not meagre, but for the 'sixties' it was worthy of remark.[13]

As a preacher, his 'aridity' must have been a welcome relief from evangelical histrionics:

> [He] rigidly avoided anything in the nature of sensationalism. He was once invited by Archbishop Benson to give the addresses to candidates during an ordination retreat at Addington, and to the surprise of those who knew him he took the subject of enthusiasm. The addresses, which were carefully written beforehand, left the impression that their author had been investigating a subject that was new to him.[14]

The content of Holland's sermons was as welcome as his delivery. Like all popular preachers, he told his audiences what they wanted to hear. When the Mutiny shook public confidence in the beneficence of the Raj, he argued that the conquest of the subcontinent by the British was consonant with God's designs; and he denounced the celibacy of the Catholic priesthood to an audience largely composed of clergymen's sons:

> There are some who look wistfully towards the Church of Rome. Her priests have not money cares, and what admirable missionaries they make! Being unmarried, with what singleness of heart can they care for the things of the Lord! The celibacy of the clergy seems best. To which conclusion three things oppose themselves. 1. The Word of God. 2. The traditions of the Church. 3. The experience of mankind.[15]

The deans who controlled prominent pulpits were mainly old-fashioned high churchmen or broad churchmen anxious to include acceptable representatives of the high church school on some balanced ticket. Holland's cathedral style made him a safe choice whenever sermons had to be delivered to particularly distinguished congregations. 1859, when he was just turned thirty, was his *annus mirabilis*. The Dean of Westminster asked him – along with nine bishops – to deliver a series of sermons in the Abbey; and Archbishop Summer made him one of the 'six preachers' of Canterbury Cathedral. *The Times*, commenting on his appointment as a 'six preacher', pointed out that he had only been in holy orders for eight years. 1873 marked another milestone: the Corporation of the Sons of the Clergy asked him to deliver the anniversary sermon at their annual festival in St Paul's. The Corporation was formed in 1655 to relieve clergymen who had been evicted from their livings, and it went on relieving the widows and orphans of poor clergymen after the Restoration. The annual festival was 'a very big show indeed'. It opened with a concert of sacred music; it reached its climax with a huge banquet in the Merchant Taylors' Hall; and it ended with a select dinner for the stewards at Lambeth Palace. The stewards were all top people who were made to pay heavily for the privilege of appearing in this annual list of pre-eminent friends of the church – and the preacher was always a distinguished clergyman, rising or risen. Two years later, Queen Victoria set the seal of royal approval on Holland's sermons. After hearing him preach in St George's Chapel, she made him one of her chaplains-in-ordinary.

As a chaplain, Holland paid regular visits to Windsor; and in the course of his visits, he met the usual assortment of courtiers and politicians. He dined with Gladstone at the deanery in April 1875. The Grand Old Man came down 'rather out of humour from the Academy dinner, when Disraeli made a good speech, and he none'. Holland soon drew him out. The two men were both good talkers, and they had so much to talk about: Eton, the Church of England, 'society'. It was 12.30 before they went to bed. Next morning, Gladstone asked Holland to go for a walk with him and saw him off at the station. Holland told his wife that Gladstone's conversation had been amazing. However *récherché* the subject, his 'fire and eagerness and tenderness and wondrous versatility' turned his comments into gold. They met a second time in 1876, over lunch at Baroness Burdett-Coutts'. Once again, Gladstone was very affable – 'no one could be afraid of him out of the House' – and talked away 'with his usual fire'. It would be interesting to know what Gladstone thought of Holland. One assumes he must have been equally impressed. Three years after he returned to power, a stall fell vacant at Canterbury. He promptly offered it to Holland. At the time, six of Holland's relatives – all Buxtons: his sister married into the clan – had just sat, or were currently sitting, or were just about to sit on the Liberal back-benches. There is no evidence to suggest that they lobbied Gladstone on Holland's behalf; but their presence confirmed that he had the right social credentials for a cathedral close.[16]

Holland's pastoral work was all of a piece with his ritual and his sermons. He took an interest in hospitals for the aged poor. But that was as close to slumming as he ever got. His real speciality was the education of the upper classes – or that half of the upper classes which was most responsive to his ministrations. He practically invented a new kind of school: the Church of England High School for Girls. The schools he founded, risking his own fortune and soliciting gifts from rich friends, educated the 'daughters of the well-to-do on definitely religious lines'. At least one of his foundations survives, on the western edge of Regent's Park: the Francis Holland School ('nice, plain, well-proportioned' – the buildings, not the girls).[17]

Thomas Darling (1816-93): The Conscientious Parish Priest

Thomas Darling was born before his time. He should have been a ritualist slum priest: he had all the right instincts. But he was twenty years too soon. The virile Protestantism of his Scottish forebears was strong enough to stop him dabbling with full-blooded Popery, and his terminal living – a tiny parish in the City of London – contained too few paupers to give him much scope for social work. Frustrated on both counts, he found other outlets for his good intentions. In the main he wrote hymns.

Darling learnt his churchmanship at his public school and his Cambridge college. In later life, he absorbed some of the Ecclesiologists' ideas about ritual and some of the Tractarians' ideas about doctrine; but all they did was add extra resonance to the religion of seemliness which he learnt in his youth. Charterhouse and St John's, like almost all the ancient foundations in the 1830s, were bastions of the old high churchmen: and the conservatives in control of the two institutions were determined to keep them that way. The governors of the Charterhouse tended to be ecclesiastical dignitaries and Tory grandees who occasionally sent their younger sons to the school and used their patronage to help deserving Carthusians get a start in life. Until his death in 1828, Archbishop Manners-Sutton was the most illustrious old boy and the most influential member of the governing body. With very few exceptions, the headmasters came from the same stable: they were old Carthusians who took high honours at the Oxford college which produced more Hackney activists than any other. When an abortive experiment with pupil-teachers produced a crisis of confidence half-way through Darling's time at the school (the number of boys fell from 460 to just over 100 in five years), the high churchmen in charge kicked the reforming headmaster upstairs (to a canonry at Canterbury) and went back to Christ Church for a safer replacement. The young tutor they appointed, Augustus Page Saunders, saved the school and taught Darling classics. He was a brilliant, if lazy, teacher. Gladstone, his student at Christ Church, said that 'he had never known anyone who carried into the relations of a tutor and pupil such kindly feelings'. The long-serving Master of St John's – when Darling won his scholarship, with Saunders' aid – was just as well-intentioned and just as high and dry. Two phrases tell one all one needs to know about James Wood. He 'never introduced the subject of religion into common conversation' and he was 'firmly attached to decent ceremonial and modern discipline, as distinguished from bigotry and enthusiasm'. The fellows felt safe with him – safe from 'any fanciful and arbitrary innovations'. He had done too well out of the system to want to change it.

He was born the son of a Lancashire handloom weaver; he left £50,000 when he died.[18]

Darling's first curacy taught him a very different lesson: the satisfaction of slumming. St Giles, Holborn, was only a few minutes walk from his parents' house in Russell Square, but it might have been on a different planet. In the 1840s St Giles-in-the Fields – to give the parish its full ironic title – was one of the most spectacular cases of spiritual destitution currently confronting the Church of England. The huge population (around 40,000) included the most notorious criminal slum in Britain: the great St Giles rookery, a no-go area in the heart of the West End. Pickpockets and whores slipped out of the maze of tortuous lanes each evening, went about their business in the night world of the theatres and brothels, and retreated into a rabbit-warren of unlit passages and yards. Burglars ventured further afield – into the grandest terraces of Bloomsbury and Mayfair; then they sold their swag in markets run by Fagin-like fences. No one could follow them into their sanctuary. If the police entered the rookery in hot pursuit, they were set upon by mobs of bystanders while the miscreants made their escape through cellars, across roof-tops, between beds in overcrowded bedrooms – by any one of a hundred routes. If they succeeded in taking captives, their prisoners were freed before they could get them away: and if a prisoner was brought to trial, a dozen perjured witnesses gave him an alibi. The clergy in their capacity as moral policemen were greeted with hooting and stones. But how could they stay away? The denizens of the rookery needed them so much: they were so delectably degraded. They constituted

> a class utterly devoid of all moral sense, who lived in defiance of religious control, in whose creed theft is no crime, immorality no disgrace, intemperance no reproach, who see nothing degrading in falsehood, persons who never use the name of God but to blaspheme.[19]

Forty years before Toynbee Hall was founded and the university settlements started stealing the headlines, the clergy of St Giles became pioneer social workers on a massive scale. The rectors – as chairmen of the select vestry, the only form of self-government – drew up scheme after scheme: schemes for sanitation; schemes for regulating lodging houses; schemes for road-widening; schemes for clearances which eventually swept the rookery away. In the meantime, the curates set up ragged schools, supervised poorhouses and distributed relief in hard winters. By the standards of the day they were immensely effective. They recruited hundreds of voluntary workers and raised thousands of pounds each year;

it was all very big business.[20] But young curates could become so engrossed in uplift that it cast a shadow over the rest of their clerical careers. Compared with the ongoing excitement of St Giles, Darling's first living – Thanington, in Kent – proved a depressing anticlimax. There was nothing to do: no sense of involvement in some great collective endeavour, just the humdrum round of Sunday services (with tiny congregations) and weekday visits (to unresponsive labourers). Christmas was particularly dispiriting: in 1847 only seventeen parishioners took communion on Christmas morning, the one service Darling could be bothered to hold:

> On the afternoon of my first two Xmas days I had such a woefully disheartening number present that I determined to give up that service for the future and for the last two years I went to the Cathedral, taking any children with me to see the beautiful effect produced by the lighting up of the Nave and Choir, which can only be witnessed once a year.[21]

Bored and frustrated, Darling toyed with the idea of accepting a living in a manufacturing district for the sake of the 'increased usefulness', but his father counselled him against 'leaving so soon the situation in which you uncle has placed you and depriving yourself of the advantage of his patronage hereafter'.[22] While he waited for the dean to find him 'a more extensive field of labour', Darling did what underemployed incumbents were doing all over the country: he engaged a smart London architect to restore the run-down fabric of his church. He must have inspected William Butterfield's first major commission: St Augustine's College was *the* great religious development in Canterbury in the 1840s and it was only two or three miles from Thanington. He may have met Butterfield through their mutual patron, the dean. In any event, he asked the Ecclesiologists' favourite architect to transform St Nicholas, Thanington on approved Ecclesiological lines. All the eighteenth-century accretions which offended the Cambridge Movement's sense of propriety were swept away. The schoolroom which took up the whole of the western end of the nave departed to new premises; the false ceiling which cut off the tops of the pointed windows was ripped down; a vestry was created in the bottom of the tower; choir stalls were installed in the empty chancel and a new set of communion plate was displayed on a proper altar. Darling was so excited when the plate arrived (in a specially-made oak box) that he insisted on carrying it into church himself. Surprisingly, given his high church client, Butterfield reserved his most inventive touches for the pulpit. With its panel tracery, its delicate pillars and 'structural honesty', it constituted 'an astonishing forecast of the much better-known furniture designed for the Morris firm by Philip Webb'.[23]

A marginally more extensive field of labour was soon forthcoming. The dean and chapter of Canterbury were patrons of two livings in the City of London and, when one of the long-serving incumbents died in 1848, Lyall nominated his nephew for the vacancy. Sadly St Michael's Paternoster Royal was no St Giles. The population of Darling's new parish was low and falling. In the eighteenth century, City congregations were much like congregations in any economically-buoyant town: there were enough worshippers to fill all the seats and every section of the community was represented. Then, in the course of the nineteenth century, the resident population of the City collapsed. As the demand for offices and warehouses grew, land values rose to the point at which accommodation was squeezed out. The commercial magnates followed the gentry into the West End; the white-collar workers started commuting to newly-built suburbs; the proletariat drifted into the slums to the east. Darling arrived in the middle of this process of depopulation. In 1842, seventy-odd City parishes had around 1,700 inhabitants apiece; by 1901, the first census after Darling's death, the resident population had fallen by three-quarters. If he started out with 500 parishioners he was lucky; when he finally resigned his living, in 1893, just 130 remained. The number of adult communicants at a typical Sunday service – if one deducts the choir and the officials – must have been down to single figures.[24]

Broadly speaking, there were two ways out of this dilemma: two ways in which Darling could make enough work to keep himself busy. He could go in for 'poaching' – attracting worshippers from other parishes. Or he could specialise: he could provide services for special interest groups scattered all over the Anglican communion whose members never entered his church. In practice he tried both. Congregations in London were fickle affairs, forever deserting their parish churches for more stirring sermons or more elaborate rituals elsewhere. The dull magnificence of the services at St Paul's drew thousands of Londoners into the City each Sunday. A natural showman could have diverted a fraction of this immense stream into his own church. Eloquent preachers – the sort of orator whose sermons were reported at length in the national press – could always draw packed audiences. All it took was enough fire and brimstone. Violent denunciation of sins described in lurid and titillating detail: that was the standard recipe. Ritualism was another draw: a good working alternative to pulpit oratory. In the 1860s and 1870s a new kind of priest started reviving the religious life of a number of difficult districts in London – parishes with no perceptible sense of community, often parishes dominated by slums. Their fortes were theatrical display and the cult of personality. They wore outré clothing – swirling cloaks, scarlet cassocks, embroidered birettas; clothes indicating that they were not as other men. They lived together in clergy houses, flaunting their celibacy as proof of their devotion and training their acolytes to address them in specially deferential ways. If the evangelical press reviled their popish ways, they revelled in their notoriety; and they posed as martyrs for their faith, if their ecclesiastical superiors charged them with breaches of clerical discipline. Their most lasting achievement was the transference to ordinary parish churches of the type of service traditionally restricted to cathdrals: the service as spectacle. The ritualists combined conventional elements – the sight of rich vestments, the smell of incense, the sound of music, the symbolism of movement – in a single overwhelming assault upon the senses; and their synthesis scored a signal triumph with their social and intellectual inferiors, with women and the working-class. In time they even developed a distinctive kind of church. An Ecclesiological interior, with all its surfaces decorated in every conceivable colour and every conceivable medium, was the English equivalent of the Baroque: 'a series of sledgehammer blows' drumming reverence for the divine into the startled spectator.[25]

Darling was too inhibited, by his 'high and dry' upbringing and his gentle personality, to match the orators' railings or the Anglo-Catholics' flamboyance; but he clearly found the ritualist alternative more congenial, once it lost its power to shock. The mainstream of Anglican practice was moving steadily towards pre-Reformation models; the City parishes acted as a sump for well-connected Anglo-Catholics; and Darling drifted with the tide. His best friend – an old Etonian, the Rev Edgar Hoskins – spent sixteen celibate years in the citadel of the Ecclesiologists, the clerical complex at All Saints, Margaret Street, compiling a series of devotional manuals which ran through many editions and included an *Horae Beatae Mariae Virginis*. Hoskins only left All Saints to become rector of St Mary Magdalene, Old Fish Street – another City living.[26] Darling's church was a sign of the times. He asked Butterfield to adapt St Michael's Paternoster Royal to 'modern requirements', because Wren's basic plan – a single box-like compartment – was poorly suited to the ritualists' *ideé fixe*, the celebration of the sacraments by priestly actors in a distant chancel. He would probably have preferred to raze St Michael's to the ground and put up a Gothic building in its place. There were no aesthetic objections to demolition. Wren's reputation, twenty years after the publication of Pugin's *Contrasts*, was at its nadir. But there were practical obstacles. The site was too constricted and too valuable: too constricted for a sprawling medieval plan, and too valuable not to be sold for development if the church ever came down.[27]

Sadly, the eighteenth-century furnishings were completely unprotected. Butterfield began with the pews. High-backed Georgian box-pews were anathema to the Ecclesiologist because they reduced the priests' control over the worshippers and stopped the poor coming to church. Ritualists set great store by two desiderata: congregations maintaining a mood of devout reverence and congregations moving and chanting in unison. Box-pews were prejudicial to good discipline on this spiritual parade-ground. Their occupants, half-hidden behind chest-high walls of wainscot, could snooze or gossip, fidget or flirt. The same walls divided congregations into economic classes. Those who could afford to pay the highest rents got the best seats, generally at the front of the nave, while the paupers were reduced to free benches at the back. The whole social hierarchy of a parish could be reconstructed from the seating-plan of the parish church. In poorly-endowed livings this had one great advantage: pew rents were a comparatively painless way of generating a large enough income to maintain the fabric and supplement the incumbent's stipend without incurring the odium of levying a church rate. But Ecclesiologists argued that the poor were too ashamed of their poverty to sit on their accustomed benches; that the only hope of luring the working-classes back into church was to make everyone else sit on benches too. The rest of Butterfield's changes were all of a piece with his massacre of the box-pews. The gallery occupying 'the whole space between the towers and the north wall' was dismantled; the organ was greatly enlarged by the best-known organ-builder of the century; and stained glass was installed in several windows, reducing the level of the lighting to the soft gloom supposedly conducive to religious experience.[28]

These concessions to the *Zeitgeist* probably reduced the rates at which Darling's congregations fell, but they failed to reverse the cumulative decline. St Michael's suffered from unfair competition. Why should anyone in search of a stirring sermon or a spiritual spectacular seek out an ordinary parish church when the dome of an immense baroque cathedral towered over the rooftops, a few minutes walk away? In a free market for religious services, Darling's fate was entirely predictable. Long before his forty-five year ministry came to an end, St Michael's was a religious dinosaur:

> The Church is open daily for private prayer, but few seem to take advantage of the privilege. On Sunday an extremely small congregation gathers. Thousands (of commuters) may pass and repass the very doors . . . but few there be who enter, though . . . any occurrence of interest – a horse down or a woman in a fit, the vagaries of a crazy woman or the capture of a thief, would

in a few seconds attract a crowd greater than most of these churches ever hold. The field of utility is thus very limited.[29]

Darling responded to his dwindling congregations by developing a number of specialities which reached outside his tiny parish. He kept up his old interest in the slums. He went on supporting the ragged schools of St Giles, and he raised funds to relieve slumps and epidemics – the regular crises of working-class life. He worked as a publicist, editing a 'Welsh Church paper' (which opposed the disestablishment of the Church of Wales) and acting as a spokesman for the Churchwardens Association (which defended Church rates). His real forte, however, was hymnology. His own compositions were fluent but anodyne. He used the right association-laden words to evoke a mood of solemn adoration. A stream of devotional diction kept bubbling up, effortlessly, into his head, but he never coined a telling phrase or described a vivid incident. Moreover, there is nothing resembling *development* in a Darling hymn: all that happens is that one pious abstraction merges blandly into another. Every line is equally static and equally opaque: a little like late Delius. Yet Darling, so poor a judge of his own work, proved an adept editor of other people's. He sifted through an enormous stock of eighteenth-century hymns, in the hope of finding half-a-dozen unsung gems; he translated hymns from Latin, the German and the French; he even emended classics like 'For All the Saints' (and authors of the stature of Bishop Waltham How accepted his suggestions). The proof of his acumen lay in his sales. *Hymns for the Church of England* was up against stiff competition. The three collections which eventually captured the entire market – *Hymns Ancient & Modern* (Tractarian), *The Hymn Companion to the Book of Common Prayer* (evangelical) and *Church Hymns* (SPCK) – all appeared between 1860 and 1870. Darling's humble offering, published at exactly the same time, ran through eight editions. Squabbles over royalties broke out after he died.[30]

William Hearle Lyall (1826-1900): The Pervert to Rome

William Hearle's mother 'dwelt much on the contentedness of his disposition' and his aunt thought that few men had so little to complain of, except 'the want of children – if it is [a want]'. He married the perfect wife – the daughter of a rich inventor, a 'most complaisant' woman who adored him; his uncle, the dean, presented him to the richest benefice in the chapter's gift; and his father, the Chairman of the East India Company, left him a small fortune. He was exquisitely happy playing with his Wren church and his tiny, undemanding parish. They were the height of his ambition; he had no desire for further preferment. Little wonder that he grew fat, 'recalling the Dean'. Yet with every reason for complacency, he was the only member of the connection to go over to Rome.[31]

The rot started at university. William's elder brother (who had been at Balliol) warned his parents '*very strongly*' against sending his sibling to Oxford. It was the 1840s: the Tractarian movement was at its height, and the hot-house atmosphere of a society dominated by celibate clergymen was leading men astray. At Oxford, William might pick up 'fine foppish notions inconsistent with the life of a country clergyman'; whereas at Trinity, the dean's old college at Cambridge, he would be much more likely to arrive at 'a sound and rational view of the duties of his profession'. Moreover, Cambridge was a better bet for a younger son with his way to make in the world. It was cheaper; there were more open fellowships; and there was less competition:

> It will be objected by people who do not know, as I do *thoroughly*, the working of these things that Oxford is the Church university and Cambridge the Law university; this is true and precisely for this reason would I send him to Cambridge; at the latter clergymen are not to be found in the same overwhelming number and the standard is not so tremendously high as it is at Oxford where nothing but the most rigid *external* sanctity and the most profound *apparent* knowledge of Divinity with first rate scholastic attainment can obtain any professional distinction. All this is mighty well if a boy is *devoted to study* and likely to eclipse his competitors, but otherwise it is apt to sour and dishearten him.[32]

William's brother might have saved his breath: his father mixed with Peelites from Oxford and sent his youngest son to St Mary's Hall.

Lyall went on flirting with ritualism after he went back to London as a curate in St Pancras. He corresponded with the leading Ecclesiologist, John Mason Neale, on the use of biers and palls, while Neale was writing a short manual on *Funerals and Funeral Arrangements* for the Cambridge Camden Society. He became the treasurer of one of the more notorious Anglo-Catholic fraternities and the president of a marginally more respectable group of high churchmen – Sion College: the charity (with almshouses and a library) which doubled as a club for City clergymen. He even dreamed of rebuilding his Baroque church on approved Gothic lines. He commissioned G.E. Street, Butterfield's great rival as a high church architect, to draw up a set of plans which were published in *The Ecclesiologist*. But that was as far as he got. There was no difficulty over money: St Dionis Backchurch owned enough land in the City to finance any conceivable building programme. It was the very wealth of Lyall's church that proved his undoing. Successive Bishops of London wanted money for church-building in the East End, and the site on which St Dionis' stood was an under-utilised asset. When the Ecclesiastical Commissioners finally sold it, it fetched £47,000: enough to build six or seven new churches, judging by the £7,000 spent on the new St Dionis Parson's Green. After thirty years of consultation and controversy, firm proposals for the church's demolition were put forward under the Union of Benefices Act. Sir Giles Gilbert Scott appealed to the Lord Mayor to save the 'forest of beautiful steeples' which dominated the sky-line of the City, and William Morris wrote to *The Times* protesting against the loss of another of Wren's masterpieces. It was all to no avail. Lyall preached his farewell sermon in September 1877, just twenty-four years after his induction:

> One blighting, crippling, disheartening disappointment has chequered the tenure of my office in this parish. It was the aspiration, the fond dream of my younger, my more ardent days here to see the parish church completely restored and made as fit as we could make it for the services of the Most High God . . . [Now] what is to follow on this spot, where we . . . meet for the last time; where congregations have worshipped for almost six hundred years, where successive generations have been interred and sent to their 'long home'? All that is sacred is to be swept away, and the place given up to secular purposes.[33]

The loss of his church made Lyall wonder whether Roman Catholics would have parted with a site sanctified by six centuries of worship for the sake of pecuniary gain. But he hesitated to take the final, fatal step until his wife showed him the way. Susan Lyall, complaisant and adoring, led him into the arms of Rome.

Robert Peter (1818-1910): The Clever Fool

After a false start, Robert Peter finally got the fat rectory which Sir Alfred Lyall felt was owing to 'a round divine with good connections'; but he had to wait until he was in his forties to get it, and his eventual good fortune owed nothing to Dean Lyall. The dean presented him to his first living; but St George's, Canterbury, was a pauper parish – and something fairly drastic had to be done to stop it turning into a permanent resting-place when Lyall died. Fortunately Peter had an alternative patron to hand: his old college at Cambridge. He went back to Jesus as a tutor while he waited for a suitable living to fall vacant. In 1860 an aged incumbent died, and

Jesus presented him to the richest rectory in its gift: Cavendish in Suffolk, worth £900 a year.[34]

In one sense, Peter was the most meritocratic of Lyall's clients. He got his fat rectory by passing a stiff competitive examination superlatively well. He was fourth classic at Cambridge in 1842, which is to say, only three candidates got higher marks in the classics tripos of that year. His contemporaries expected great things of him – the *third* classic became Master of Clare – and Jesus were glad to have him back. Yet, with all his intellectual ability, he achieved remarkably little. There is reason to suppose that he made a mediocre parish priest; and he never acted as an administrator, except for a short spell as Rural Dean of Clare. He could have been a scholar-publicist on the same lines as the Lyall brothers: the author of weighty works of divinity and hard-hitting polemics. But all he published was a small manual of prayer for students and two letters to his diocesan. The manual was heavily derivative, being based on a collection of prayers originally intended for boys at Winchester; and the letters to the Bishop of Ely read like watered-down versions of Lyall's charges, when he was discussing dissenters in his most statesmanlike vein.[35]

Peter achieved so little because he was a fool. His religious obsessions exhausted visitors to the rectory at Cavendish. The continuous services – conducted in an 'atmosphere of ascetic mysticism' – reduced Barbara Webb to a trance-like state: 'I have been listening, as in a dream, to R.G.P. telling me his reasons from a catholic point of view for disapproving of the new version of the New Testament'. He lost the £25,000 his sister left him, through 'an absurd investment'; and he quarrelled with his elder brother, who disinherited him, leaving the Peters' ancestral estates to a distant relative of his wife's. The feud was so bitter that Peter's sister-in-law refused to send for him as his brother lay dying. He only got to know that his brother was dead when the son of an old retainer sent him a telegram. He started for Chyverton the same day, but there was no reconciliation: his sister-in-law refused to receive him, except once in a darkened room.

Peter's relatives may have had right on their side. He was notoriously impulsive, and his recklessness made him a standing danger to everyone around him. He had a short way with choirboys who refused to sing:

> 'Please Sir, I've got a pain', [one] said.
> 'Ah! a pain', said Peter, 'We'll soon settle that', and dashing into his rooms he seized a bottle of castor oil . . . and poured it down the unfortunate boy's throat. Rumour said the boy's screams could be heard all over the Court.[36]

Peter's horses were the worst victims of his cruelty. He offered to drive two of the fellows of Jesus over to Cavendish to inspect his new living; and one of them, at least, never forgot the terror of the journey:

> The horses were young and fresh, and Peter, who had not the vaguest idea how to drive, lashed them up to full speed. We galloped through the town. Bump! went Dr Westmorland and myself on a seat as hard as stone, and all the time we could hear Peter on the box, urging [the horses] on. Coming down the far side of the [Gog Magog hills, just outside Cambridge] was even worse. The carriage rocked from side to side, sometimes on two wheels only. Westmorland and I rode with our heads hanging out of the windows, one each side, shouting at the tops of our voices:
> 'Stop, Peter! Stop! Stop! Stop!'
> All Peter did was to shout back, 'Have faith, man! Have faith!'
> At the cross roads from sheer exhaustion [the horses] slackened a little and we leaped out. Peter continued his mad career to Cavendish. We walked back to Cambridge.
> Some time later I went over to spend a Sunday with him at Cavendish, and eventually naturally asked to see [the horses]. He put the matter off.
> 'No, Morgan', he said, 'No Morgan. You can't see them.'
> I insisted, however, and went round to the stables. To my horror and disgust Polly was standing in the stable with both her knees broken. It filled me with pity to see a beautiful horse so damaged.
> 'How did you manage that, Peter?' I asked.
> 'Well', he said, 'I was driving down the Gog Magog Hills *musing on Switzerland*, when quite suddenly Polly fell down and broke both her knees.'[37]

Henry Carrington (1814-1906): The Dilettante Dean

Unless the valuations in *Crockford's* are even more misleading than usual, Henry Carrington made more money out of the Church than any two of Lyall's clients put together – and he made it in the simplest possible way. His uncle, Archbishop Howley, gave him a rich living while he was still a young man, and he hung on to it for more than sixty years. Given the initial presentation and the subsequent longevity, anyone could have done it. Sadly, Carrington did very little to justify his good fortune. He had plenty of opportunities: Bocking needed nursing, just as Hadleigh needed nursing, because the town was dominated by a particularly pugnacious set of dissenters. Seventeenth-century Puritans, eighteenth-century Congregationalists and nineteenth-century Unitarians all attacked the Anglican incumbents. Unitarian meetings – 'shorn of mystery, deprived of dogma and deficient in emotion' – had little appeal for the masses; but they were a way of being rationalist without incurring the stigma of being irreligious, and they had 'a peculiar charm for shrewd [and] knowing men'. The ruling class in Bocking, the clothiers and the professionals, were nothing if not shrewd and knowing; and the shrewdest of them all was the great silkmaker, Samuel Courtauld. Courtauld's mill towered over the parish church, blocking out the light; his influence cast a long shadow over the entire parish. He would have been a formidable opponent for any clergyman, let alone a feeble dilettante.[38]

Courtauld's monopoly of the manufacture of black crepe, coupled with the Victorian vogue for extravagant mourning, made him a millionaire. In the 1870s his annual income averaged around £70,000 a year: as much, one imagines, as the largest landed magnates. If it had been £70,000 a year in interest on gilt-edged stocks, it would still have made him a power in the parish. The fact that it was derived from giving employment enormously increased his political leverage. His mills were far and away the largest employers of labour for miles around; and as his rivals went out of business, his firm became almost the only employer outside agriculture – an island empire in a sea of farms paying some of the lowest wages in the country. Courtauld's relations with his work force were thoroughly patriarchal. He gave them model cottages, model schools, model institutes, but he expected absolute obedience in return. Any difference of opinion was regarded as proof of degeneracy, and the slightest show of opposition was ruthlessly suppressed. Strikers were dismissed: junior partners were humiliated; Unitarian ministers were openly upbraided. The Bible itself attracted Courtauld's self-righteous contempt:

> Robertson [a local minister] has given me a stupid Psalm to read . . . I get very tired of this scrap-reading . . . I have been two hours looking through all the old Bible for something to read, and can find nothing that can be read. To be sure that Book as a worship is the most monstrous thing in all history of mankind; it is a huge mass of rubbish, trash and abomination, with some truly venerable writings collated with it.[39]

Courtauld's connections outside Bocking reinforced his local power base. Unitarians were heavily over-represented in every radical cause in the 1840s, and the leading activists were linked to one another. Sometimes the bonds consisted of nothing more concrete than a community of sentiment; sometimes they were members of the same voluntary organisations; sometimes they belonged to dynasties bound together by interlocking marriages. In any event, a Unitarian with a cause to advance – especially a cause as attractive as the abolition of church rates – could convert a personal grievance into a metropolitan *cause celèbre* by activating his web of contacts. Courtauld became a national leader of a national campaign thanks to the support given him by his co-religionists.[40]

With such a parish and such an opponent, the titular deans of Bocking should have been exemplary parish priests. Nothing less would do; nothing less could contain the dissenters' attack. In practice Howley's nominees exemplified all the worst faults of the old high churchman. Carrington's immediate predecessor probably precipated the anti-church rates campaign single-handed, by systematically snubbing all his most influential parishioners. Sir Herbert Oakley was a baronet married to the granddaughter of a duke, and he never let the local tradesmen forget it. If they called at the deanery, he ostentatiously turned his back on them. They resented his hauteur as only parvenus anxious for acceptance can do. Even a millmaster as successful as Samuel Courtauld was socially insecure. He remembered the shifts to which his family were reduced when his father went bankrupt; he worked very hard supporting the local Whig politicians during the agitation over the Great Reform Act; and he was bitterly disappointed when his erstwhile allies refused to make him a magistrate.[41]

Carrington was too courteous to repeat Oakley's mistake, but his many accomplishments – as a poet, a painter and a musician – did nothing to impress his parishioners. They thought that he was a gentle dreamer, ill-suited to the routine work of an Anglican parson. He was a poor preacher in a town which judged non-conformist ministers by their sermons. His carefully-written disquisitions were too long and too subtle for his congregation, and they were delivered in the driest possible way, 'punctuated by sighs and . . . embarrassing pauses when he was unable to read his writing'. He read the lessons, on the other hand, at breakneck speed: his nickname was 'Dean Swift'. He allowed – allowed being the operative word – a religious society to build a chapel-of-ease in a part of the parish which was miles from his church, but he opposed the subdivision of Bocking into two more manageable parishes. His pastoral work was equally unsatisfactory. He took a perfunctory interest in the local schools, but that seems to have been the full extent of his commitment.

Worst of all, he was an annual absentee. He used to spend each winter in Italy, escaping the English climate. The curates left in charge were chosen for their cheapness, and often left in disgrace. One was a pederast, another was a lunatic, a third was an alcoholic. In time their conduct became part of the folklore of the place. The ostensible justification for Carrington's absenteeism was his delicate health. When he first arrived in Bocking he was rumoured to have only one lung, and no one expected him to live very long. In the event, he lasted sixty-one years and his longevity may well have been his greatest service to the Church of England. It turned him into a local institution. An age fascinated by gerontocrats revered him as 'the oldest beneficed clergyman in Essex'.[42]

The truth is that Carrington earned his preferment in the time-honoured way: by being the right man's nephew, and marrying the right man's niece. His marriage to Juanita Lyall consolidated a crucial connection by turning the dean's working relationship with Archbishop Howley into a dynastic alliance. Carrington's reward for his compliance in this dextrous piece of social engineering was one of the richest livings in the archbishop's gift. But his sacrifices were proportionately great. Juanita Lyall was as strong as he was weak; he practically had to ask her permission to leave the room:

> By all accounts she was a strange person, and there were many weird stories about her. For one thing, she rarely came to Church and was hardly ever seen in the district. It was said that she was extremely passionate; that she used to beat her three daughters unmercifully; that it was she who chose the curates, invariably taking the cheapest she could get to fill the post. Towards the end of the dean's life, it was generally acknowledged that it was she who ran the parish. [She dominated meetings of the parochial church council and] when any document was brought to the deanery for the dean's signature, she would take the paper out of the room, sign it herself and then bring it back.[43]

The wear and tear of marriage to Juanita seems to have increased with advancing age. Towards the end of his life, Carrington only left the deanery to take 'carriage exercise' in his brougham. On these daily sorties, 'he spoke to no one . . . and was often seen by his parishioners to be in tears'.[44]

George Pearson (1814-94): The Recluse of St Margaret's Street

The client who did worst out of Lyall's patronage was the least deserving. George Pearson spent twenty years revolving round poorly-paid parishes in Canterbury. His stipend averaged £59 a year, and £59 a year was about what he was worth. He was far too absent-minded and far too anti-social to make a good parish priest. He had difficulty turning up for services:

> I well remember one Sunday after the bells [of his church in Canterbury] had long ceased tolling in, when I volunteered to ascertain why he had not put in an appearance. I ran off to the cathedral precincts, where he was living at the house of Dean William Rowe Lyall. I was ushered in, and there in front of a roaring fire stood, in his dressing gown, the rector, lost in thought. Quoth the

narrator, 'Please Sir, the people are waiting for you at church.' The answering rector – 'Bless me, Wiltshire, is it Sunday?'[45]

Pearson's cousin, Sibylla Holland, was surprised to see him in his stall during an ordination service – surprised that he had found his way to the right place at the right time. He looked 'quite bewildered' and was nearly left behind when the procession left the choir. As he got older, he got worse. By the 1880s his relatives were referring to him as 'the recluse of St Margaret Street'. He shut himself up in his library, and took to staying at seaside resorts in the off-season to reduce the risk of meeting casual acquaintances in the street:

> He came back to Canterbury for a night to procure a relay of books, but retired again to Folkestone next morning. 'Master is forced to go away', says Stickels [his butler], 'because he can't take any fresh air in Canterbury. If he goes out he meets ladies and they will stop him – so he has to sit indoors till it's dark. At Folkestone, bless you, he's out all day long, amusing hisself by hisself'.[46]

Pearson's well-wishers thought that he might make a scholar. He must have seemed an obvious choice as sub-warden of St Augustine's College and a six preacher at the cathedral. He was well-read and he loved displaying his esoteric knowledge:

> He lunched here yesterday and discoursed at length. As Mamma was in bed, he had the field clear. I joyfully let him talk on. Mamma would have taxed him and had a slight battle I know. She has a way of saying it is all trivial and ridiculous etc. in a sorrowful way, which makes G.C.P. writhe and gnash, and they get quite *enragé* together. At least [he] does. Mamma keeps her temper more, but adds fuel to the fire in G's heart by her occasional contemptuous laughter and very *de haut en bas* ways of treating his arguments.[47]

But much as he liked talking, Pearson was reluctant to *write*. With all the leisure in the world, the sum total of his publications was a new edition of Dean Lyall's *Propaedia Prophetica*. It came out when Pearson was seventy-one, like a ghost from the past. The methodology – the use of Jewish prophecies to prove the divinity of Christ – was impossibly old-fashioned, and Pearson's introduction made matters worse by defiantly defending Lyall's anachronisms instead of explaining them away.

Pearson's basic problems were his constitutional cynicism and his incorrigible laziness. He settled into a sybaritic routine while he was a young man, and there was no reason why he should ever step outside it. He inherited enough money to keep up a bachelor establishment without working, and his faithful retainers protected him from the outside world.

Towards the end of his life the Lyalls got into the habit of using his inertia
as a kind of absolute zero, against which other people's exertions could be
measured. When Sir Alfred Lyall felt that he should be doing more 'in the
literary way', he complained that 'the old G.C.P. indolence' was creeping
over him. Sibylla Holland, who lived in the precincts and had first-hand
experience of cousin George's little ways, was positively scathing:

> Give Gladstone another fifty years, and one's imagination dare not follow him.
> Give Carlyle fifty years and he would wear a halo round his fine old head. Give
> the same to G.C.P. and he would be found with eyes hermetically closed, a
> mutter on his lip, and a half-sarcastic smile fixed for ever.[48]

William Pearson (1817-67): The Unknown Quantity

William Pearson, George Pearson's younger brother, has disappeared
into the mists of antiquity. Very few of his papers survive, and the
references to him in the correspondence of his relatives tell one next to
nothing about his personality or his ministry. The bare outlines of his life
can be recovered from the usual collective biographies. He went to Exeter
College; he served as Dean Lyall's curate at Great Chart; he inherited his
first living from Thomas Darling; and he stuck in Thanington, on a
stipend of £60 per annum, for fourteen years. In 1862 he exchanged
Thanington for a better living in Warwickshire. Five years later he was
dead. He never married and he may have suffered from a debilitating
illness – he was known in the family as 'poor William'. On such slim
evidence, it seems impossible to arrive at any judgment on his
'professional services'.[49]

At first sight, a failure rate of two – possibly three – out of eight seems a
poor return on an investment of almost a quarter of a million pounds: the
Lyall connection's income from all their preferments. But two or three out
of eight is an exaggeration. The most complete failure, George Pearson,
never held a living worth more than £60 and resigned his last parish in his
forties. His gross income from all preferments came to less than a
hundredth of the Lyall connection's aggregate income from the church: as
a consumer of resources he hardly counted. Carrington was a different
matter: he made more out of the church than any other member of the
connection, with the possible exception of Dean Lyall. It could be argued,
with some justification, that his sixty-year tenure of Bocking deanery did
nothing to vindicate patronage. But *any* system of selection was bound to

Table 5
Merit and Reward: Professional Competence and Gross Stipend

	Average Stipend [1]	Lifetime Earnings
Outstanding		
William Rowe Lyall	£1,850	£64,000
Specially Talented		
Francis Holland	£540	£29,000
Alfred Lyall	£415	£10,800
Conscientious Parish Priests		
Robert Peter	£505	£29,800
William Hearle Lyall	£250[2]	£11,800[2]
Thomas Darling	£225	£11,500
Definitely Unsatisfactory		
Henry Carrington	£1,000[3]	£64,000[3]
George Pearson	£37	£1,900
Unknown		
William Pearson	£90	£1,600

[1] Total income from all preferment divided by the number of years between first presentation and death.
[2] £445 and £21,000 if he went on drawing his pension (£400) until his death, despite his conversion to Roman Catholicism.
[3] At his death the gross value of Carrington's living at Braintree was £880; the net value was only £350.

produce a certain number of duds. The most experienced judges had difficulty predicting how well a clergyman would do a particular job, before he tried to do it. The parson's freehold, rather than patronage per se, protected failures from the consequences of their failure. It was Carrington's legal right to his living that stopped his patrons transferring him to a post better-suited to his undoubted accomplishments. Considering the immobility of Lyall's clients, the wonder is that his system of training and selection worked so well and the efficiency of the connection was so high.

The other surprise which the Lyall connection has in store is the existence of a rough correlation between merit and reward. Such a correlation is not supposed to exist under a system of patronage. But if one ignores Carrington (who was grossly over-rewarded) and Peter (who got his terminal living by passing a competitive examination), the members of the Lyall connection got what they deserved. The star performer – Dean Lyall – took home an average gross stipend (£1,850) three-and-a-half times his best-paid client's; his most efficient protégé (Francis Holland) earned about nine times as much as his least-efficient nephew (George Pearson); and the runt of the litter (William Pearson) hardly recovered the cost of his expensive education. Put another way, the two protégés with something special to offer (Francis Holland and Alfred Lyall) got £540 and £415 a year; the conscientious parish priests (William Hearle Lyall and Thomas Darling) got £445 and £225; while the Pearson brothers – the one dubious, the other definitely unsatisfactory – got £60 and £37. Gross lifetime earnings tell the same tale. If one excludes Carrington and Peter, the dean's £64,000 was more than double the life-time earnings of his best-paid client; the best-paid client, once again, was Francis Holland; and the Pearson brothers, with £1,600 and £1,900, were firmly at the bottom of the earnings league.

Chapter 7

The End of The Connection

The Cathedral body has gained a little by the coming of the Rawlinsons – but is in no respect superior to the time when I first knew it. The present Dean and his family are really *grievously* below par socially. I could not dine at the deanery when asked, but I went to [a] party there – and I assure you Mrs Burridge[?] looked quite 'aristocratic' compared with the greater part of the assembly as well as the host and his family.

Mary Drummond Lyall, widow of the Rev Alfred Lyall,
to her son, (Sir) Alfred Lyall, 16 January 1873

When the Church of England loses its social rank . . . it will sink rapidly.

(Sir) Alfred Lyall to Mary Drummond Lyall, 9 February 1873

The Lyall connection was a long time dying. More than fifty years (1857-1910) separated Dean Lyall's final stroke from the death of his longest-lived client. But the connection's extinction was only a matter of time, once it ceased to attract new recruits; and the last recruit, Francis Holland, married into the clan in 1855. The sons of Lyall's clients resolutely refused to follow their father's example by taking holy orders. They became civil servants, army officers, lawyers – anything rather than submit to ordination. The daughters of the connection staged their own boycott: they married into every profession except the church. This flight from the cloth had some obvious economic and cultural causes. By the time the third generation came to choose their occupations, at different points between the 1870s and 1900s, the connection was running out of patrons. Most of Dean Lyall's clients were wholly dependent on his access to episcopal and decanal advowsons. When he died, there was no one to take his place; the connection was decapitated. Even if Lyall had lived for ever, the value of his patronage would have gone down. The agricultural depression reduced the prices at which crops were commuted into tithes, and the tenants of glebe land demanded rent abatements. The long-term effects on some of the connection's richest livings were catastrophic; and there were limits to the Lyalls' ability to supplement their dwindling stipends from their private resources. Clients with children, the obvious source of fresh recruits, were particularly hard hit. If they once dipped into their capital – perhaps to educate their sons – they had no hope of replenishing it; and if they had several heirs, their modest fortunes were certain to be subdivided through multiple inheritance.

The non-economic compensations for low stipends, the real reasons Dean Lyall's clients took holy orders, were also in decline. Ordination still held out the prospect of assured status and considerable job satisfaction, but it offered these incentives to a different class of ordinand – to men from humbler social backgrounds with a highly-developed sense of vocation. The redefinition of the clergyman by the religious militants – the new emphasis on the priest's sacred character and the holding out of the busy social worker as the *only* model for emulation – threatened to turn the Anglican clergy into a separate sacerdotal caste with stronger claims to popular respect on spiritual or moral grounds, but a much weaker title to gentility. The constant assertion that clergymen were 'not as other men' raised the dread possibility that they might not be *as other gentlemen*. One by one the characteristics which they shared with the ruling-class were whittled away. The gradual extrusion of the clergy from local government and the breakdown of the system of dependency in the countryside deprived parsons of most of their power over their parishioners. The pressure to maximise congregations and contain the spread of dissent had the same effect: it put incumbents in a much weaker position vis-à-vis the consumers of their services. Like doctors and solicitors, they had to give satisfaction in highly competitive markets; something which seriously compromised their rugged independence. The inchoate mass of social work which they were expected to undertake drastically reduced their leisure, and the loss of leisure destroyed the axiomatic association of the clergy with learning: the great attraction of the cloth for at least three members of the Lyall connection. All these changes deterred ordinands from upper-middle class families, men who had the capital and the connections to enter a wide range of genteel professions. The rising ideological qualifications for ordination hit the best-educated hardest. In the early nineteenth century, graduates drifted into holy orders in much the same spirit in which they read for the bar. It was a profession, like any other. Ordinands might develop a sense of vocation afterwards, as they learnt how to do the job – or they might not. By the end of the century, candidates for holy orders were expected to show signs of possessing a real inward call before bishops accepted them for ordination, and just as the demand for ideological commitment reached its peak, the 'high honours men' discovered more attractive alternatives to their ancestral Anglicanism. Families like the Lyalls and their allies had difficulty swallowing the Thirty-Nine Articles, once they were exposed to the Scylla of Catholicism and the Charybdis of Doubt.

The Diminishing Returns to a Clerical Career

Are things . . . getting very bad? The answer is they are already very bad indeed. Anyone who opens a Clergy List will find the income of each living given in the forms, *gross* and *net*, with a considerable difference between them.

Rev. H.C. Beeching, 'The Poverty of the Clergy',
Cornhill Magazine (1897)

The flow of patronage through Dean Lyall's hands was the only bond holding his clients together. Without the dean, they ceased to be a connection and became a random assemblage of more or less distantly-related clergymen. Something might have been saved from the wreckage. If one of the members of the connection – just one – had become a dean or a bishop, he could have perpetuated the connection for another generation. Sadly, none of Lyall's clients had Lyall's ability, and it may be that none of them had his opportunities either. The ladder which he had climbed was falling down. The destruction of the old high church party, a process which began twenty years before Lyall's death, inhibited the emergence of Lyall-style patrons and the construction of Lyall-style connections.

The high churchmen's 'valued friends', the Tractarians and Ecclesiologists, did far more to divide and discredit the old high church party than their ostensible enemies. While the bishops were developing their strategy of cooperating with the Peelites, the Oxford Movement's brilliantly-publicised intransigence was hopelessly upstaging the Hackney Phalanx's accommodation with their political masters. As propagandists, the Tractarians captured the high ground of principle. They succeeded in persuading a significant proportion of the Phalanx's natural recruits, the best Oxbridge graduates, that no government, not even a Tory government, could be trusted to protect the Church's vital interests. Alongside their heroic defence of the priesthood's divinely-ordained autonomy, the high and dry dignitaries – with their comfortable incomes and their docile submission to the politicians who promoted them – seemed suspiciously opportunist. The ablest ordinands, who would once have rallied to the Phalanx's leadership, learnt to despise their ecclesiastical superiors; and once they started drifting into ritualism, the Protestant backlash kept them out of high office. The resurgence of partisan religious controversy on a seventeenth-century scale changed the whole way in which appointments to bishoprics and deaneries were made. In 1805 – when the royal family made Manners-Sutton Archbishop of Canterbury, despite Pitt's preference for Tomline – the choice of primate was a private matter arousing very little public interest. In 1848, when Howley died, the press furiously debated the merits of the rival candidates and the crucial decision-takers were far more responsive to outside pressures. Queen Victoria's realisation that party men disturbed the peace of the church by stirring up controversies coincided with the discovery by her liberal premiers that the extension of the franchise made 'No Popery' a major political force. In distributing crown patronage, they might as well have hung out a sign saying 'Broad Churchmen Preferred'.[1]

For more than forty years, from Lyall's ordination till his installation as dean, all the primates, all the bishops of London and a clear majority of the most forceful personalities on the bench were Hackney men. So were many of the deans, archdeacons and heads of Oxbridge colleges. The entire *modus operandi* of the Phalanx, their network of personal contacts, was predicated on this preponderance. Then, in the 1840s, the unthinkable happened. The high churchmen began losing their hold over the hierarchy. The highest pinnacle of all, the primacy, was the first to go. Howley's successor was the most prominent evangelical bishop. The 'Canterbury Party', the quondam members of Howley's household, were aghast. They knew that Sumner's patronage would be redirected towards evangelicals, and they wondered how he would react to high church ventures like St Augustine's. The college was explicitly, even aggressively, Ecclesiological. The evangelical press campaigned against it, and Howley only lent his name to the appeal for funds on the strict understanding that the college's constitution would give the primate, as Visitor, almost unlimited powers over the committee of management. Would Sumner use these powers to suppress the college? Would he pack it with low churchmen? In the event, he did the statesmanlike thing: he left St Augustine's alone, provided the college kept a low profile.

Blomfield's see was the next to go. His successor as Bishop of London, Archibald Tait, was the broadest of broad churchmen. Howley used to say he would sooner die than consecrate Arnold a bishop, and Arnold chose Tait to continue his 'great work' at Rugby. As Bishop of London, Tait defended F.D. Maurice – the totem of the latitudinarians – against the high churchmen's accusations of heresy, and as Archbishop of Canterbury he piloted the Public Worship Regulation Act through parliament. The act made deviations from the traditional liturgy criminal offences, with a view to suppressing ritualist excesses. At root, Tait opposed the Anglo-Catholic revival because he never understood it. The deep historical and theological motives which underlay the Oxford Movement were outside his experience. 'This mimicry of antiquated garments' is how he described them. When Lyall died, his deanery went the same way. Henry Alford, the next dean, was 'educated privately' in the bosom of the Bickersteth family: a dynasty which nurtured three generations of evangelical bishops. Then he came in contact with the old high churchmen at Cambridge, more especially the Wordsworths, and his low church convictions were never quite the same again. In his great edition of the Greek Testament, Alford reiterated 'a liberal belief in inspiration' somewhere between 'the mechanical and verbal theory' and 'the free handling of Testament writers such as Professor Jowett'. In other words, he trimmed.[2]

In this deteriorating environment, the members of the Hackney Phalanx lost the ability to perpetuate their species. The hand-picked acolytes – carefully-groomed for high office by a small self-conscious coterie – were overtaken on the rails by a mob of liberal Anglicans who attracted the attention of the politicians by attracting the attention of the general public. They 'hit off in the pulpit and in publications that particular tone of thought and writing which the public [were] prepared to recognise as at once pious and reasonable'. The chances of the high churchman's protégés obtaining much promotion in this more impersonal and competitive scrimmage were comparatively slim. The sons of a few of Lyall's closest collaborators managed to get to the top of the greasy pole. Christopher Wordsworth the Younger became Bishop of Lincoln in 1869 and Alfred Blomfield became Bishop of Colchester, his father's old archdeaconry, in the 1880s. They were the exceptions.

The fate of Benjamin Harrison was a terrible warning to potential recruits to the Phalanx. Under the *ancien régime* Harrison was transcendently deserving. He had all the qualifications for a bishopric or a deanery. His father, the treasurer of Guy's Hospital, moved in exalted Anglican circles, 'being closely connected with the Clapham Sect'. He took high honours at Christ Church – the college favoured by the high churchmen *and* the political elite; Gladstone was one of his contemporaries. He proved his dexterity as a publicist, by writing four of the *Tracts for the Times* on suitably politic themes (mainly the scriptural authority for episcopacy). As select preacher to the university, he showed that he could deliver brilliant sermons, and he demonstrated his 'statemanship' by sticking to the Church of England when the rest of his Oxbridge associates went over to Rome. So the Phalanx took him up. Howley made him his domestic chaplain; the last in a long line of chaplains which included Lyall and Rose. When Peel gave Lyall his deanery, Howley gave Harrison the offices which Lyall vacated: the archdeaconry of Maidstone and the canonry at Canterbury. And there he stuck: no more preferment came his way. He was only thirty-seven; he had another forty-two years to live – and he was vigorous to the end. Contemporaries praised 'his intimate knowledge of the clergy, his regularity at the cathedral services, his activity in the business of various church societies . . . his geniality, wit and tolerance . . . his readiness to take part . . . in the gatherings like County Cricket Week or the meetings of the agricultural . . . societies'. But he was still an archdeacon and a canon when he died.[3]

Even if the high churchmen had kept control of the dignitaries' patronage, it would have been a diminishing asset. Between 1833 and the end of the century, the number of advowsons controlled by the bishops doubled, but the net value of the richest livings halved – and it was the more valuable preferments that reconciled Dean Lyall's clients to their clerical careers. The agricultural depression which started in the 1870s and lasted till the Second World War hit the cathedral clergy and the rural clergy as badly as the landlords and the farmers. When Lyall took holy orders, the deanery at Canterbury was worth more than many bishoprics. Lyall's immediate predecessor *was* a bishop: a Bishop of St Asaph's, a see so poor that its occupants invariably held other preferments *in commendam* to make their aggregate income up to an acceptable level. After Bagot's resignation, the Ecclesiastical Commissioners reduced the dean's stipend to £2,000 – and the £2,000 was a maximum, not a minimum. The deans kept control of estates which were supposed to be large enough to yield their allotted income, but the agricultural depression falsified all the Commissioners' calculations, and the difference between the deans' nominal incomes and their actual receipts became a yawning gap.

The canons were caught in the same trap. Francis Holland's stall at Canterbury was valued at £1,000 a year in 1883, when Gladstone made him a member of the chapter. In 1906, at the time of his death, it was valued at £600. The parochial clergy escaped the Ecclesiastical Commissioners' net, but there was no escaping the imports of North

American grain. When Howley presented Henry Carrington to the rectory at Bocking in 1845, it was worth £1,400 a year gross; sixty years later, when Carrington died, it was worth £350 net. Over the same period, the nominal value of many of the poorest livings actually increased, because the church commissoners spent a large part of their surplus income augmenting pauper parishes, but enhancements of a few pounds a year in the kind of parishes in which the members of the connection began their clerical careers was no compensation for the loss of all the comfortable berths in which they were wont to spend their middle age.[4]

The steady increase in the clergy's inescapable expenses also eroded their financial position. The depression, which was concentrated in the wheat-growing counties where Lyall's clients held their livings, did nothing to reduce their parishoners' claims on their largesse. The rectory was expected to provide relief in times of trouble, and there was popular disaffection if it failed to do so. In the middle of the century, a Darling or a Carrington could afford to restore a church or build a school largely at their own expense. By the 1890s their subscriptions to local charities were drying up. At the same time, incumbents were coming under pressure to employ a better class of curate. When the connection first came into being, parsons could delegate their 'duty' to a succession of poorly-paid derelicts. The parochial revolution put a stop to this kind of low-cost absenteeism. Curates were expected to be competent – as competent, in some cases, as the incumbents – and competent curates expected a living wage.

The clergy's expenditure on their children's education was also rising. Their sons *had* to attend a recognised public school, or run the risk of falling out of their caste, and the public schools were charging higher fees to finance a higher standard of tuition. The majority of Dean Lyall's clients had economical educations. Four of them went to Charterhouse while it still occupied its original buildings and educated a large number of poor day-boys paying nominal fees or no fees at all. A fifth member of the connection went to Repton while it was still an obscure country grammar school teaching the sons of local tradesmen and farmers. In the 1870s Charterhouse moved out of London to a grandiose Gothic complex in the middle of vast playing-fields. The boarders moved to Surrey with the school; the poor boys were left behind. Repton passed through the same metamorphosis; the tradesmen and the farmers were squeezed out. In any event, neither the new Charterhouse nor the new Repton was good enough for the children of Lyall's clients. Every member of the connection who had sons to educate sent them to Eton, the most expensive school in the country, and a clear majority of the Etonians went on to complete their education at two of the most expensive colleges at Cambridge. The author of one of the best known manuals for parents, *The Choice of a Profession*, put the cost of a clergyman's education at £1,100 (including interest) in 1857; by 1877 it must have been higher still.[5]

The inherited capital which made it possible for the Lyalls to maintain upper middle-class life styles, despite their low and falling stipends, was a wasting asset. Sooner or later, the dean's clients were bound to exceed their incomes, and once they started spending capital, there was no possibility of their making good their losses. Large families were the greatest threat to the connection's modest fortunes. The cost of setting children up in life – of shoe-horning sons into suitable professions and daughters into suitable marriages – could easily exceed an incumbent's total stipend, and the subdivision of a parson's inherited capital through multiple inheritance automatically impoverished the succeeding generation. The four clients who got married and reproduced themselves had, on average, six children apiece. The most prolific, the Rev Alfred Lyall, had eleven. Three of them died in infancy, leaving him with four sons and four daughters to support. One can understand his anxiety when his eldest son, an incorrigible ne'er-do-well, threw up his commission in the army, contracted an unsuitable marriage, lost a large sum of money mismanaging plantations in India – and finally abandoned his wife and children to their relatives' charity. George Lyall's offers of Indian appointments for the second and third sons must have come as a heaven-sent relief. At the age of nineteen they were taken care of for life, and once they got to be commissioners on £3,000 a year, they could actually accumulate savings: something a clergyman could hardly hope to do.

The declining social attractions of a clerical career loomed just as large in the Lyalls' refusal to take holy orders. When Sir Alfred Lyall compared the Indian civilian's lot with the career of 'a fat cleric with good connections', he had his brothers-in-law in mind. As rector of Cavendish, Robert Peter was one of the rulers of mid-Victorian Suffolk, and Francis Holland's canonry gave him plenty of leisure to devote to scholarship. What Sir Alfred overlooked – and the next generation realised all too well – was the ephemeral nature of the power and the leisure: the traditional perquisites of the gentleman. A large part of the parsons' power over their parishioners was derived from their alliance with the landowners. In closed parishes – parishes in which all the land and all the houses were owned by a single landlord (or a small number of landlords acting in collusion) – the landowners' will was law, and landowners generally insisted on their dependents deferring to the parson's wishes, in the the reasonable expectation that the parsons would insist on their congregations 'rendering unto Caesar . . .' Inculcating obedience to properly-constituted authority and acceptance of the existing distribution of wealth was part of the incumbent's role: it was written into the Prayer Book and it was built into the fabric of the normal parish church. Industrialisation undermined this cosy axis. First, the landed interest lost control of the central government to the towns; then the agricultural depression hit them and they lost control of the countryside also. The *ancien régime* persisted on a few estates until the First World War, but the gentry as a whole were in decline, and their erstwhile allies shared their fate.[6]

The other bulwark of the parsons' power – their possession of office – broke up at much the same time, for similar reasons. As chairman of the vestry, the incumbent ran the smallest unit of administration: the only form of self-government at the level of the village. As governors and trustees and guardians, clergymen controlled a host of local institutions: schools, hospitals, workhouses, and charities. The education of children, the treatment of the sick, the relief of the poor, were in their hands. Above all, they dominated the rural bench in counties with too few landowners to go round. If a clerical magistrate held enough overlapping offices, his writ extended to every aspect of his parishioners' lives. He could reward regular communicants and punish evil-livers with the whole force of the state at his back. But the days of the parson-as-despot were numbered.

The Victorian Revolution in Government may not have led to the emergence of an army of full-time bureaucrats, but it did replace the general-purpose justice of the peace with a host of more specialised agencies, and it was difficult for a single individual to accumuate the range of offices which would give him the same wide-ranging power over a community that a simple magistrate once enjoyed. The growth of centralised control was another nail in the paternalist's coffin: it tended to deprive local office-holders of the discretion to reward their favourites and penalise their opponents. They became unpaid functionaries mechanically applying written codes to specific cases. Then the growth of class-conflict and the new conception of the clergyman's role pushed the parsons out of local government altogether. The agricultural depression pitted the farmers against the labourers. The farmers were desperate to screw down wages, to avoid bankruptcy; the labourers were determined to protect their customary standard of living. Whichever side the clergy took in this revolt of the field, they lost out. Either they lost the support of the farmers, their crucial allies in the management of every parish; or they antagonised the labourers, the majority of their congregation. Robert Peter, caught in the crossfire in Suffolk, equivocated: he weighed the claims of both sides and preached reconciliation, but it did him no good.

The farmers felt that they had been betrayed by their traditional ally, while the labourers realised that the parson was part and parcel of the system of deference by which they were oppressed. Clerical magistrates were trapped in a particularly invidious dilemma. Should they appeal to the farmers to pay established wage-rates, risking insolvency, or should they appeal to the strikers not to destroy the harmony of the countryside and jail trade unionists whenever mobs assembled and ricks were burnt? There was only one escape from this impasse: resignation. There was a feeling that clergymen had hopelessly compromised their true role, as bringers of men to God, by accepting secular offices; and one by one they slipped off the bench. They took very little part in the county councils which superseded the old Quarter Sessions in the 1880s because they would have had to stand in contested elections.[7]

The parson's leisure was a casualty of the insatiable demand for religious services and the popularity of social work. The new model incumbents responsible for the parochial revival provided a much larger number of more elaborate acts of worship. In some parishes three services on Sundays and daily evensong became the norm. But the greatest demands on the young idealists' energies lay elsewhere, outside their churches. The revival of the clergy's traditional social role could have absorbed a profession ten times as large. The scope for good works was almost infinite. Parsons relieved poverty, improved rural sanitation, and set up village schools. They worked with women (through the Mothers' Unions); they worked with youth (Boy Scouts and Girl Guides). They threw themselves into the provision of savings banks, allotments, playing-fields and reading-rooms – until the 'rational recreations' of countless villages revolved around the church. In the course of this great uplift drive, the clergy won back a large part of the respect they had lost.[8]

Delight in acting as surrogate social workers had one drawback: it precluded thought. Once the incumbent's day was fragmented by a myriad petty distractions, there was no possibility of his making 'an original contribution to knowledge'. The Lyall brothers could never have produced their heavy-weight tomes on metaphysics or theology if they had modelled themselves on the ideal parish priest of the 1880s. They belonged to an older tradition, which associated the clergy with learning and promoted scholars for their contributions to scholarship. It was still possible for great historians to write great works in their parsonages in the second half of the century – one thinks of Stubb's *Constitutional History* or Creighton's *History of the Papacy*; but they were the last representatives of a dying breed. A friend of the Lyalls lamented their passing, just as the connection acquired its last recruit:

In times not very remote the Church might be called, by way of distinction, the learned profession. A clergyman and a scholar went together, as naturally as an officer and a gentleman. The obvious thing for a man to do who wanted to lead a studious life, was to take orders. This is no longer the case. Men are [not] made bishops in the present day merely for the sake of scholarship. It does a man no harm to know Greek, but Greek is not what it was thirty or forty years ago as a stepping-stone towards the mitre. The road to being a bishop in the present day is to get a large parish into good order. It appears to be thought almost indispensable that a good clergyman should be engaged in a whole network of schemes for the general improvement of the parish in which he lives. He is full of a mass of small engagements which cut his day to pieces and dissipate his mind even more than his leisure.[9]

The end results of the diminishing economic and social returns to a clerical career were perfectly predictable. Oxbridge graduates with the wherewithal to enter rival professions and the drive to make a success of them stopped entering the church. In practice, this meant graduates with rich parents and graduates with first-class degrees. The sons of landowners were the first to go. The number of Cambridge graduates (with honours degrees) from landed families who went on to take holy orders fell away to almost nothing in the 1880s. The flight of the first-class men was almost as pronounced. In 1841-43 two-thirds of the Cambridge graduates who got firsts were ordained; in 1871-73 less than one-third found that they had a vocation; by 1900 the numbers were negligible. As there was no diminution in the church's demand for manpower – it actually increased, due to the multiplication of urban parishes – the social standing of prospective ordinands went down. After the 1860s a third of all ordinands were non-graduates, and by the First World War, Oxbridge graduates were in the minority.[10] Contemporaries were well aware of this dilution and lamented the decline:

The Church of England [was once] supported by the private resources of her officers, the income-tax returns [showing] that the total income of the clergy [was] nearly treble their official income. [Now] there is a large and increasing class of really indigent clergy – cultured men whose wives and daughters do the housework, whose boys have to earn their bread at fifteen, who eat meat but once or twice a week, and who are grateful for gifts of cast-off clothing. The laity must be prepared to see an impoverished clergy recruited from a lower social and intellectual [level]. Already, scarcely half the newly-ordained come from Oxford or Cambridge. Many elementary schoolmasters are seeking ordination, clerks in commercial houses and even the higher class of artisans are ambitious that the cleverest of their sons shall enter the sacred ministry. An underbred priesthood would be almost as great a calamity as an unlearned one. There is a real danger of the clerical office being sought by inferior men . . . to whom £180 a year and a house are not poverty, but affluence.[11]

Clearly a clergy without its upper-class leaven – a profession full of the sons of clerks and artisans – did nothing to help the sons of opulent merchants and manufacturers gain acceptance in polite society. At some point around 1870, the church started losing its ability to launder new money at the apex of the social pyramid. At most, it sanitised the petty bourgeoisie – and a petty bourgeois profession was no place for the Lyalls. In 1902, when the last child of one of Dean Lyall's clients graduated from King's College, Cambridge, only one in twenty of his contemporaries entered the church. King's combined an upper-class intake with a brilliant academic record. It was notorious for its atheism.[12]

The Scylla of Catholicism

The sons of Lyall's clients were more concerned with the ideological objections to ordination than their parents' cost-benefit analysis of the clerical profession. Once they were presented with attractive spiritual alternatives, unquestioning submission to the faith of their fathers was a thing of the past; and just as the third generation were choosing their careers, they were exposed to two particularly seductive substitutes for the Church of England. At least half a dozen of Dean Lyall's relatives became Roman Catholics, and many more lapsed into disbelief.

The great majority of the converts, five out of six, were female. Susan Lyall, the wife of William Hearle Lyall, led the stampede in 1880. Henry Carrington's daughters were the next to go. Mary Carrington became a nun in France; Evelyn Carrington married a Catholic, an Italian count. Sibylla Holland lapsed in 1889, abandoning her husband, the canon of Canterbury, for a convent in York. Mildred Darling saved her husband from a similiar humiliation by waiting until he died. The Lyall women were exposed to a different range of influences from the Lyall men. They never met Tractarians at Oxford or Ecclesiologists at Cambridge, because they never went to university. Their interest in theology began at home. Their male relations – fathers, brothers, husbands – drew them into the theological debates of the day; and once they got into the habit of asking large questions, it was only a matter of time before they started arriving at the wrong answers:

> What do you understand by 'Objective Presence' in the Sacrament? It surely means more than a special spiritual presence beyond that in the heart of the worthy receiver, which would be merely subjective. Is this correct? And does our highest doctrine of the Sacrament differ so materially from that of God?[13]

The more intelligent women, deprived of any other outlet for their intelligence, threw themselves into doctrinal controversies with all the ardour of undergraduates discovering how intoxicating speculation can be. It was their only escape from the mindless round of housekeeping and good works and socialising with the same narrow set of friends and relations:

> It so riles me to feel intelligent and to know so few people who can improve my little talent. I know how lucky I am in my mother, who keeps one wonderfully rubbed up. When I reflect on the *tone* of the conversation in the homes of most people – nearly everybody *here* [in Dover], and that of my own house – I am thankful and surprised. When one thinks of the millions of families sitting round their little dining tables, waited on by their little domestics, shut in their own little castles, all utterly *stupid* and *mean* in their ideas, without one grain of loftiness in them, not one twinkle of divinity – I ask myself, where *will* all these good people go to? What are they here for? Why cumber they the earth?[14]

The male members of the Lyall connection not only argued with the weaker sex, they let their wives and daughters read the kind of books which no evangelical would have allowed into his home. Scott's novels were bad enough. They made Barbara Lyall identify with Jacobites and Cavaliers, because 'I do so *instinctively* and almost spitefully hate the old horrid Covenanters. There is something in that sort of fanatic conceit that I detest'. La Motte Fouqué was even worse. His romances stimulated Sibylla Holland's imagination, and her imagination was already too active for her own good:

> As a young girl of fifteen she was staying at the house of her uncle, the Dean of Canterbury. She stole down to his study one night when the house was asleep, took possession of his cathedral key, fearfully let herself into the dark, empty, vast and mysterious church, and passed almost the whole night prostrate before the altar.[15]

Soft novels led inexorably to hard-core divinity. Sibylla Holland worked her way thorugh the 'French divines' and the Tractarians' apologias en route to her own apostasy. At one time she saturated herself in the history of the Port Royal movement – Port Royal being the Cistercian convent near Paris which became the great powerhouse of Jansenist theology in the seventeenth century. The envy of the Jesuits led to the convent's suppression. The buildings were razed to the ground and the nuns' corpses were dug up and scattered, but the memory of the movement lingered on in the works of its greatest sympathisers, Pascal and Racine. The publication of St Beuve's *Port Royal* (1840-59) – an immense, imaginative reconstruction of the Jansenist cast of mind – revived interest in the Cistercians' struggles. As Sybilla packed St Beuve's eight volumes, to send them back to the London Library, she said how much she would have liked copies of her own. Her seven-year-old son overheard her:

> and two or three days after he came into the drawing-room with a large parcel and a frightened look. I said, 'What have you got there?' He hesitated and blushed, and at last put the parcel into my lap, and with a sob said, 'Mamma, it is the book, but I am so afraid you will be angry; I've spent all the money which I saved'. And when he found that I was not going to scold him he was radiant, and hardly seemed to touch the ground for joy. He had been by himself to half-a-dozen shops, and at last all the way down to Hatchard's; but what frightened him was the enormous price. He had never imagined that any book could cost 3*s*., and his little soul was torn with various emotions.[16]

Absorption in St Beuve's masterpiece of historical empathy heightened Sybilla's receptivity to Port Royal's nineteenth-century counterpart: the Oxford Movement. 'There is something', she told her sister, 'so incisive and clear as crystal in Newman's way of putting things'. As for Ward's *Ideal of a Christian Church*, it stated 'so neatly all my old difficulties as to the Anglican Church being identical with that of the Fathers'.[17]

Foreign travel was almost as subversive as a little knowledge of theology. The coming of the railways made an immense difference to the amount of time which the Lyall clan spent on the Continent, more especially the female members of the clan, and the farther south they went, the more attractive Catholicism appeared. Unmarried daughters and recently-married brides faced the rigours of lumbering berlins and squalid hostelries in the 1830s, but as soon as they had children to look after they tended to stay at home. As a result they only nibbled at the fringes of Europe, and their first encounters with northern European Catholicism reinforced their Protestant prejudices. When Thomas Darling's sisters first went to France, they got no further than Normandy and stayed in a Protestant household. They paid a visit to a little Catholic chapel and attended mass in the cathedral at Rouen. Neither house of God impressed them:

> There was an image of the virgin and child decked out with trumpery beads and artificial flowers of satin and before the altar, though in broad daylight, tallow candles were burning; it all seemed such a mockery of what *we* esteem religion. I can't conceive how in the present enlightened day it is kept up. It seemed a sort of mummery which I would not connect with real religion.[18]

The Alps were the crucial turning-point; the wives and daughters who crossed the Alpine passes and got down into the north Italian plain were never the same again. The great heartland of Catholicism seduced them. Sibylla Holland visited Italy in 1885 and had difficulty ever after in believing that it was not heaven; Mildred Darling spent the autumns of 1889 and 1890 at Lugano and lived in Rome for months together after her husband died; Evelyn Carrington married an Italian nobleman with a *palazzo* on Lake Garda.[19] The attractions of the Mediterranean were basically aesthetic. The Lyall womenfolk were overwhelmed by the sheer beauty of it all:

> Now I have at last seen Italy, the thing that I am most bent upon in life, is to see her more. Oh! the loveliness and the peace of that country! I never can say how much I felt its beauty. The ochre-covered hills, the broad valley of the Arno, studded with red Tuscan willows, and the course of the river marked out by the slender poplars tipped with gold in the afternoon sunlight – and the little old cities on the hills . . . I went to your S. Giorgio in the Seaweed and looked at the sun setting behind the blue Eugenian hills and then at Venice lying flooded in the rosy light. The campanile is gone and the little island looks very desolate – but there is still the high wall and the gracious madonna leaning forward to bless. On bad days I am quite happy if I find one church, one of the large ones, *en fête* – with a lighted altar and people kneeling and standing here and there. I sit and think.[20]

Works of art reinforced the works of nature:

> Please remark the statue of Sophocles in the Lateran Museum – I thought it so wonderful. So is the head of the young Augustus in the Vatican and, among the pictures, the Transfiguration of Raphael and Domenichino's Last Communion of St Jerome. But the Sistine Chapel pleased me beyond all things. Everything of Michael Angelo's [sic] is beyond all others in power of conception.[21]

The Eternal City – the seat of Anti-Christ – was the natural climax of the Lyalls' pilgrimage. It is left them with

> a profound impression of the grandeur and force of the great unbroken Roman tradition; there is a savour of the antique pre-Christian ceremonial overlaid and sublimated by the medieval presentation of Christianity, and decorated by the pomp of the Renaissance – the imagination is carried back 1800 years.[22]

On Good Friday 1896 Mildred Darling attended services in three different churches in Rome. She heard an English Jesuit preach and watched a cardinal plenipotentiary blessing the people with a long rod. The high spot of her visit was a mass conducted by the Pope in a chapel in the

Vatican. Her exultation infected her children. They regarded Rome as 'quite the most enchanting, delightful place in the whole of Italy'. 'I am dreadfully Rome-sick,' her sixteen year-old son wrote from Eton, 'I long to go there again.' Sibylla Holland preferred Florence. There was no jarring conflict between the old pagan world and the 'evidences of Christianity' – between the Colosseum and St Peter's. But she still fell in love with 'the little Christian basilicas and the gardens on the heights round Rome', with the *campagna* lapping like a sea at their feet. Her brother Alfred, the arch-sceptic, thought he was proof against religion; but even he felt the city's decadent charm.[23]

Italy had much the same effect as a ritualist service. A cumulative assault on the senses heightened the traveller's receptivity to the dramatic *certainty* of Catholic piety. The 'vast mixed multitude' who attended mass on Easter Day

> came crowding up hour after hour to the altars to be fed by the pale patient priests. A dense crowd [formed] in a side aisle, and it was the same at three other altars in the cathedral, and at all the other churches. Old crippled people, young children, big boys and girls innumerable, rich and poor of all ages pressing steadily forward and streaming back with clasped hands and downcast eyes.[24]

Inevitably the Calvinists suffered in comparison:

> We spent the day at Lausanne and saw the cathedral, which is considered the finest in Switzerland. It is *never used*. Within is neither altar, nor font, nor pulpits, nor seats. It seems there is no sort of sign of outward worship to be discovered in this country. Anything more miserable than the afternoon service which we attended in the *Staatliche Kirche* of Montreux cannot be imagined, a sort of service so much better suited to a white-washed meeting-house.[25]

Mildred Darling walked up an Italian hillside, for four hours in pouring rain, to make a pilgrimage to a Marian shrine with some interesting stations of the cross – just two days after attending an Anglican communion in a hotel in Lugano, 'a very miserable muddle: only one lady beside ourselves'.

The Victorian cult of death also propelled the female members of the Lyall connection into the arms of Rome. Wives who lost husbands and mothers who lost children demanded ever-increasing doses of religious consolation of a sort which the standard-issue Anglican parson was ill-equipped to supply. Women like Sibylla Holland and Mildred Darling saw themselves as grief-stricken heroines; they wanted spiritual advisers who were willing to accept supporting roles in soap operas of their own devising. 'Attentive celibates', Catholic or Anglo-Catholic, with a histrionic streak and a taste for religious ceremonial were much more likely to make convincing actors in the kind of affecting tableaux their female parishioners had in mind. Muscular Christians were embarrassed by demands for emotional intimacy; and there was always the terrible danger that they would tell the mourners to pull themselves together instead of being so feeble – not at all the kind of response they required. Even the kindest high and dry clergyman failed to give satisfaction:

> Talked with Dr Sheppard in the library till nearly 1 p.m. He is very kind and has a large tender heart . . . under his rough old body and face. But his religion has no symbols, no system, nothing but the sense of the power and love of the Father. This is the religion of the scientific man.[26]

The death of Sibylla Holland's second son – he drowned in a river when he was nine – left her with nothing worse than a tendency to commune with God at his graveside. Each Sunday morning she used to take the rest of her children to put a cross and crown of flowers on his grave:

> Mrs Deacon sends me the loveliest creamy roses and large lilies. I put moss between each flower and the dew keeps them alive for days. I wish you could see the deep peace of my Alfred's resting place. The little churchyard bosomed round with great lilacs in full bloom and rhododendrons coming into flower, and in the old orchard behind the apple blossoms almost [sweeping] the top of the long grass, which is full of cowslips and bluebells. I [sit] there for a long time [because] the place is [so] lovely, but it half kills me to know that my boy's bright hair is under the turf. I wind and twine and arrange the flowers in a dream out of which I awake to unspeakable anguish. I could never have imagined how sharp and terrible would be the pain of mere absence, for I certainly would not bring the child back, nor do I struggle against God's decree.[27]

Seventeen years later, when Sibylla's eldest daughter caught a fatal disease, solitary communion ceased to be enough. The essential loneliness of Protestantism – the obligation to seek out the truth for oneself, the impossibility of relying on authority – oppressed her. Sitting in a high-backed box-pew which concealed all the other members of the congregation, she reflected on

> the virile [patriarchy of the] Protestant religion, in which the master of the house is the teacher, and where each man fights his own way out of his own Egypt. Nothing mystic is here. I wonder who is right . . . Controversy in this age does not lie between the angels of heaven on the one side and the powers of

evil on the other; but it is a sort of night battle, where each fights for himself, and friend and foe stand together.[28]

As her daughter lay dying, Sibylla reverted to the religion of the unscientific woman. She dressed Lucy in a Carmelite habit and had her carried into Harbledown Lodge on a stretcher, looking 'exactly like a white nun on her bier, her hands folded, her face still, only her large eyes moving gently'.[29]

Mildred Darling's bereavement brought out another of the recurrent strains in the cult of death: the use of grief to manipulate close relations. Mildred used her husband's death to coerce her children:

> Last year you had a very precious birthday greeting from one of the best of Fathers, I hope his words are still fresh in your mind, if not read his letter over again. It is a comfort to feel sure that he is still praying for you, and I hope you will ever bear his lovely example in mind, and try your hardest to be what he so earnestly desired. I trust . . . you will never do anything or listen to anything or say anything you would be ashamed for Father to know about. I look to you . . . to help and cheer and support me in my great loneliness. Distinction in work is much thought about, but you know Father cared little as to that, as long as you strove earnestly to do everything to God's honour and glory.[30]

Catholicism, with its mariolatry, offered Mildred more scope for oppressive maternalism than virile patriarchy was ever likely to do.

The gradual acceptance of Catholics by polite society facilitated the desertions from the Lyall connection. It was one thing for the Tractarians to sever the bonds that connected them to their friends and relations. As bachelors or widowers they could sink into new institutional settings, and carry on with their clerical careers. It was quite another thing for a woman, especially a woman married to an Anglican priest. She not only repudiated her old faith, she repudiated her husband also; and she ran the risk of her family repudiating her. When the connection was in its prime, it would have boycotted apostates, and it would never have allowed an apostate mother to keep her child. Fifty years on, the social sanctions against conversion were much weaker. Sybilla Holland's desertion embarrassed her husband, the canon of Canterbury; and her subsequent retreat to a convent in York must have embarrassed him still further. He actually submitted a written explanation of his wife's vagaries to Archbishop Benson. George Pearson remonstrated with Sibylla; her sisters disapproved; and her brother Alfred denounced her selfish credulity:

She has done wrong; she should have sacrificed herself to her husband. But my opinion is irrelevant, for I cannot place myself in the mental attitude of a highly-intelligent person who believes in the vital importance of doctrinal differences in matters of pure metaphysical speculation. [How can anyone suppose] that he has or can require any knowledge whatever regarding the propositions in the Athanasian Creed? At present my ruling feeling is strong resentment against those Canterbury Jesuits – especially Père Du Lac. I wonder Frank so long allowed him the run of the house.[31]

After a while the ripples settled. None of Sibylla's relatives cut her off and her life went on much as before. Mildred Darling's conversion triggered off another family row, still remembered ninety years later; but once again there were no irreparable breaches.

The exact origins of this social acceptance are difficult to determine. Catholic Emancipation undoubtedly raised the status of the religious minorities. The acts of 1828-34 not only removed a series of legal disabilities; they also removed a social stigma. As long as the law disapproved of Catholics, it was difficult for law-abiding citizens to approve of them. Theological uncertainty also made for toleration. The impossibility of arriving at conclusions which were sufficiently certain to be worth enforcing paved the way for the conviction that religious opinions were best left to individuals. The development of Catholic chic was more important still. As long as the English middle class only came across one kind of Catholic, the Irish immigrant, there was no possibility of Catholicism becoming fashionable. The new Tractarians and the old recusants changed all that. Men like Newman and Manning were not just intellectual giants; they were transparently genteel. At the same time, old recusant families emerged from their historic obscurity and took up prominent positions in English society, as leaders of the Catholic revival. No one in that intensely class-conscious age needed to be ashamed of belonging to the same church as the dukes of Norfolk or the earls of Shrewsbury. For the first time since the Glorious Revolution, it was possible to become a Catholic without automatically falling out of one's class. When Mildred Darling met Cardinal Vaughan on the doorstep of the William Lyalls – and Cardinal Vaughan *bowed* to her – she positively purred. Father Benson was the son of Archbishop Benson, so she listened to his sermons with particular respect. Canon Scott Holland, in comparison, was 'vulgar, coarse and irreverent'.[32]

Canterbury, the great seat of the connection, was a microcosm of this social change. The Catholics in Canterbury were mainly Irish immigrants; and had they been the only papists in town, Sibylla Holland would have remained an Anglican. But the social leaders of the Catholic community were the Jesuits of Hales Place. After Napoleon III's defeat and deposition, the Second Republic stopped the Society of Jesus running schools or colleges in France, so they looked round for a new site for one of their most exclusive *lycées*. Canterbury was only a day away from Paris; it had a religious ambience; and the last representative of one of the oldest recusant families in Kent, Miss Hales of Hales Place, put her historic mansion at their disposal. Sybilla got to know the Jesuits through Miss Hales; then she got to know the parents of the pupils through their teachers. The Jesuits, she discovered, were more 'finished' than the average bog-trotting secular priest – and the parents tended to be members of the French nobility. Soon Père Du Lac, the principal of the Jesuit College, was a regular visitor at her house in the precincts; and Sybilla was dining at Hales Place with the leader of the Catholic party in the French Assembly, Comte Albert de Mun. One wonders what the clergy wives thought of it all. Were they envious of Sybilla's acceptance in such aristocratic circles? Or did they regard her as a religious collaborator, treating with the enemy? Or both?[33]

The Charybdis of Doubt

I got a book parcel by last mail, tore it open eagerly, as one does in the jungle. Tracts, by Jingo! A translation from some German on the evidences of Christianity. Alack, I am far beyond the evidences by special pleading of learned Europeans: you cannot imagine the disintegrating effect upon one's religious faith in Paley's *Evidences* and Butler's *Apology* of a careful study of religions in the East. Every nation form[s] its own religion, according to its own pecular idiosyncracy, and it is idle to think of engrafting the rigid and simple faith of the Saxons upon the Hindus. I have often thought that, as every nation has its own form of Christianity, it can really matter little whether a Christian be Protestant, Roman Catholic or Greek.

(Sir) Alfred Lyall, ICS, the son of the Rev. Alfred Lyall,
A composite quotation from three letters, 1859-72

Last Sunday in church the clergyman and his sermon got 'on my nerves' till I could hardly sit still. Every word he said [bored into] my brain [until] he and the church and the surplices and the banners appeared so stifling. I am constantly shocked to find how far you and I have drifted from the faith of most of my friends. Sometimes I have nights of anguish. I was oppressed by having denied my God from a strong wish to agree with you. The truth is I have an extraordinary belief in you as a seer – nobody that I ever met comes near you in that line – and I can hardly believe you are *not* right in the main.

Barbara Lyall to her brother, (Sir) Alfred Lyall,
2 April 1869 and 3 March 18??

In the 1880s and the 1890s Dean Lyall's most distinguished nephew exercised as much influence over his younger relatives as the dean had done, forty years before. But Sir Alfred Lyall (1835-1911), the son of the Rev. Alfred Lyall, undermined the faith his uncle sustained. He turned his cousins – the sons and grandsons of Dean Lyall's clients – into agnostics, by sheer force of example. The third generation of the Lyall connection, the generation which was lost to the church, looked up to Sir Alfred, because the entire Victorian establishment looked up to him. He was the kind of superman they loved to honour: a man of action *and* a man of mind. As a soldier, he fought his way through the Indian Mutiny. As an administrator, he rose as high as an Indian civil servant could go. He ruled one of the most important provinces in the subcontinent; he became the secretary of state's most influential adviser; he turned down offers of colonial governorships; he was in the running for the viceroyalty. As a laureate of Anglo-India, he was only surpassed by Kipling; his verses ran through edition after edition. And as an analyst of Indian politics and Indian religions, he was never surpassed at all. His *Asiatic Studies* were so much subtler and so much more realistic than any of his rivals (Max Müller and Sir James Frazer being the obvious comparisons) that one wonders how their 'solar myths' were ever taken seriously. On every side a chorus of acclamation went up. Journalists remembered his heroism; statesmen besieged him with offers of appointments; Tennyson acclaimed him as a fellow-poet; ancient universities showered him with honorary degrees. He scored a 'specially remarkable' social success. The Athenaeum welcomed him with open arms; London hostesses lionised him; landed magnates invited him to all the right country house-parties. But none of it went to his head; he remained as approachable as ever. He could be reserved with strangers. In fact, it was said that he had 'the manners of an ambassador'. But with those he knew, 'he threw aside all reserve and overflowed with quizzical fun'. His conversation and his 'singular personal charm' opened every door. He could talk, with great vitality and wit, on almost every subject under the sun; he told the most delightful jokes, often jokes against himself; and he won the hearts of the younger members of his family with his quick and warm sympathy.[34]

The keys to Lyall's intellectual originality were the interaction between his two careers and his pervasive scepticism. Without his Indian experience, he would have degenerated into an elegant but essentially light-weight author of belles-lettres; a skilled writer with too little to say. Without his analytic acumen and literary flair, he would have been just another Anglo-Indian. As things were, his two careers enriched one another. His experiences in the Mutiny and his membership of a ruling caste gave point and purpose to all his sociological inquiries. Once he had seen all the unreconciled conflicts in Indian society blow up in his face, he was obsessed by the possibility of a second great uprising destroying the fragile fabric of British rule. Hence his enduring preoccupation with the maintenance of social order. How, he wondered, would the 'decentralised vitality' of primitive animism affect the stability of Indian society? Would some great religious revival act as a unifying force, amalgamating previously unconnected groups in a single moral community? Or would the destruction of traditional beliefs exacerbate the existing state of anomie, in which apathy alternated with outbursts of fanaticism?

Lyall's freedom from religious or philosophic preconceptions gave his answers to these questions a special authority. When evangelicals such as Grant or Utilitarians like Mill examined Indian ideas and Indian institutions, they examined them through the distorting mirrors of fashionable shibboleths. If India failed to conform to Protestant or Benthamite blue-prints, India stood condemned. In fact, the only object of the exercise was to point out India's defects and pave the way for the introduction of Anglocentric norms. The Hindu religion and the caste system were the most conspicuous victims of this kind of reportage. On the Grant-Mill interpretation, they were the outcome of a sacerdotal plot. 'Crafty priests' imposed on their congregations' ignorance; then they used their spiritual supremacy to perpetuate superstition, from fear of losing their privileges. This Brahman conspiracy theory was a re-run, on a different continent, of the Protestant-Utilitarian explanation of the stranglehold of the Roman Catholic church. Lyall's explorations of the genesis of new cults were far more rewarding, because they were far more sympathetic. He never asked whether primitive animism was true or false. The issues which absorbed him were the issues that anthropologists and historians – especially French anthropologists and historians, disciples of Bloch and Lévi-Strauss – tackle today: how do ideas and institutions interact, and how do they evolve over time?[35]

The ultimate source of Lyall's astonishingly modern outlook was his restless dissatisfaction with received ideas. Successive viceroys complained about his readiness to criticise and his reluctance to come to a decision:

> He will not give you a positive opinion upon any question, but he will put all aspects of it before you with wonderful analytic acuteness . . . He is a man of very subtle intellect, who sees so much to be said on both sides of every question that he often finds it hard to make up his mind which side to take; and when he comes to put pen to paper he balances and balances until it is not easy to discover at what conclusion he arrives.[36]

Lyall's hereditary faith dissolved in the acid of this endless balancing. There was no sudden trauma of deconversion, because there was no conversion to reverse. The notorious Oxbridge agnostics – the Stephens and the Sidgwicks and the Greens – were the sons of evangelicals. They went through agonies while they fought their way free from their childhood conditioning. Lyall was the son of a speculative philosopher; he simply came to the conclusion that the balance of probability had shifted against a set of traditional propositions. He soaked up the 'triple assault' on revealed religion, even in remote outposts in the Central Provinces. Historians like Renan, deists like Maurice and scientists like Darwin gave him some of his 'deepest pleasures'. Renan's *Life of Christ* – which treated the Son of God as if he were merely mortal – demolished his belief in the divinity of Jesus; Maurice's *Religion of the World* persuaded him that the differences between Christian denominations were immaterial; and after reading *The Origins of the Species*, he was 'haunted by Darwin's struggle for existence'. He thought that Protestantism was a 'stout useful creed' when it came to promoting popular moralities, and he wished that he could find his way out of 'the dreary desert of scepticism' in which he was wandering; but 'the peremptory exercise of the right of private judgment' had undermined the element of a priori certainty in a dogmatic theology, and 'without dogmas you can't hold a religion long'.[37] When his mother reproached him with infidelity, he reasserted the right his father claimed; the right to pursue the truth, wherever it might lead:

> The great object of education is to learn to think for oneself, to clear the mind of illusion, to see things as they really are, and to understand that we did not find out everything that is to be found out 2,000 years ago . . . I always saw that you had too good an intellect to be able to solace yourself satisfactorily with religious commonplaces. I am not sneering at real religion, but I believe that none but dull and self-complacent people of the incapable sort ever really manage to console themselves for the drawbacks in this life by a sense of fitness for the next, about which, say what you will, we know nothing distinct whatever.[38]

Lyall's loss of faith rubbed off on his relatives, when they sought his advice on spiritual matters. They asked him for guidance because he was an authority who refused to lay down the law. As his sister Sibylla put it, 'He is a person from whom one can differ without a shade of bitterness'.[39] The only drawback to his tendency to see all sides of a question was the indecision the viceroys deplored:

> I begged your uncle Alfred to mark me out a course of reading which [would] track the way by which the intellectual men of his younger. generation have

arrived at the point where they perceive that the old creed is lifeless. He replies
that it would be very difficult, etc. But why should it be difficult? I have an
entire desire for the truth, and I am not afraid to inquire. If prayer and a firm
belief in God and a future state is no longer of avail, why should not a woman
of average understanding be enlightened if she *can* be enlightened? It is this
reluctance [to give] grounds for unbelief that makes so many women suspect
that the true reason for the leaving of the former ways of life is a dislike in the
minds of men to the exercise of prayer, and to the irksomeness of trying to live
by spiritual rules . . . Also a certain pride which has overflowed men's hearts in
consequence of the progress of science. But we may be wrong; only I should
think there ought to be some explanation which I could be made to
understand.[40]

In all probability, Lyall's evasiveness was a more effective solvent of his
family's faith than aggressive atheism would have been. His very
reluctance to proselytise was a message in itself: it demonstrated the
sincerity of his perplexity. On the few occasions on which he did form
definite judgments, his praise could be as devastating as his
condemnation. He approved of the Church of England, but he approved
of it on the wrong grounds. He praised erastian churches as convenient
fictions, eminently suited to the simple-minded and the highly intelligent.
The simple needed 'a comparatively safe channel for canalising [their]
religious feeling'; the intelligent could sit 'lost in dreams' while the priests
got on with their mumbo-jumbo.[41]

The clearest-cut examples of Sir Alfred's influence on his younger
relatives were his favourite nephew and his ward. Bernard Holland and
Malcolm Darling might have been programmed to become late Victorian
agnostics. Their fathers, Francis Holland and Thomas Darling, Dean
Lyall's clients, were well-educated high churchmen with London livings;
they belonged to the class which thought seriously about the evidences of
Christianity and reacted to the arguments of the sceptics. Their mothers,
Sibylla Holland and Mildred Darling, both deserted the Church of
England for the greater certainty of Rome. They went to a school, Eton,
which tolerated a greater diversity of religious sentiment than any other;
and they took respectable degrees at two of the most aggressively secular
colleges at Cambridge. Trinity was worldly, King's was cerebral; the end-
result was the same. Holland absorbed the rationalist ethos of his peers,
Darling became the disciple of a fellow who asked his pupils to have the
courage to face the possibility that there might be no God; and they both
hero-worshipped Sir Alfred Lyall. Holland admired his uncle's social and
literary success, and tried to emulate it. He became a civil servant
specialising in the kind of assignments – as a secretary to ministers or royal
commissions – which brought him into contact with Whig and Tory

grandees. He was private secretary to the Duke of Devonshire (1892-4) and the Earl of Elgin (1903-8). In his spare time, he was a man of letters. He dabbled in poetry, history and biography, producing a slim volume of verse, a detailed account of the tariff reform movement, and a fat life and letters. Darling revered his guardian's attainments as an administrator and an anthropologist; so he went out to India (after taking Sir Alfred's advice) to replicate his career as an Indian civilian and an expert on the peasantry.[42]

Both men, as one might expect, misplaced their faith at a fairly early stage. When Bernard's doubts became too definite to be concealed, Sibylla Holland asked him for reassurance. She wanted to be quite certain that he had not become an amoral sensualist:

> I should think you were a Benthamite. It would comfort your poor mother did she know that you read every day half a page in the Book of Books. I love to know your mind, and may God in His mercy keep you free from the slough of materialism in which a man is given up to follow his own heart's lusts and left to his imagination without a sting of conscience. This, and perhaps this only, would break my heart.[43]

When Mildred Darling realised what was afoot, she sent her son a death-bed appeal:

> In your last letter you said, 'I hope and pray'. Do you really mean literally what you wrote? It seems too good to be true, and I can hardly believe it, because when in India I asked you merely to say three words, 'God bless Mother', to my unfeigned sorrow you replied, 'You put too much on me'. It did seem hard to bear. Can you reassure me in my illness by saying truthfully, 'Yes, it was not a *façon de parler*, I really did pray for you, Mother?' How I should rejoice. I have never alluded to your lack of faith, but as you began I could but enquire to make sure! You will never guess how I pray for you, dear Malcolm, and I am quite sure 'it will come'. I shall not live to rejoice with you in your new-found joy, but that will not matter, as I shall be able to do more for you when dead.[44]

'Dear Malcolm' had enough assurance to resist his mother's emotional blackmail. He insisted on the rising generation's right to pursue the truth, just as Sir Alfred had done, in reply to a similar missive, thirty years before:

> Margaret was a little hard on me if she said that my attitude towards 'religious views' was indifference and not tolerance. I do still at bottom feel a great indifference to religious forms, but not to religious views. These have always interested me enormously – nothing more so. I feel a very keen sympathy with

the real religious spirit whenever I meet it, whether it is in Arthur Cole or in the Raja. [But] anything so definite as a creed it still beyond me. Creeds are the expression of organised theology, that is of Churches, which have a way of slipping between the individual and God, showing him some glimpses of the great mysteries, but obscuring by the mechanical processes that belong to all organisations the full splendour of the real vision. I am afraid I have been verbose and obscure. It is so difficult to express some things.[45]

Chapter 8

The Hackney Phalanx

The English Church now shows corruption in a new form; the rich aspiring tradesmen have perceived that it is fashionable; therefore, instead of sending their sons into the Army, they turn some of them into Anglican curates, and they insist on having them licensed to London churches, so as to be in society, invited to garden-parties at Lambeth, caressible for Ladies who pique themselves on founding every summer some new ephemeral 'charity', i.e. an institution for the maintenance of tame cat secretaries [and] 'Society Curates'.

William Cory to A.D. Coleridge, 21 August 1890

Mr Gladstone used to quote [Archbishop Howley] as one of the persons of high authority who dated the revival of religion in England from the horror aroused by the excesses of the French Revolution

G.W.E. Russell 'William Howley',
A Dictionary of Church History (1948)

Such significance as the Lyall connection possesses lies in the interaction between the commonplace ambitions of upper middle-class families and the needs of a Church threatened with disestablishment and disendowment. The families wanted secure incomes, assured status and rewarding vocations; the church wanted talented scholar-publicists, diligent parish priests, competent administrators and dextrous politicians. The two sides of this implicit bargain have been treated separately by historians. Social historians have looked at the assimilation of the *nouveaux riches* and religious historians have dissected the Anglicans' rearguard action; but no one has ever put the two phenomena together. As soon as one begins to examine the interaction between them, the Church of England's co-option of the upwardly mobile leaps out of the sources.

Britain's political stability has always been attributed to the ease with which new men were absorbed by an open upper class. There was no revolution comparable with the revolutions of the liberals on the Continent, no 1848, because the natural leaders of such a revolt – the rich businessmen, the professional elites, the intelligentsia – were divided amongst themselves. Enough of the dominant townsmen were persuaded that the existing system satisfied or could be made to satisfy their interests and aspirations. The role of the Church in this reconciliation of the potential revolutionaries has never been explored. If anything, it has been seen as a reactionary provocation: an additional source of resentment on the part of the excluded bourgeoisie. The great radical force in nineteenth-century England was middle-class dissent, so the property and privileges of the 'church by law established' were running sores, estranging urban oligarchs from Tory squires. The textbooks imply that this religious discontent was assuaged by a combination of appeasement and revival. The clergy surrendered untenable positions – their monopoly of higher education, their right to levy church rates, their pluralism and non-residence – and stepped up the quality and quantity of the spiritual services they supplied. The Lyall connection suggests that another mechanism may have been at work: the selective recruitment of ordinands and the promotion of meritocrats. If the rich aspiring tradesmen and the affluent professionals sent their sons into the Church, ordination must have neutralised some of the most dangerous supporters of the anti-clerical cause; and if enlightened patrons used their patronage to reward meritorious climbers, the Church must have tapped the talents of one of the ablest and most ambitious sections of English society.

Research on the co-option of new men has tended to concentrate on the topmost pinnacle of the politically-active class, the large landowners. One can understand why: the sources of information on the owners of great estates are so much richer and more accessible than the sources on any other section of society. But this obsession with the ownership of land is an anachronism. Victorian arrivistes had no need to sink large sums of capital in such an unprofitable and illiquid investment. They could break into an expanding ruling class by joining the urban elite, the co-adjutors of the territorial magnates. Dean Lyall's relatives – the Chairman of the East India Company, the Director of the Bank of England, the editor of the *Annual Register*, the barristers and solicitors, the fashionable physicians, the Indian governors – belonged to the class of landless businessmen and professionals who dominated the cities and the empire; who ran the chartered companies, the financial institutions, the influential reviews, the law courts, the hospitals, the civil service. They represented national interest groups in parliament and sat in aristocratic cabinets; and if they wanted to consolidate their eminence, they sent their sons into the Church.

The upper clergy, especially if they had private means, could claim a rough parity of status with the lesser landowners and were constantly drawn into contact with them. They went to the same schools and the same colleges. They shared the problems of estate management and the business of government. Bishops were territorial magnates with seats in the House of Lords; parsons, with their glebes and their tithes, were magistrates and poor law guardians, trustees of local schools and governors of local hospitals. They were the rulers of the Victorian countryside; and in the absence of resident squires, they ruled their subjects in splendid isolation. In the towns they were weaker. The urban clergy were one profession among many. But they still took their place among the city fathers. None of their rivals enjoyed the same prominence or exercised the same influence. Moreover, the Church held out the possibility of incorporation on a massive scale. With 10-14,000 livings to fill, it could launder new money as effectively as the armed services; and it only took a single ordinand – one public commitment to the established church – to ease an entire dynasty into conformity

The Lyall connection can be seen as a classic instance of this kind of co-option. Dean Lyall's father was immigrant in trade; his father-in-law was a successful physician in Liverpool. The shipowner was born and bred a Presbyterian; the Lancashire physician was the stuff that Unitarians were made of. John Lyall and Joseph Brandreth should have joined the opposition to the Anglican domination of British religion and the aristocratic domination of British politics. In the event, they joined the establishment. They bought their residential estates – at Findon near Brighton and Hall Green near Liverpool – and sent four of their sons to Eton and Trinity: the kind of education which virtually guaranteed that some of them would go into the Church. The fathers and fathers-in-law of Lyall's clients were similar sorts of men: upwardly-mobile businessmen and professionals anxious for acceptance. They included a City tycoon who got into the House of Commons; the most famous manufacturer of pianos in an age with an insatiable appetite for domestic music-making; one of the most fashionable doctors in London and one of the richest doctors in Bloomsbury. The piano-maker's father, a Scots Presbyterian, married a Swiss Calvinist and was buried in a Methodist cemetery. The physician in Bloomsbury, another Scottish immigrant, was a close friend of the leading Presbyterian divines in London and wrote a Utilitarian treatise on medical reform. There was even a radical ideologue with a weakness for free thought who died in self-imposed exile in the United

Table 6

The Lyall Connection as a Middle Class Melting-Pot: The Social Origins and Education of its Members

Father's Occupation	Father's Education	Members	School	College	Highest Office Held	Sons' Education
THE DEAN AND HIS BROTHER						
London Shipowner	None	William Rowe Lyall (1788-1857)	Eton	Trinity, Cambridge	Dean of Canterbury	None
London Shipowner	None	Alfred Lyall (1795-1865)	Eton	Trinity, Cambridge	Parish Priest (Good Living)	Eton and Haileybury; Marlborough
THE DEAN'S NEPHEWS						
London Solicitor	None	George Pearson (1814-94)	Charterhouse	Exeter, Oxford	Parish Priest (Poor Living)	None
London Solicitor	None	William Pearson (1816-67)	Charterhouse	Christ Church, Oxford	Parish Priest (Poor Living)	None
London Physician	Edinburgh U	Thomas Darling (1816-93)	Charterhouse	St John's, Cambridge	Parish Priest (City Living)	Eton and King's, Cambridge
London Tycoon and MP	None	William Hearle Lyall (1826-1900)	Eton	St Mary's Hall, Oxford	Parish Priest (City Living)	None

THE DEAN'S NEPHEWS-IN-LAW						
Colonial Judge and MP	Winchester	Henry Carrington (1814-1906)	Charterhouse	Caius, Cambridge	Dean of Bocking	None
Landowner and MP	Christ Church, Oxford	Robert Peter (1818-1910)	Repton	Jesus, Cambridge	Parish Priest (College Living)	None
London Physician	Edinburgh U	Francis Holland (1828-1907)	Eton	Trinity, Cambridge	Canon of Canterbury	Eton and Trinity, Cambridge
NEPHEWS WHO REJECTED ORDINATION						
London Solicitor	None	John Pearson (1806-40)	Eton	Balliol, Oxford	Barrister	None
London Tycoon and MP	None	John Edwardes Lyall (1811-45)	Eton	Balliol, Oxford	Barrister (India)	None
London Tycoon and MP	None	George Lyall II (1819-81)	Unknown	None	Director, Bank of England (Family Firm)	Eton and Trinity, Cambridge; Wellington
London Physician	Edinburgh U	John Darling (1821-58)	Charterhouse	Christ Church, Oxford	Barrister	None
Parish Priest	Eton and Trinity	Sir Alfred Comyn Lyall (1835-1911)	Eton	Haileybury	Lt-Gov. (India)	Eton
Parish Priest	Eton and Trinity	Sir James Lyall (1837-1916)	Eton	Haileybury	Lt-Gov. (India)	None
Parish Priest	Eton and Trinity	Walter Tschudi Lyall	Unknown	None	Consul	Unknown
Parish Priest	Eton and Trinity	Henry William Lyall (1852-1925)	Marlborough	None	Solicitor	None

States. Yet all their children ended up in the same orthodox fold.

The Church of England's role in the assimilation of the Lyalls (and the families with which they intermarried) went far beyond the provision of Anglican services and Anglican rites of passage. John Lyall, the Scottish shipowner, had seven children and twenty-one grandchildren. All of them were safely installed in upper middle-class or upper-class niches; and at every stage in their penetration of the establishment, their rapprochement with the clergy was a major enabling factor. Twelve of Lyall's sons and grandsons (an overwhelming majority) were educated by clerical corporations – by schools and colleges staffed and controlled by Anglican clergymen. Seven, the largest single contingent, went to Eton; four went to Charterhouse; and nine went to Oxbridge, generally to the most fashionable colleges. It was the same with the Lyalls' choice of occupation: the Church was their first preference. Six of the nine graduates – Dean Lyall and his clients-by-birth – took holy orders; the rest of the sons and grandsons were dispersed over the services and the law. Only the two teenagers taken straight into the family firm entered socially equivocal occupations. Their wealth and political eminence – they became MPs and directors of the East India Company and the Bank of England – silenced their kinsmen's reservations; but one of them, at least, took out an insurance policy by marrying a clergyman's daughter. The Lyall's marriages complemented their education and careers. There was a close parallel between the female Lyalls' choice of a husband and the male Lyalls' choice of an occupation. Male Lyalls could become patrons by occupying offices which had patronage attached to them; John Lyall's daughters and granddaughters had to marry into families which already possessed patrons. Four of the granddaughters, a majority of those who got married, accepted proposals from well-connected clergymen. One granddaughter married the younger brother of a vice-chancellor at Oxford; another married the nephew of an archbishop of Canterbury (and the son of an MP); a third married the son of a West Country squire (who also sat in the Commons); the fourth married the son of a baronet (and the younger brother of a cabinet minister). One can only assume that the Lyalls made appropriate settlements on their brides, or offered the dean's influence in lieu.[1]

This kind of trade-off – wealth and influence against status and influence – was one of the fastest ways in which rising families could extend their connections into the heart of the upper-class. The Broadwoods of Lyne, who intermarried with the Lyalls two or three times over, were an even clearer-cut example of integration in the establishment through the capture of clerical husbands. Socially and economically the

Broadwoods were on exactly the same trajectory as the Lyalls. The founder of the family fortunes, John Broadwood (1732-1812), was born at Cockburnspath in Berwickshire; a few miles along the Great North Road from John Lyall's birthplace at Greystone Lees. Family tradition holds that he walked to London in search of employment as a cabinet-maker and persuaded an immigrant Swiss harpsichord maker to take him into his workshop. He married his master's daughter, inherited the business – and revolutionised the manufacture of the piano. John Broadwood was the perfect entrepreneur: technical innovation, the organisation of an assembly-line, the building up of a network of distributors, the control of the company's finances – he was equally adept at them all. He was also lucky. The middle-class market for pianos was expanding indefinitely: possession of a piano was evidence of gentility, the ability to play it a necessary feminine accomplishment. Within a few years, Broadwood's firm became the largest manufacturer of pianos in the world. By the time their output peaked, in the middle of the nineteenth century, they were producing around 2,500 instruments a year. No workshop had produced a tenth as many pianos before, and Broadwoods were able to charge high prices for them: fifty or sixty guineas for a simple square piano: the annual income of a clerk.

The social aspirations of John Broadwood's descendants were the greatest threat to his firm's survival. His sons made competent managers, because they were taken into the firm at an early age; but they developed expensive tastes after their father died. Two of them bought estates in Sussex; the third, a bachelor, set himself up in chambers in the Albany; and all of them went in for the kind of public service which costs money and confers prestige – one was a magistrate, one was a sheriff and one was an MP with a post at court (Gentleman of the Bedchamber to the Prince Regent). The firm's assembly-line techniques – based on the specialisation of labour, rather than the use of machinery – were sufficiently profitable to withstand the constant haemorrhage of capital, as they withdrew large sums of money to meet the high cost of their genteel lifestyle. But no management could resist the progressive loss of interest, once they started sending their sons to public schools and Oxbridge colleges. John Broadwood's eldest son, James Tschudi Broadwood (1773-1851), bought the Lyne estate, served as High Sheriff of Surrey and sent his eldest son to Oxford. The outcome might have been predicted. The son and heir refused to take an active part in the business and took holy orders instead. There is no reason to suppose that James' son had a vocation; he never served a parish. He simply stayed at home, living the life of a scholar-gentleman and collecting folk-songs. He became a clergyman

Table 7
Marriage to Clergymen as a Means of Extending Connection:
The Five Daughters of James Tschudi Broadwood

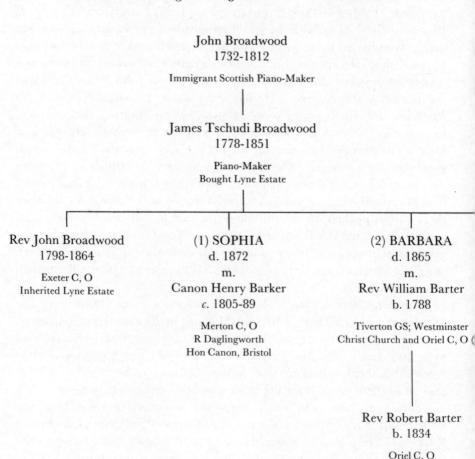

John Broadwood
1732-1812

Immigrant Scottish Piano-Maker

James Tschudi Broadwood
1778-1851

Piano-Maker
Bought Lyne Estate

Rev John Broadwood 1798-1864	(1) SOPHIA d. 1872	(2) BARBARA d. 1865
Exeter C, O Inherited Lyne Estate	m. Canon Henry Barker *c.* 1805-89	m. Rev William Barter b. 1788
	Merton C, O R Daglingworth Hon Canon, Bristol	Tiverton GS; Westminster Christ Church and Oriel C, O (

Rev Robert Barter
b. 1834

Oriel C, O
R Greinton

ABBREVIATIONS:
C   College or Cambridge
F   Fellow
m.   married
O   Oxford
R   Rector
S   Scholar
V   Vicar

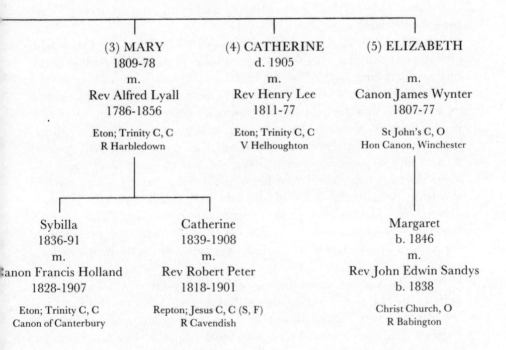

(3) MARY
1809-78
m.
Rev Alfred Lyall
1786-1856

Eton; Trinity C, C
R Harbledown

(4) CATHERINE
d. 1905
m.
Rev Henry Lee
1811-77

Eton; Trinity C, C
V Helhoughton

(5) ELIZABETH

m.
Canon James Wynter
1807-77

St John's C, O
Hon Canon, Winchester

Sybilla
1836-91
m.
Canon Francis Holland
1828-1907

Eton; Trinity C, C
Canon of Canterbury

Catherine
1839-1908
m.
Rev Robert Peter
1818-1901

Repton; Jesus C, C (S, F)
R Cavendish

Margaret
b. 1846
m.
Rev John Edwin Sandys
b. 1838

Christ Church, O
R Babington

because it was the thing to do – for serious-minded young men with scholarly interests. His five sisters married clergymen, for much the same reason; it helped integrate the family in the upper-middle class. Mary Broadwood married the Rev Alfred Lyall, linking two *nouveaux riches* dynasties; Elisabeth Broadwood married into a dynasty of West Country parsons, Balliol graduates for four generations; Catherine Broadwood married a Welsh squarson, a Lee of Dinas Powis; and Sophia Broadwood married into a family of landowners in the Cotswolds – the Barkers of Fairford Park. In the next generation, three of the sisters' daughters married priests belonging to the right kind of family. Sibylla Lyall married Viscount Knutsford's younger brother; Catherine Lyall married the eventual heir of the Peters of Chyverton; and Margaret Wynter concluded an alliance with another dynasty of squarsons, the Sandys of Kingston. They could hardly have done better. The Broadwoods suddenly woke up to the fact that they had little caches of well-connected relatives all over the establishment.

The price of assimilation was neglect of the family firm. A partner who died in 1881, leaving £424,000, 'took no share in the active portion of the business'; he simply lived on his estate in Carmarthen, waiting for the dividends to roll in. The last Broadwood to join the board – after Eton and Cambridge – was described in the normally deferential trade press as a keen farmer, an accomplished oarsman and a heroic swimmer; anything, in fact, except an entrepreneur. As a result, the family firm missed the boat in a rapidly-expanding market. They refused to adopt iron frames or overstringing, long after they became *de rigueur*; and they refused to substitute machinery for skill. Broadwoods relied on their name, a network of distributors kept sweet with long-term credit, and the high standard of craftsmanship which made their products exorbitantly expensive. By the 1890s production was down to 1,000 instruments a year.[2]

An analysis of the social origins of the most prominent members and allies of the Hackney Phalanx shows that the behaviour of the Lyalls and Broadwoods was representative of a large class of upwardly mobile tradesmen and professional men, who were using the church to insinuate their children into the ranks of older-established families. Out of the thirty members and allies analysed, half were the sons of tradesmen or professional men; and a majority of these distinctly bourgeois recruits were the offspring of conspicuously successful tradesmen or professional men in London. Two of the Phalanx's founders, the Watson brothers, were the sons of a wine merchant who made a fortune out of government contracting during the Napoleonic Wars. The third member of the triumvirate, Henry Norris, was the son of a merchant in Hackney. Thomas Sikes' father was a banker; Robert Gray's was a silversmith; William van Mildert's was a distiller; and Charles Le Bas' was a shopkeeper in Bond Street. Benjamin Harrison Senior turned one of the most famous medical institutions in the country, Guy's Hospital, into a personal fief; Percival Pott was the foremost surgeon of his age. (His obituaries credited him with 'raising the social standing of the surgeon in this country'.) The other half of the Phalanx – the established half – consisted of the sons of landowers, Anglican dignitaries and parish priests. Paradoxically enough, they seem to have worked harder than the sons of the tradesmen and professionals. The London plutocrats could afford to pay the full cost of their sons' education and were prepared to buy them suitable presentations (if not entire advowsons). The clergymen's sons, especially the sons of parish priests, had to pay their own way by winning scholarships and fellowships. Out of the six sons of ordinary incumbents, five won scholarships to Eton or Winchester; all six won scholarships to Oxbridge colleges; and five of them became fellows.[3]

Table 8

The Hackney Phalanx as a Meritocratic Melting-Pot:
The Social Origins and Education of Thirty of its Members and Allies
(Summary)

Father's Occupation		*Preferred Schools*		*Preferred Colleges*	
Landowners	4	Eton	9 (3S)	*Cambridge*	*16 (14S)*
Upper Clergy	6	Charterhouse	4	Trinity	8 (8S)
Parish Priests	6	Winchester	3 (3S)	King's	3 (3S)
Tradesmen & Professionals		Provincial GS	4		
(London)	9	Proprietary	2-4	*Oxford**	*14 (5S)*
(Provinces)	5			Christ Church	7 (3S)
				Oriel	3
				Queen's	3

*Some double-counting due to migrations between colleges

The Hackney Phalanx as a Meritocratic Melting-Pot: The Social Origins and Education of Thirty of its Members and Allies

	Father	School	University	Highest Office Held
Sons of Landowners (4)				
Henry Bayley (1777-1849)	Lancashire Landowner[1]	Eton	TCC (S,F)	Archdeacon of Stow
George Cambridge (c. 1756-1841)	Dilettante in Twickenham[1]	Not known	Queen's and Merton, O (F)	Archdeacon of Middlesex
Charles Manners-Sutton (1755-1828)	Nottinghamshire Landowner[2]	Charterhouse	Emmanuel, C (1st)	Archbishop of Canterbury
George Tomline (1750-1827)	Suffolk Landowner	Bury St Edmund's Grammar School	Pembroke, C (S,F)	Bishop of Winchester
Upper Clergy (6)				
Edward Churton (1800-1874)	Archdeacon of St David's	Charterhouse	Ch Ch, O	Archdeacon of Cleveland
William Churton (c. 1801-1828)	Archdeacon of St David's	Rugby	Queen's and Oriel, O (F)	Domestic Chaplain
George D'Oyly (1778-1846)	Archdeacon of Lewes	Not known	Corpus, C (S,F)	Rector of Lambeth
Thomas Rennell (1754-1840)	Prebendary of Lincoln	Eton (S)	KCC (S,F)	Dean of Winchester
John Spry (1777-1854)	Prebendary of Salisbury	Eton	Oriel, O (1st)	Canon of Canterbury
Christopher Wordsworth (1807-1885) (the Younger)	Master of Trinity	Winchester (S)	TCC (S,F,T)	Bishop of Lincoln
Parish Priests (6)				
Christopher Bethell (1773-1854)	Rector of Wallingford, Berks.	Eton (S)	KCC (S,F)	Bishop of Llandaff
William Howley (1766-1848)	Vicar of Bishop's Sutton, Hants.	Winchester (S)	New and Ch Ch, O (S,F,T,P)	Archbishop of Canterbury
Charles Lloyd (1784-1829)	Rector of Aston-sub-Edge, Gloucs.[3]	Eton (S)	Ch Ch, O (S,F,T,P)	Bishop of Oxford
John Lonsdale (1788-1867)	Vicar of Darfield, Yorks.	Eton (S)	KCC (S,F,T)	Bishop of Lichfield
Richard Mant (1776-1848)	Rector of All Saints, Southampton[4]	Winchester (S)	Trinity and Oriel, O (S,F)	Bishop of Down and Connor
Hugh Rose (1795-1838)	Vicar of Glynde, Sussex[5]	Uckstead School	TCC (S, 1st)	Principal, King's College, London

	Father	School	University	Highest Office Held
London Tradesmen (7)				
Robert Gray (c. 1762-1834)	London Silversmith	Not known	St Mary's, O	Bishop of Bristol
Charles Le Bas (1779-1861)[6]	London Shopkeeper[6]	Hyde Abbey School	TCC (S,F)	Principal, Haileybury College
William Lyall (1788-1857)	London Shipowner[7]	Eton	TCC (S)	Dean of Canterbury
Henry Norris (1771-1850)	London Merchant[8]	Dr Newcome's School	Peterhouse, C	Prebendary of St Paul's
Thomas Sikes (c. 1766-1839)	London Banker	Not known	Pembroke, O	Vicar of Guilsborough
William Van Mildert (1765-1836)	London Distiller	Merchant Taylor's	Queen's and Ch Ch, O (S,F,T)	Bishop of Durham
John Watson (1769-1839)	London Wine Merchant	Charterhouse	University, O	Prebendary of St Paul's
London Professionals (2)				
Benjamin Harrison (1808-1887)	Treasurer of Guy's Hospital[9]	Not known	Ch Ch, O (S,F)	Archdeacon of Maidstone
Joseph Pott (1759-1847)	Surgeon	Eton	St John's, C (S, 1st)	Archdeacon of London
Provincial Tradesmen and Professionals (5)				
William Carey (1769-1840)	Poor Tradesman in Worcester (?)	Westminster (S)	Ch Ch, O (S,F,T)	Bishop of St Asaph's
Richard Jelf (1798-1871)	Rich Tradesman in Gloucester (?)	Eton	Ch Ch, O (1st)	Principal, King's College, London
Charles Blomfield (1786-1857)	Schoolteacher in Suffolk	Bury St Edmund's Grammar School	TCC (S,F,T)	Bishop of London
James Monk (1784-1856)	Army Officer	Charterhouse	TCC (S,F,T,P)	Bishop of Gloucester
Christopher Wordsworth (1774-1846) (the Elder)	Attorney in Cockermouth	Hawkshead Grammar School	TCC (S,F,Master)	Master of Trinity

Abbreviations

C	Cambridge
Ch Ch	Christ Church
F	Fellow
GS	Grammar School
KCC	King's College, Cambridge
O	Oxford
P	Professor
S	Scholar
T	Tutor
TCC	Trinity College, Cambridge
1st	1st Class Degree

[1] Cambridge was the grandson of a London merchant

[2] Manners-Sutton was a grandson of the 3rd Duke of Rutland, a brother of Lord Manners (a Lord Chancellor of Ireland) and father of Viscount Canterbury (a Speaker of the House of Commons).

[3] And a schoolmaster in Great Missenden, Bucks.

[4] And a Master of King Edward's Grammar School.

[5] And a schoolmaster at Uckfield.

[6] He was the grandson of a London brewer; he married the daughter of the brewer who invented India Pale Ale.

[7] William Lyall's father was an immigrant Scotsman.

[8] Norris's grandfather on his mother's side was a parish priest.

[9] Harrison married the daughter of a London banker and prominent member of the Clapham Sect – Henry Thornton, MP.

The implications of the Lyall connection for the reform of the Church of England are just as wide-ranging. Historians have largely lifted their accounts of Anglican religious renewal from Tractarian or evangelical propaganda. Publicists proclaiming the importance of the Oxford Movement and the Clapham Sect claimed that the years between 1828 and 1845 marked a great discontinuity in the history of the Church of England. A crisis of overwhelming proportions arose, as the enemies of the Anglican establishment seized control of the state and turned its power against 'true religion'. Only a handful of far-sighted and dedicated men realised the full extent of the danger, and launched crusades which forced the hierarchy's hand – a hierarchy stuffed with worldly placemen.

Dean Lyall and his clients gave very little support to these sensational and self-serving interpretations. Neither the conventional chronology nor the conventional denigration of the old high church party fits the Lyall connection. The Hackney Phalanx adopted the future dean before Catholic Emancipation rose to the top of the political agenda, and his clients were still perpetuating his high and dry churchmanship fifty years after Newman's 'perversion' to Rome. At their level, the level of the working clergy, the stress is all on continuity; on religious evolution, rather than religious revolution. Moreover, the prime movers during the first phase of the Anglicans' spiritual renewal were the despised high churchmen. The most conservative wing of the church, the high and dry dignitaries, initiated their counter-revolution forty years before the terms Tractarian and Ecclesiologist were invented. The differences between the generations were mainly differences of emphasis and style. The old high churchmen were dignified and emollient; the young militants were exhibitionist and provocative, so they made a much bigger splash in the media.

With one vital exception (the Ecclesiastical Commissioners), all the components which made for the Anglican revival were already in place when the political crisis of the 1820s and the 1830s broke out. There was no need to create a new theology or a new ritual. The high churchmen preserved Laudian doctrines and practices through the tunnel of the eighteenth century: all the Tractarians and Ecclesiologists did was thrust them down the evangelicals' throats, with great shows of gratuitous hostility. Two of the Hackney Phalanx's favourite voluntary associations, the SPC and the SPCK, were inherited from an earlier age; and their greatest creation, the National Society, was launched in 1811. Above all, the network of personal relations, which made the high church party such a formidable lobby, was already in existence. The 'clerical employment agency' was steering promising clients towards sympathetic bishops, long before Joshua Watson accelerated the tempo. Out of the thirty members and allies of the Phalanx, twenty-five got first-class degrees and twenty-three graduated before 1810. Clearly, the first phase of this meritocratic reaction was part of an establishment-led revulsion against the French Revolution; it was only at a much later stage that the outsiders – the religious militants and the politicians – got in on the act.

It is possible that Howley's predecessor as primate, Archbishop Manners-Sutton (1755-1828), was the real pioneer. Manners-Sutton (Bishop of Norwich, 1792-1805; Archbishop of Canterbury 1805-28) was the personification of aristocratic influence. His grandfather, the third Duke of Rutland, was a semi-permanent fixture at court; his brother, a Lord Chancellor of Ireland, was raised to the peerage as Lord Manners; his son, a Speaker of the House of Commons, became Viscount Canterbury. He owed all his preferment to his relatives' political pre-eminence and the favour of the royal family. Yet he worked hand-in-glove with the Phalanx, just as Howley did. His chaplains, like Howley's, were in the van of the church movement. Two examples will make the point: Christopher Wordsworth (1774-1846) and Hugh Rose (1795-1838) – two classic middle-class scholarship boys.

Wordsworth, the brother of the poet, was the orphan son of an impoverished attorney in Cockermouth, who left practically nothing when he died, except a 'claim' on Lord Lonsdale which Lord Lonsdale promptly repudiated. He went to the grammar school at Hawkshead, did brilliantly at Cambridge (tenth wrangler) and got a fellowship at Trinity (1798-1802). At that point he was spotted. Manners-Sutton, currently Bishop of Norwich, took him into his household as tutor to his son. When Manners-Sutton moved to Lambeth in 1805, he took Wordsworth with him as his domestic chaplain. Between 1804 and 1812 he presented Wordsworth to four livings and in 1826 he persuaded Liverpool to appoint him Master of Trinity. Wordsworth repaid his patronage. As an author, he published *Ecclesiastical Biography* (1819) – a collective eulogy of selected high church heroes. As a member of the Phalanx, he helped Joshua Watson found the National Society. As Dean of Bocking, he befriended dissenters; he even married a Quaker. As Master of Trinity, he kept the largest and richest college at Oxbridge firmly in the high church camp; and as Vice-Chancellor, he tried to rationalise the classics and divinity examinations. He even founded a dynasty of divines: two of his sons and one of his grandsons became bishops.

Rose was the son of a schoolteacher in Sussex. He won a scholarship to Trinity from Uckfield School, took high honours (fourteenth wrangler; Chancellor's Medalist) and just failed to get a fellowship. Lord Sheffield helped him pay his way through Cambridge and the Duke of Argyll employed him as tutor to his son, but Rose's aristocratic patrons soon gave way to a high church collective. In 1819-21 George D'Oyly, one of Manners-Sutton's former chaplains, tried Rose out as a curate. It soon became apparent that he was the most gifted champion of traditional theology against the Biblical Critics, and over the next fifteen years the Phalanx carefully stage-managed his career. They put together a package of preferment which gave him a high enough income to concentrate on theological controversies, and a succession of public platforms to propagate his ideas. Manners-Sutton presented him to a living at Horsham in Kent, had a hand in his original appointment as a select preacher at Cambridge, and got him a stall at Chichester. After Manners-Sutton's death, it was up to others to provide. Blomfield (currently Bishop of London) made Rose his domestic chaplain; Howley (currently Archbishop of Canterbury) presented him to the deanery at Hadleigh; Van Mildert (currently Bishop of Durham) gave him the chair of divinity in the newly-created University of Durham; the Governors of St Thomas's Hospital appointed him perpetual curate of St Thomas's, Southwark, and the Trustees of King's College, London, elected him the first Principal. Rose lived up to this sponsors' expectations. He went to Germany to beard the Biblical Critics in their lair, preached brilliant sermons against infidelity, and published the most effective refutations of the Tübingen school. His reputation stood so high in the 1830s that the Tractarians hoped he would assume the leadership of their movement.

Pursuing the high church party forward in time has much the same effect as tracing the origins of the Phalanx: it shows how central the old high churchmen were, in the whole process of reformation. They gradually lost control of the bench, but a high and dry tradition survived in the Phalanx's best-fortified strongholds: the self-perpetuating clerical corporations. Lyall's earliest experiences of the high churchmen's measured ceremonial were the chapel services at Eton and Trinity. A century later, they were very little changed; the dean's great-nephews were in safe hands. Neither low church enthusiasm nor ritualist excess set the tone of the most aristocratic institutions; good taste was all, and good taste was the monopoly of the high and dry. The cathedrals were more vulnerable to attrition because the chapters were the playthings of bishops and premiers, but half a century after the Irish Church Bill, there were still plenty of high churchmen in the cloisters. For thirty years after Lyall's death, one of his closest collaborators was the most prominent member of the chapter at Canterbury. Deans came and deans went, but Archdeacon Harrison went on forever. When he finally died, in 1887, he had claims to be the last surviving member of the Hackney Phalanx. Outside the clerical corporations, high church parsons remained loyal to their old patrons. Carrington and Darling inserted stained glass windows to Howley's memory in their churches. They simply waited for the mainstream of Anglican sentiment to catch them up – and in two vital respects that was what happened. The standard Anglican service moved towards the high churchmen's cathedral norms without arriving at the Anglo-Catholics' histrionics; while evangelical theology, with its emphasis on conversion and the community of all believers, lost ground to some of the Phalanx's favourite doctrines, notably the importance of the sacraments and the apostolic succession.

There was some surprise when the Church of England reached the end of a century of reform with so many of its privileges and so much of its property intact. Loyal churchmen, as well as dissenters and Catholics and rationalists, wondered how the trick was done. Patronage may well have been the key: the crucial link between social mobility and religious reform. The patrons' readiness to reward merit drew the thrusting sons of self-made businessmen and professionals into the orthodox fold. As a result, patronage not only contained the latent conflict between priesthood and bourgeoisie which produced such virulent anti-clericalism on the continent, it coopted enough of the natural leaders of the religious opposition to revitalise the church. The most powerful motive that the nineteenth century knew worked in the Church of England's favour. Not sex, not money, not even religious enthusiasm, but the desire for social acceptance. Snobbery was on the side of the Anglicans, and patronage kept it there. In 1873 the great luminary of the Lyall family, Sir Alfred, predicted that the Church of England would 'sink rapidly' once ordination ceased to be a channel of upward social mobility. The twentieth century proved him right.

Chapter 9

Patronage

I believe with you that the days when great prizes and distinctions could be got by those who had the spirit to aim at them and [the] courage to pursue are fast passing away, to be replaced by a more general distribution of fortune's gifts on as very diluted scale; but this is not taking place in your service alone – it is the same in the Church and in other professions. You, however, who advocate progress and the break-up of the old 'Tory' abuses which kept in comparatively few hands power and patronage, ought not to regret the changes. I may more consistently do so. I am not, as you have so often asserted, a Tory; but I do not expect unmitigated good from any change that *men* can make. I believe [every] state of society [has] had its compensations – I might even say its advantages – which are lost in passing to another. Perhaps each state of things was the best that could be in that particular state of mankind. I do not know that I should have asked to live in any previous age – yet *this* sometimes appears to me to lack the strength and vigour and simplicity of its precursors. Diffusion and weakening seem its characteristics.

Mary Drummond Lyall, the wife of the Rev Alfred Lyall,
to her son, (Sir) Alfred Lyall, ICS, 7 April 1863

Until the system went into terminal decline at some undefined point in the nineteenth century, patronage was the organising principle of English society. Compared with the vibrant realities of patronage, class looks suspiciously like a grand abstraction: an explanatory device invented by historians, which had very little influence on the everyday ambitions of individuals who knew that their fates turned on their ability to commend themselves to effective patrons. Patron-client relationships, as much as class relationships, allocated resources on a massive scale, and every institution adapted itself to their allocative function. The middle-class family, the basic microcosm of the dominant class, operated as a patronage-maximising collective.

Like some species threatened with extinction in a hostile environment, kinship groups continually tested the full range of patrons to whom they had access and concentrated their resources – human and financial – on the most responsive. Individual inclinations were subordinated to the common struggle for survival. Sons spent the first half of their life-cycle commending themselves to patronage-bestowers in the hope that they would become patrons in their turn. Daughters made similar sacrifices for the common weal: they were married off to well-connected clients. More complex organisations – the Church of England, say – became confederations of connections which imposed their own dynamic on their symbiotic hosts. Clusters of clients grouped round rival patrons competed for offices, and their competition explains the organisations' departures from impersonal bureaucratic norms. One could even argue that connections stabilised the class system by acting as a safety-net and a safety-valve. Influence reduced the speed at which upper-class drop-outs fell out of their castes: preferential access to undemanding jobs was one aspect of patronage. At the same time, the pursuit of patrons turned ambitious (and potentially disruptive) arrivistes into assiduous sycophants.

Clerical patronage has particular claims on the attention of historians. Clergymen made up a significant proportion of the intelligentsia; they supplied religious services to half the population; they dominated local government, as justices of the peace and poor law guardians; they were widely credited with maintaining a high standard of popular morality; they exercised a pervasive influence over public opinion. With its 10,000 ordinands, the church was the largest employer of graduates: a larger employer than all the other professions put together. Yet we know next to nothing about the appointment and promotion of this vast work force. Slim shafts have been sunk into the selection of bishops, but very little of the research on the working clergy looks at the operation of the system of patronage from the inside. The few studies which have been undertaken tend to treat patronage in the way the parliamentary papers treated patronage, as statistical exercises rather than dynamic processes. There is no Namierite dissection of the 'parties' within the church. There is no detailed study of a clerical connection. More surprising still, there is no monograph on the Hackney Phalanx. The best book on the Phalangists – indeed, virtually the only book on the Phalangists – is the two-volume biography of Joshua Watson, the Phalanx's lay leader, written more than a century ago. Except for a handful of doctoral dissertations, the old high churchmen and their pervasive influence have been consigned to the dustbin of history. This neglect of a once powerful elite is all of a piece with the neglect of patronage as a whole. Historians have explored the *political* implications of patronage, as a means of winning elections and mobilising majorities in the Commons; but the social dimension of patronage – patronage as the matrix in which professional families had their being, permeating every aspect of their lives – is a gaping hole in the historiography.[1]

There are obvious reasons for this omission. The current preoccupations of the intelligentsia set the agenda of historians, and patron-client relationships hardly feature in the after-dinner conversation of the chattering classes. Patronage is a dragon which has been slain. Class, the great rival of patronage as a mode of explanation, may be momentarily in eclipse; but it still appeals to romantic conservatives, and history is written by backward-looking men. *Clerical* patronage is an even deader duck since organised religion stopped exercising any leverage over society aeons ago. It takes a real effort of the imagination to appreciate the power wielded by the great ecclesiastical patrons, or the importance of the Church of England in early nineteenth-century society. The educated layman sees the clergy of the early nineteenth century through Trollope's eyes, and the divines of Barchester are marginalised men – picturesque figures in picturesque settings, already on the sidelines of history.

Another obstacle inhibiting research on clerical patronage is methodological. It is comparatively easy to obtain information on institutional reforms. The sources are accessible and the context is familiar. Hansard, blue books, the royal archives, the papers of the relevant ministers, the files of official bodies; records such as these are the stuff of life to mainstream political historians. The context is equally comprehensible: parliament, the cabinet, commissions and committees – none of them drive the working historian to the limits of his ability to comprehend. As a result, researching the Peelites reforming the Church of England instead of the Peelites abolishing the Corn Laws involves a slight change of focus, not an intellectual revolution. The very ease with which policies can be researched has led to the neglect of processes; and the further down the clerical hierarchy one goes, the more difficult research becomes. One can find out why bishops were appointed from major collections in the public domain. The real problem is finding out why an ordinary incumbent was presented. The relevant letters have almost always been destroyed, because presentations were so commonplace, and such references as survive tend to be scattered through a mass of very low-grade ore. It is, therefore, almost impossible to reconstruct the full extent of an individual clergyman's allies: the entire range of patrons and clients with whom he was in touch; the first step towards discovering the way his connection worked. The more decentralised forms of patronage were so diffuse that one can never be sure that every strand in the chain of influence has been unravelled. The most that one can do is exploit chance survivals – survivals like the letters on which this book is based.

Problems of evaluation exacerbate these difficulties. Three great issues dominate the study of patronage. Did patronage unite or divide society? Did it give poor meritocrats a chance to rise in the socio-economic scale, or keep them in their lowly places? Did it make institutions more or less efficient? None of these questions has been subjected to particularly rigorous analysis. Historians have generally been content to regurgitate contradictory arguments developed in the course of the great nineteenth-century controversies over the redistribution of patronage.

Patronage undoubtedly had divisive implications. Every connection – every cluster of clients around their patron – was in competition with all the other connections for a limited number of good things, and every member of a connection was in competition with all the other members of the same connection for the favour of the patron. Faction and servility were the inevitable results. Yet patron-client relationships also made for integration. The advantage of hunting as a pack held higher-order kinship groups together, long after they would have been broken up into their nuclear constituents, and unrelated 'friends' were drawn into alliances through marriage or godparenthood (the 'pseudo-kinship' of the anthropologists). Similar bonds cut across the lines of class in a highly-stratified society. The emergence of class consciousness and class conflict was inhibited when patrons and clients in structural opposition to one another recognised reciprocal obligations and claimed that they belonged to a single moral community. Patronage produced clerical dynasties and bound petty-bourgeois clerks to the landed magnates who presented them to livings.[2]

The effects of patronage on social mobility were equally contentious. Radicals saw 'influence' in much the same light that they saw the empire – as a vast system of outdoor relief cushioning the undeserving rich from the harsh realities of the labour market. The well-connected few monopolised all the prizes of life, while the poorly-connected many waited hungrily in the wings. Apologists for the old order wavered between saying that this was only as it should be – given the inherent superiority of the well-bred gentlemen – and exaggerating the frequency with which enlightened patronage raised poor clients in the social scale. The church was one of their favourite examples of upward social mobility. Even in the eighteenth century, the golden age of aristocratic patronage, there was a trickle of bishops from comparatively humble origins.[3]

Of course the apologists overlooked the fact that the most meritocratic members of the bench only got their feet on the ladder of preferment by passing examinations superlatively well. It was only *after* the poverty-stricken sizar financed his education by winning scholarships and became a fellow of some Oxbridge college, that he began to attract the attention of landed magnates or leading politicians or members of the royal family by coaching their sons. Victorian reformers casting round for some objective test of ability fell on the first part of this selection process – the open competitive examinations – as the ideal portal to the service of the state. But they also had their blind spot. Examinations could just as easily narrow the social spectrum from which recruits were taken. After the directors of the East India Company lost their rights of nomination, the Indian Civil Service was swamped by the sons of clergymen, because successful examination-wallahs needed a highly specialised and highly-expensive education, which the sons of Oxbridge graduates were far more likely to receive than any other section of society. Far from regretting this financial barrier, the Macaulays and the Trevelyans of this world positively welcomed it. The rising cost of a public school-cum-Oxbridge education was seen as a rough and ready guarantee of a candidate's gentility: a substitute for 'connection' as a means of weeding out individuals without the necessary moral qualities and savoir faire to command the respect of their inferiors, if they were entrusted with public office. There was a general panic, which threatened the existence of the entire examination system, when it was discovered that a handful of poor men's sons were making their way into the ICS, thanks to the higher efficiency and lower charges of the London crammers.[4]

Institutional efficiency – the third great issue – was clearly a function of the suppression or promotion of talent. Radicals blamed patronage for the underperformance of every complex organistion, from the army's failure to trounce the Russians in the Crimea to the church's failure to trounce the dissenters at home. Their critique ran on familiar lines: favouritism deprived soldiers and clerics of all incentive by divorcing merit from reward. Only impersonal tests could encourage 'ability and exertion'. The champions of patronage were less certain of the advantages of objectivity. They insisted that patrons were better judges of their clients' deserts than anonymous examiners or remote personnel officers. A patron had more data on an individual's competence, because he knew him personally, and he had a powerful motive not to advance the undeserving because his reputation was at stake. If a patron's protégés habitually let him down, they made him look a fool; and his peers soon learnt to distrust his judgment. Examiners had far less to go on when they predicted an examinee's probable performance 'in the field' – only his ability to write polished essays or perform abstruse calculations under wholly artificial conditions; and no examiner lost face if his hot tips turned into bad bargains.[5]

It would be absurd to suggest that the study of a handful of nineteenth-century clergymen could resolve questions of this order of magnitude. An entire school of historians could hardly do justice to the complexities and ramifications of patronage if they devoted a lifetime to its study. *The Passing of Barchester* is only a beginning. It suggests lines of enquiry, rather than arriving at definitive conclusions. But this first study of a clerical connection does represent a historiographical breakthrough, in a modest way. It shows – if nothing else – the potential for 'connection-reconstitution' among the clergy. What Namier did for political history, when he published his *Structure of Politics at the Accession of George III*, could be done for the Church of England also. Church and state are amenable to the same kind of analysis. If other historians pursue this possibility, they may yet rescue the clerical connection, that vital microcosm of patronage, from the blind alley of the blue books – and the great patronage-mongers, the old high churchmen, from the 'massive condescension of posterity'.

Appendix

The Hackney Phalanx: Thirty Members and Allies

Identifying the members and allies of the Hackney Phalanx raises problems of data-retrieval and definition. The leaders proper – the three activists permanently resident in Hackney – have basked in a historiographical spotlight ever since Edward Churton published his life of Joshua Watson.[1] But they would have been pious angels struggling ineffectively in a void without their extensive network of contacts with sympathetic high church dignitaries. The concentric circles of 'members' and 'allies' revolving around the stable core were as essential to the operations of the Phalanx as the triumvirate at the centre, and the personnel making up those circles are still a hodge-podge of odd names. Ideally one should reconstruct all the relationships of the triumvirs, then concentrate on the most important collaborations. Sadly, most of the leaders' papers have been destroyed – and chasing up the scattered references to them in the collections which do survive would produce some very hit-and-miss results. Moreover, even if every fact ever committed to paper was still available, it would still be difficult to determine the exact point at which a clergyman became an ally of the Phalanx or the exact point at which an ally became a member.

Patronage provides a way of cutting both these Gordian knots. Reasonably systematic data on preferments is readily available – in registers of Oxbridge graduates, lists of old boys, individual obituaries

---

[1] The Phalanx's houses in Hackney have been demolished, but their churches survive. John James Watson was rector of St John's, Lower Clapton Road, for forty years (1799-1839): a vast classical church, in the middle of a huge graveyard, on the plan of a Greek cross, by James Spiller, 1792-97. More than any other building, it gives an impression of what a desirable residential area Hackney must have been, when it was dominated by the spacious villas of well-off City merchants. Henry Handley Norris was perpetual curate and rector of St John of Jerusalem, in Lauriston Road, for forty-one years (1809-50): a large 'Early English' church on a large island site, by Hakewill, 1845-48.

and the *Dictionary of National Biography*. Wives and children are frequently ignored, but preferments never. This contemporary preoccupation with pelf makes it comparatively easy to reconstruct the flows of preferment between patrons and clients, and patron-client relations take one straight to the heart of the Phalanx. In a sense, the whole Hackney movement can be seen as an extremely successful patronage-hunting cooperative. A few members and allies stood outside the network of patronage, neither receiving nor conferring preferment; but the great majority knew that their effectiveness as a party depended on their candidates capturing high offices in the church. So they chose particularly able protégés, lined up opportunities for them to display their talents, and launched little lobbies whenever suitable appointments fell vacant. Their activities divided the old high church party into small clusters of clients – higher-order Lyall connections – attached to particular patrons. Some of the clusters were comparatively stable; a given group of clients retaining the same patron until death did them part. Sadly, most of the connections making up the Phalanx were more complex. The highest-flying members and allies had to attract new patrons, if they were to keep on climbing the ecclesiastical hierarchy, until they eventually emerged as patrons themselves; and there was a certain amount of protégé-swapping among the big men – the bishops, deans, and archdeacons at the head of the Phalanx. When they planned the young men's careers, they put their heads together.

The thirty clergymen anatomised in this appendix are the outcome of a first trawl through the most obvious sources. Churton mentions the triumvirate's clerical associates in his life of Watson. I followed his nominations, adding extra names as they cropped up in obituaries and *DNB* entries. A really systematic search of the surviving private papers, the records of the Phalanx's favourite voluntary associations and the small mountain of ecclesiastical biographies would undoubtedly increase this total. It might also correct two built-in biases. Churton concentrated on big names – the names his readers might recognise – when he discussed Watson's collaborators; the smaller fry got left out. The second lacuna is mine: although the Phalanx did a great deal to encourage the establishment of colonial bishoprics, I have ignored their collaborators among the colonial clergy.

The Hackney Phalanx: A Checklist Showing
Fathers, Families, Education, Preferment and Services*

BAYLEY, *Ven Henry Vincent (1777-1844): Archdeacon of Stow, 1823-44*

Father: Lancashire landowner interested in agricultural improvement, prison reform and urban sanitation.

Family: Brother, Chairman of the East India Company 1840 (immediate predecessor of *William Lyall*'s brother).

Education: Winwick Grammar School; Eton; Trinity College, Cambridge (Scholar, 1802 Fellow).

Preferment: Like *Charles Le Bas*, Bayley acted as tutor to one of *Bishop Tomline*'s sons, and obtained all his preferment from Tomline as Bishop of Lincoln and Winchester.

Examining Chaplain to the Bishop of Lincoln; 1804-6, Rector of Stilton, Hants; 1805-28, Sub-Dean and Prebend of Lincoln; 1806-14, Vicar of Hibaldeston, Hants; 1810-26, Vicar of Messingham and Bottesford, Lincs; 1812-44, Vicar of Great Carlton, Lincs; 1823-44, Archdeacon of Stow; 1826-44, Rector of West Meon, Hants; 1828-44, Prebend of Westminster.

Services: A distinguished classical scholar; restored Lincoln Cathedral; built a new church at West Meon.

BETHELL, *Right Rev Christopher (1773-1859): Bishop of Gloucester, 1824-30 and Llandaff, 1830-59*

Father: Rector of Wallingford.

Family: Two brothers, King's Scholars at Eton and Fellows of King's College, Cambridge; one Master and Fellow of Eton; the other a Yorkshire landowner.

Education: Eton (King's Scholar); King's College, Cambridge (Scholar, 1794-1808 Fellow).

Preferment: May have acted as tutor to a member of the Percy family; the *DNB* gives no hint as to how he obtained his deanery or his bishoprics.

1808-30, Rector of Kirkby Wiske, Yorks (Duke of Northumberland); 1814-24, Dean of Chichester (Lord Liverpool); 1824-30, Bishop of Gloucester (Lord Liverpool); 1830-59, Bishop of Llandaff (Duke of Wellington).

Services: Works on theology.

*Individuals whose names appear in italics have separate entries of their own.

BLOMFIELD, Right Rev Charles James (1786-1857): Bishop of Chester, 1824-28 and London, 1828-56

Father:	Schoolmaster near Bury St Edmunds.
Family:	Brother, Fellow and Tutor of Emmanuel; son, Bishop of Colchester.
Education:	Bury St Edmunds Grammar School (rejected a scholarship at Eton); Trinity College, Cambridge (Scholar, Third Wrangler, 1809 Fellow, 1810 Tutor).
Preferment:	'A protégé of Whig lords' – the Marquis of Bristol 'took an interest' in the local child prodigy and gave him his first livings; then *Archbishop Howley*, dazzled by his prodigious energy, took him up.

1800-20, Vicar of Quarrington, Lincs; 1811, Rector of Dunton, Bucks; 1817-20, Rector of Tuddenham, Suffolk (all Bristol family livings); 1820, Rector of Little Chesterford, Essex; 1820-28, Rector of St Botolph's, Bishopsgate, in succession to *Richard Mant* (*Howley*); 1822-24, Archdeacon of Colchester (*Howley*); 1824-28, Bishop of Chester (Lord Liverpool); 1828-56, Bishop of London (George IV and the Duke of Wellington).

Services:	An accomplished Greek scholar (edited Aeschylus, Herodotus and Euripides); a hyper-active parish priest and bishop ('he performed his duties with immense energy, and, on the whole, with sound common sense and moderation'); a champion of church extension (he consecrated two hundred new churches); 'always an effective speaker' in the House of Lords; the moving spirit behind the Ecclesiastical Commission; he offended Tories by supporting the Reform Bill and evangelicals by ordering the clergy of his diocese to observe the articles of religion of 1562. *William Lyall* worked with him as Archdeacon of Colchester, 1828-41.

CAMBRIDGE, Ven George Owen (c. 1756-1841): Archdeacon of Middlesex

Father:	A dilettante with a small estate and a villa at Twickenham.
Family:	Grandfather a London merchant.
Education:	Queen's College and Merton College, Oxford (Fellow?).
Preferment:	Chaplain to *Archbishop Manners-Sutton* (possibly while he was Bishop of Norwich); Archdeacon of Middlesex (Bishop of London); Prebendary of Ely (Bishop of Ely).

CAREY, Right Rev William (1769-1846): Bishop of Exeter, 1820-30 and St Asaph, 1830-46

Father:	Poor tradesman in Worcester (?).
Education:	Westminster (Scholar); Christ Church, Oxford (Scholar, Fellow, Tutor).
Preferment:	Carey had two crucial patrons: Dr Vincent, who got him a nomination to Westminster after his father died, and Cyril Jackson, the Dean of Christ Church, who sent him back to Westminster as headmaster.

1784, Vicar of Cowley; 1801, Whitehall Preacher; 1803-14, Head-master of Westminster; 1804, Canon of York and Vicar of Sutton-in-the-Forest; 1809, Prebend of Westminster; 1820-30, Bishop of Exeter (Lord Liverpool); 1830-46, Bishop of St Asaph (Duke of Wellington).

Services: A classical scholar; a philanthropist who left £20,000 to endow scholarships at Christ Church for intending ordinands from West-minster; an energetic and popular bishop.

CHURTON, *Ven Edward (1800-74): Archdeacon of Cleveland, 1846-74*

Father: Archdeacon of St David's (the orphaned son of a Cheshire yeoman taken up by the Rector of Malpas: he wrote biographies of high church dignitaries).

Family: Brother *Ralph Churton*, Fellow of Oriel, became Domestic Chaplain to the Bishop of London (*Howley*) *c.* 1826/7, but died in 1828; Churton edited his *Memoirs*. Another brother, Fellow of Brasenose and Pre-bend of Chichester; a third brother, Fellow and Tutor of Brasenose; son, Bishop of Nassau.

Education: Charterhouse; Christ Church, Oxford.

Preferment: Churton went back to Charterhouse as an assistant master; moved to Hackney as *John Watson*'s curate – capitalising on his brother's contacts – and married Watson's daughter. Three of the Phalanx's most highly-placed patrons clubbed together to help him on his way.

1834, Vicar of Monks Eleigh (*Archbishop Howley*); 1835-36, Rector of Crayke Hill, Yorks (Bishop of Durham, *William Van Mildert*); 1841, Prebend of York and 1846, Archdeacon of Cleveland (Archbishop of York, Hon Edward Harcourt).

Services: A prolific author (articles in the *British Critic*, books on theology and the standard biography of Joshua Watson – still the best account of the work of the Phalanx).

CHURTON, *Rev William Ralph (c. 1801-28)*

Father: Archdeacon of St David's.

Family: Brother *Edward Churton*, Archdeacon of Cleveland.

Education: Rugby; Lincoln and Queen's Colleges, Oxford (Scholar, 1st in classics); Oriel College (1823-28, Fellow).

Preferment: *Archbishop Howley*, currently Bishop of London, made Churton his Domestic Chaplain about a year before he died of consumption at the age of twenty-seven.

D'OYLY, *Rev George (1778-1846): Rector of Lambeth, 1820-46*

Father: Archdeacon of Lewes and Rector of Buxted, Sussex.

Family: Brother, Sir John D'Oyly, Bart, Fellow of Corpus Christi and Resident in Ceylon; brother, Sir Francis D'Oyly, killed at Waterloo; son, Rector of Great Chart (*William Lyall*'s old living).

Education: Corpus Christi College, Cambridge (Scholar, Second Wrangler, 1801-13 Fellow).

Preferment: Attracted *Archbishop Manners-Sutton*'s attention as Select Preacher (1809-11) and Christian Advocate (1811) at Cambridge; Manners-Sutton was the source of all his livings.

1813, Domestic Chaplain to the Archbishop of Canterbury; 1815-16, Vicar of Herne Hill, Kent; 1815-20, Rector of Buxted (in succession to his father); 1820-46, Rector of Lambeth, Surrey, and Sundridge, Kent.

Services: Attacked Sir William Drummond's deism (1813); annotated a popular edition of the Bible (with *Richard Mant*) for the SPCK (1814); many articles in the *Quarterly Review*; biographer of Archbishop Sancroft; a long-serving official of the SPG and SPCK; the virtual founder of King's College, London; an admirable parish priest.

GRAY, *Right Rev Robert (1762-1834): Bishop of Bristol, 1827-34*

Father: London silversmith.

Family: Son, Bishop of Cape Town, excommunicated Bishop Colenso.

Education: St Mary's Hall, Oxford.

Preferment: Gray's great patron was Shute Barrington, Bishop of Durham; the *DNB* gives no hint as to how they came into contact.

1790-1800, Vicar of Faringdon, Berks; 1796, Bampton Lecturer (on the Reformation); 1800-5, Rector of Crayke, Yorks (Barrington); 1804-34, Prebend of Durham (Barrington); 1805-27, Rector of Bishop Wearmouth (Barrington); 1827-34, Bishop of Bristol (Lord Liverpool).

Services: An efficient and liberal bishop.

HARRISON, *Ven Benjamin (1808-87): Archdeacon of Maidstone, 1845-87*

Father: Treasurer (i.e. chief administrator) of Guy's Hospital; lived at Clapham in close connection with the leaders of the Sect.

Family: Grandfather also Treasurer of Guy's; Harrison married the daughter of one of the most prominent members of the Clapham Sect, Henry Thornton, MP and banker.

Education: Christ Church, Oxford (Scholar, 1st in classics, 1828-48 Fellow).

Preferment: Harrison's reputation as a scholar and a preacher attracted *Archbishop Howley*'s attention, and Howley gave him all the preferment he ever received.

1835-37, Select Preacher, Oxford; *c.* 1842, Warburton Lecturer, Lincoln's Inn (*William Lyall* in 1827); 1842-45, Six Preacher, Canterbury Cathedral; 1843-48, Domestic Chaplain to Archbishop of Canterbury; 1845-87, succeeded *William Lyall* as Archdeacon of Maidstone and Canon of Canterbury.

Services: A Hebrew scholar; a Tractarian who wrote four of the 'Tracts for the Times' (mostly on the scriptural authority for episcopacy); saved from Rome by 'his ecclesiastical connections and a conservative temperament'; helped *Joshua Watson* found the Additional Curates Society, 1837; co-operated with *William Lyall* in managing Archbishop Howley and the Chapter at Canterbury; a zealous and popular archdeacon ('his intimate knowledge of the clergy, his regularity at cathedral services, his activity in the business of various church societies, . . . his geniality, wit and tolerance').

HOWLEY, Most Rev William (1766-1848): Bishop of London, 1813-28 and Archbishop of Canterbury, 1828-48

Father: Vicar of Bishops Sutton, Hants.
Family: Married the daughter of Warren Hastings' private secretary; presented his son-in-law and nephews to several livings.
Education: Winchester (Scholar, Fellow); New College, Oxford (Scholar, Fellow, Tutor).
Preferment: Howley became the royal family's favourite clergyman while he was acting as tutor to the Prince of Orange (later William II). He owed all his preferment to George III and George IV.

1796, Vicar of Bishops Sutton (in succession to his father); 1802, Vicar of Andover (technically the Lord Chancellor; almost certainly George IV); Canon of Christ Church (George III and Pitt); 1809, Regius Professor of Divinity, Oxford (George III and Spencer Perceval); 1811, Rector of Bradford Deverall (George III/IV); 1813-28, Bishop of London (George IV and Lord Liverpool); 1828-48, Archbishop of Canterbury (George IV and the Duke of Wellington).

Services: Howley had a local reputation as a Greek scholar, but he never published anything which would have put it to the test; he was neither an eloquent preacher nor an effective speaker; as Bishop of London, he displayed only 'regulated energy', and as Archbishop he 'hid from business'. He opposed Catholic Emancipation and the Reform Bill, but he helped *Charles Blomfield* make the Ecclesiastical Commission work. *Joshua Watson* – who acted as one of his talent scouts – claimed that Howley redeemed his deficiencies through his noble use of his vast patronage. His chaplains included *Charles Blomfield, Benjamin Harrison, William Lyall* and *Hugh Rose. Edward Churton, Herbert Norris, John Pott* and *James Watson* all received preferment from him; *John Lonsdale* and *John Spry* may have done so.

JELF, Rev Richard William (1798-1871): Principal of King's College, London 1842-67

Father: Rich merchant (?) in Gloucester.

Family: One brother, a Tutor of Christ Church, compiled a celebrated Greek grammar; another became a Canon of Rochester; a third, a Colonel in the Royal Engineers, edited Jewel's works. Jelf married a German aristocrat, one of the Duchess of Cumberland's ladies-in-waiting.

Education: Eton (a friend of Pusey); Christ Church, Oxford; Oriel College (1821-30 Fellow, Tutor).

Preferment: Like *William Howley*, Jelf made a career out of acting as tutor to a royal personage – Prince George of Cumberland, cousin of Queen Victoria and subsequently King of Hanover.

             1826-39, Preceptor of Prince George ('lived much in Berlin'); 1830-71, Canon of Christ Church (George IV and William IV, Prince George's uncles); 1844-68, *John Lonsdale*'s successor as Principal of King's College, London; 1844, Bampton Lecturer.

Services: Jelf never took a prominent part in the Oxford Movement, but he was so much respected for his impartiality that both Newman and Pusey addressed their letters on the Thirty-Nine Articles to him. Jelf's most memorable publication was a sermon entitled '*Via Media*, the Church of England's Providential Path between Romanism and Dissent'. As Principal of King's he preserved the college's high church character, not least by depriving F.D. Maurice of his Chair of Divinity.

LE BAS, Rev Charles Webb (1779-1861): Principal of Haileybury College, 1837-43

Father: London linen draper.

Family: Grandfathers, a London brewer and a captain in the East India Company's Marine; married the daughter of the London brewer who invented India Pale Ale; his son became preacher at the Charterhouse.

Education: Hyde Abbey School; Trinity College, Cambridge (Scholar, Fourth Wrangler, 1808 Fellow).

Preferment: Like *Henry Bayley*, Le Bas acted as tutor to *Bishop Tomline*'s sons, and obtained preferment from Tomline. His other patron – thanks to his family's business connections and his grandfather's employment in their service – was the East India Company.

             1812-43, Rector of St Paul's, Shadwell (Bishop of London); 1812-25, Rector of Darfield, Yorks; 1812-61, Prebendary of Lincoln (*Tomline*); 1813-37, Professor of Mathematics 1837-43, Principal of the East India Company's College at Haileybury.

Services: A voluminous author (contributed eighty articles to the *British Critic* and four biographies to the *Theological Library* co-edited by *William*

Lyall); a popular preacher; an antidote to the evangelicals in the seminary which trained Indian civilians.

LLOYD, *Right Rev Charles (1784-1829): Bishop of Oxford, 1827-29*

Father: Schoolmaster at Great Missenden, Bucks, and Rector of Aston-sub-Edge, Gloucs.

Education: Eton (King's Scholar); Christ Church, Oxford (1st in classics, 1804-22 Fellow, Tutor).

Preferment: A two-patron man: acted as tutor to Sir Robert Peel at Oxford and chaplain to *Archbishop Manners-Sutton*.

1817, Peel's election agent at Oxford; 1819-22, Preacher at Lincoln's Inn; *c.* 1820, Chaplain to the Archbishop of Canterbury (*Manners-Sutton*); 1822, Vicar of South Berstead, Sussex (*Manners-Sutton*); 1822-27, Regius Professor of Divinity, Canon of Christ Church and Rector of Ewelme (Lord Liverpool); 1827-29, Bishop of Oxford (Lord Liverpool at Peel's insistence).

Services: Lloyd's ambition was to make himself a great divine, presiding over a school of theology at Oxford. R.H. Froude, Newman, Pusey and Frederick Oakley attended his seminars. He taught, to the surprise of many of his hearers, that the Prayer Book 'was but a reflection of medieval and primitive devotion, still embodied in its Latin form in the Roman service books'. Like Peel, he changed his mind over Catholic Emancipation and voted for it in 1829; his conversion 'exposed him to the reproaches of his friends'.

LONSDALE, *Right Rev John (1788-1867): Bishop of Lichfield, 1843-67*

Father: Vicar of Darfield, Yorks.

Family: Married the daughter of an MP; one son Tutor of Balliol and Professor of Classics at King's College, London; another son Canon of Lichfield and secretary of the National Society; a daughter married Lord Grimsthorpe.

Education: Eton (Scholar, Fellow); King's College, Cambridge (Scholar, 1809-15 Fellow, Tutor).

Preferment: Three of the Phalanx's most prominent patrons – *Archbishop Manners-Sutton, Archbishop Howley* and *Bishop Blomfield* – were sufficiently impressed by Lonsdale's learning, preaching and administrative skills to patronise him.

1815-16, Chaplain to Archbishop of Canterbury (*Manners-Sutton*) and Assistant Preacher at the Temple (Master: *Thomas Rennell*); 1821-22, Christian Advocate at Cambridge; 1822-27, Rector of Merstham, Kent (*Manners-Sutton*); 1827-28, Prebend of Lincoln (Bishop of Lincoln); 1828-31, Precentor of Lichfield; 1828-34, Rector of St George's, Bloomsbury (*Howley* or *Blomfield*); 1831-43, Prebend at St Paul's (*Blomfield*); 1836, Preacher at Lincoln's Inn (Benchers); 1836-43, Rector of South Fleet, Kent (Bishop of Rochester); 1839-42, Principal of King's College, London; 1842-43, Archdeacon of Middlesex (*Blomfield*); 1843-67, Bishop of Lichfield (on the recommendation of *Howley* and *Blomfield*).

Services: A Latin scholar (Goodall, headmaster of Eton, thought him the best Latinist he had ever taught); a popular preacher; King's College 'prospered greatly' under his direction; 'there was but one opinion of [his] episcopate – he was the best bishop the diocese had ever had'; founded the Theological College at Lichfield.

LYALL, Very Rev William Rowe (1788-1857): Dean of Canterbury, 1845-57

Father: London shipowner (an immigrant Scotsman).
Family: Grandfathers, a small farmer in Berwickshire and a merchant in Newcastle-upon-Tyne; elder brother, MP for the City of London and Chairman of the East India Company; married the daughter of a Liverpool physician; redistributed *William Howley*'s patronage to at least eight of his relations.
Education: Eton; Trinity College, Cambridge (Scholar, probably a pupil of *James Monk*; two years behind *Charles Blomfield*).
Preferment: Lyall owed all his preferment, up to his deanery, to a single patron: *Archbishop Howley*. His Trinity contacts and his attacks on Dugald Stewart in the *Quarterly Review* got him two literary jobs, as editor of the *British Critic* (proprietors *Joshua Watson* and *Henry Norris*) and the *Encyclopaedia Metropolitana* (*Charles Blomfield* and *William Howley*).

1817, Chaplain to St Thomas's Hospital and Assistant Preacher, Lincoln's Inn; 1822-24, *Blomfield*'s successor as Examining Chaplain to the Bishop of London; 1823-33, Rector of Weeley, Essex; 1824-41, *Blomfield*'s successor as Archdeacon of Colchester; 1827, Warburton Lecturer, Gray's Inn (the lectures grew into *Propaedia Prophetica*); 1827-33, Rector of Fairstead, Essex; 1833-42, exchanged Weeley and Fairstead for Hadleigh, which had proved too much for *Hugh Rose*; 1841-45, Archdeacon of Maidstone and Prebend of Canterbury; 1842-52, Rector of Great Chart, Kent; 1845-57, Dean of Canterbury (Sir Robert Peel).

Services: An accomplished theologian and publicist, best-known for his reviews of Dugald Stewart's metaphysics, his charges defending the property and privileges of the clergy, and his *magnum opus*, *Propaedia Prophetica* (which proved the divinity of Christ by appealing to Jewish prophecy). As editor of the *British Critic*, the *Encyclopaedia Metropolitana* and the *Theological Library*, he came into contact with Hugh Rose and the Tractarians. A virile preacher; an exemplary archdeacon; one of the founders of St Augustine's College, Canterbury; a member of the Episcopal and Capitular Revenues Committee of 1850.

MANNERS-SUTTON, *Most Rev Charles (1755-1828): Bishop of Norwich, 1792-1805 and Archbishop of Canterbury, 1805-28*

Father: Nottinghamshire landowner.

Family: Grandfather, Duke of Rutland; brother, Lord Chancellor of Ireland, raised to the peerage as Lord Manners; son, Speaker of the House of Commons (1817-35), raised to the peerage as Viscount Canterbury.

Education: Charterhouse; Emmanuel College, Cambridge (Fifteenth Wrangler).

Preferment: Manners-Sutton owed all his preferment, up to and including the deanery of Windsor, to his relatives' political prominence; he owed his archbishopric to George III, whose great favourite he became.

          1785, Rector of Kelham, Notts and Whitwell, Rutland (Lord Manners and the Duke of Rutland); 1791-1805, Dean of Peterborough; 1792-1805, Bishop of Norwich; 1794-1805, Dean of Windsor (George III and Pitt in all three cases); 1805-28, Archbishop of Canterbury (George III despite Pitt who wanted *Tomline*).

Services: 'A staunch supporter of the small but very active band of High Churchmen' (i.e. the Hackney Phalanx); his chaplains were 'in the van of the church movement' (e.g. *George Cambridge, George D'Oyly, Charles Lloyd, John Lonsdale, Richard Mant, Christopher Wordsworth*); gave *William Van Mildert* and *Hugh Rose* livings; 'guided and animated' the SPCK; presided over the first meeting of the National Society in 1811.

MANT, *Right Rev Richard (1776-1848): Bishop of Down and Connor, 1823-48*

Father: Master of King Edward's Grammar School and Rector of All Saints, Southampton.

Family: Mant made his eldest son, a leading Orangeman, Archdeacon of Down and Connor.

Education: Winchester (Scholar); Trinity College, Oxford (Scholar); Oriel College, Oxford (1798-1804 Fellow).

Preferment: Probably got his first living by acting as a tutor to a member of the Du Cane family; attracted *Archbishop Manners-Sutton*'s attention with his 1811 Bampton lectures (defending Anglican preaching against dissenters).

          1810-13, Vicar of Coggeshall, Essex (a Du Cane living); 1813 Domestic Chaplain to the Archbishop of Canterbury (*Manners-Sutton*); 1815-19, Rector of St Botolph's, Bishopsgate (Bishop of London, *William Howley*; *Charles Blomfield* was the next incumbent); 1818, Rector of East Horsley, Surrey (Dean and Chapter of Canterbury); 1820-23, Bishop of Killaloe and Kilfenoragh (Lord Liverpool); 1823-48, Bishop of Down and Connor (Lord Liverpool).

Services: An 'indefatigable writer'; annotated a popular edition of the Bible for the SPCK (with *George D'Oyly*); produced an authoritative and readable *History of the Church in Ireland* (1840); as a bishop, he resided in his diocese, opposed Catholic Emancipation and built churches.

MONK, Right Rev James Henry (1784-1856): Bishop of Gloucester, 1830-56

Father: Army Officer.
Family: Son became Chancellor of Bristol and MP for Gloucester.
Education: Charterhouse; Trinity College, Cambridge (Scholar, Seventh Wrangler, 1805 Fellow, 1807-23 Tutor).
Preferment: As Tutor of Trinity 'his pupils carried off the greater part of the high classical honours at Cambridge'; he attracted Lord Liverpool's attention as Whitehall Preacher in 1812.

                1808-23, Regius Professor of Greek; 1822-30, Dean of Peterborough; 1822-32, Rector of Fiskerton, Lincs; 1829, Peakirk, Northants (all Lord Liverpool); 1830-56, Canon of Westminster and Bishop of Gloucester (Duke of Wellington).

Services: A great Greek scholar (Regius Professor at twenty-five) who taught several high churchmen (e.g. *William Lyall, Hugh Rose* and *Christopher Wordsworth*); a member of the Ecclesiastical Commission.

NORRIS, Rev Henry Handley (1771-1850): Perpetual Curate and Rector in Hackney, 1809-50

Father: London merchant (in Hackney).
Family: Grandfather, Vicar of Warton, Lancs.
Education: Dr Newcome's School, Hackney; Pembroke and Peterhouse Colleges, Cambridge.
Preferment: Endowed his own church, St John of Jerusalem, Lauriston Road, in Hackney; Perpetual Curate, 1809-31; Rector, 1831-50.

                1816, Prebendary of Llandaff (Bishop of Llandaff); 1825, Prebendary of St Paul's (Bishop of London, *William Howley*); Chaplain to the Earl of Shaftesbury.

Services: One of the triumvirate responsible for the day-to-day direction of the Phalanx, with the Watson brothers; shared *Joshua Watson's* house in Hackney. From 1793-1834 he 'largely ruled' the proceedings of the SPCK. Generally thought to be Lord Liverpool's confidential adviser in ecclesiastical patronage. 'Rumour secured for him the title of Bishopmaker'.

POTT, Ven Joseph Holden (1759-1847): Archdeacon of St Albans and London, 1789-1842

Father: London surgeon ('the first surgeon of his day', he 'helped to raise the surgeon's social standing in this country').
Family: Grandfather, a London scrivener, left his widow penniless; a distant relative, Bishop of Rochester, helped apprentice Pott's father to a

barber-surgeon.

Education: Eton; St John's College, Cambridge (Scholar, Medallist).

Preferment: 1784, Chaplain to Lord Chancellor, Lord Thurlow; 1785-88, Prebend of Lincoln (Bishop of Lincoln); 1787-1824, ran through six livings, including St Martin's-in-the-Fields and Kensington (Bishop of London); 1789-1813, Archdeacon of St Albans (Bishop of London); 1813-42, Archdeacon of London (*William Howley*); 1822-47 Prebend of St Paul's (*Howley*); 1826-47, Prebend of Exeter (Bishop of Exeter).

Services: An exceptionally efficient administrator; a good preacher.

RENNELL, Very Rev Thomas (1754-1840): Master of the Temple, 1797 and Dean of Winchester, 1805-40

Father: Rector of Barnack, Northants, and Prebend of Winchester.

Family: Married to a judge's daughter (Sir William Blackstone); son, Fellow of King's College, Cambridge, and Vicar of Kensington.

Education: Eton (Scholar); King's College, Cambridge (Scholar, 1776-79 Fellow).

Preferment: May have acted as tutor to the Marquis of Buckingham's son; caught Pitt's eye while preaching a sermon on the French Revolution (Pitt called him 'the Demosthenes of the pulpit').

1787-95, Vicar of Alton, Hants; 1795, Rector of St Margaret's, London Bridge (Pitt: through the influence of the Marquis of Buckingham); 1797, Master of the Temple (Pitt); 1798, Prebend of Winchester (his father resigned in his favour); 1802-40, Prebend of St Paul's (Bishop of London); 1805-40, Dean of Winchester (Pitt); 1814, Vicar of Barton Stacey, Hants.

Services: Brought leading lawyers of the day (eg Eldon, Stowell, Erskine) into the high church camp; one of *Henry Norris*'s closest collaborators; a great preacher.

ROSE, Rev Hugh James (1795-1838): Principal of King's College, London, 1836-38

Father: Schoolmaster at Uckfield and Vicar of Glynde.

Family: Grandfather, a Scots Jacobite laird; brother, Fellow of St John's College, Cambridge and Archdeacon of Bedford.

Education: Uckfield School; Trinity College, Cambridge (Scholar, Fourteenth Wrangler, First Chancellor's Medallist).

Preferment: Like *Charles Blomfield*, Rose was a child prodigy patronised by the local territorial magnate. Sheffield Park was only a few miles from Uckfield, and Lord Sheffield encouraged Rose to play with his heir. Rose also acted as tutor to the Duke of Argyll's son, after he graduated. But his aristocratic patrons seem to have done less for him, in the long run, than his tutors at Trinity: *Charles Blomfield* and *James Monk* (Rose's 'constant friend').

1819, Curate at Buxted (Rector: *George D'Oyly*, Chaplain to *Archbishop Manners-Sutton*); 1821-30, Vicar of Horsham, Kent (*Manners-Sutton*); Select Preacher at Cambridge, 1825, 1826, 1828, 1829, 1830, 1833, 1834; 1827-33, Prebend of Chichester (Bishop of Chichester); 1829, Domestic Chaplain to the Bishop of London (*Blomfield*); 1830-33, Dean of Bocking and Rector of Hadleigh, Essex (*Archbishop Howley*); 1833, exchanged Hadleigh for Fairstead, Essex (with *William Lyall*); 1833-34, Professor of Divinity, University of Durham (Bishop of Durham, *William Van Mildert*); 1834, Domestic Chaplain to Archbishop of Canterbury (*Howley*); 1835, Perpetual Curate of St Thomas's, Southwark (Governors of St Thomas's Hospital); 1836-38, Principal of King's College, London.

Services: A Greek scholar (he corrected Blomfield's edition of *The Two Against Thebes* while he was still a schoolboy); the most influential theologian of the day, and the most effective spokesman for high church party. Six times select preacher at Cambridge, he 'drew to himself the most intellectual of his contemporaries' by delivering 'intemperate, uncompromising, high church sermon[s]. The language was very beautiful and eloquent, and the delivery admirable, but more inflammatory party sermon[s have] hardly been preached since the days of Sacheverell'. Published a rejoinder to Bentham's 'pedantic scurrilities against the Church of England' (1820); 'a powerful and justly severe article' on Hume's 'spurious' *Apocrypha* (1821); a series of refutations of the German Biblical Critics (starting in 1825) which 'brought [him] prominently before the public outside his own university as a fearless champion of Catholic truth'; and four sermons on the duties of the clergy (1828) which anticipated the Tractarians' idealisation of the priesthood. Founded the *British Magazine* (a popular monthly) to supplement the *British Critic* (a heavyweight quarterly). His brother edited the *Theological Library* with *William Lyall* (1831-32). The search for contributors made him the crucial link between the London-based Phalanx and the Oxford-based Tractarians; he set up the historic conference at Hadleigh in 1833, which supposedly marked the birth of the Oxford Movement; Newman eulogised him in his *Apologia Pro Vita Sua* as 'the leading spirit in the great Church revival'.

SIKES, *Rev Thomas (c. 1766-1839): Vicar of Guilsborough, 1792-1834*

Father: London banker (in Hackney).
Family: Sister married *Joshua Watson*; uncle, Archdeacon of Salisbury, was 'one of the leading churchmen of his day'.
Education: St Edmund's Hall and Pembroke College, Oxford.
Preferment: 1792-1834, Vicar of Guilsborough, Northants.

SPRY, Rev John Hume (1777-1854): Rector of St Marylebone, 1825-54

Father: Vicar of St Mary's, Bristol and Prebendary of Salisbury.
Family: Grandfather, Archdeacon of Berkshire; two uncles, Prebendaries of
               Salisbury.
Education: Eton; Oriel College, Oxford.
Preferment: 1815, Bampton Lecturer; 1816-25, Vicar of Hanbury, Staffs (Bishop
               of Lichfield); 1825-54, Rector of St Marylebone (Lord Liverpool);
               1828-54, Canon of Canterbury (probably *Archbishop Howley*).

Services: A Greek scholar.

*TOMLINE, Right Rev Sir George Pretyman (1750-1827): Bishop of Lincoln, 1787-1820
and Winchester, 1820-1827*

Father: Suffolk gentry.
Family: Tomline showered preferment on his immediate family. His younger
               brother became Archdeacon and Precentor of Lincoln; his second
               son became Chancellor of Lincoln and Prebendary of Winchester;
               his third son became Precentor of Lincoln. He married a Bucking-
               hamshire heiress, prosecuted a claim to a dormant baronetcy and
               sent his eldest son into parliament.
Education: Bury St Edmunds Grammar School; Pembroke Hall, Cambridge
               (Scholar, Senior Wrangler, Fellow).
Preferment: Tomline's great patron was William Pitt. Tomline became Pitt's
               tutor when he went up to Cambridge (aged fourteen): he acted as
               Pitt's chief confidant and private secretary until he died in 1806; and
               he went on serving Pitt after his death, as his literary executor.

               1782, Rector of Corwen, Merioneth; 1784, Prebend of Westminster;
               1785, Rector of Sudbourn; 1787-1820, Bishop of Lincoln and Dean of
               St Paul's; 1820-7, Bishop of Winchester (Lord Liverpool). George III
               vetoed Pitt's attempt to make Tomline Archbishop of Canterbury in
               1804 and insisted on *Manners-Sutton*.

Services: Tomline was 'a supporter of the prerogative and an uncompromising
               friend to the existing order of things'. He persuaded Pitt to drop
               Catholic Emancipation; advised him on ecclesiastical patronage
               (1787-1806); used his own resources to reward his sons' tutors (*Henry
               Bayley* and *Charles Le Bas*); compiled a textbook for ordinands,
               Elements of Christian Theology (1797), which ran through many editions
               and 'justified his episcopal appointment'.

*VAN MILDERT, Right Rev William (1765-1836): Bishop of Llandaff, 1819-26 and
Durham, 1826-36*

Father: London distiller.
Education: Merchant Taylor's School, London; Queen's College, Oxford.

Preferment: Van Mildert's cousin (who married Van Mildert's sister) bought
                 him his first presentation; his uncle persuaded the Grocers' Company
                 to present him to one of their City parishes. His lectures and sermons
                 brought him to *Archbishop Manners-Sutton*'s notice, and Manners-
                 Sutton recommended him to Lord Liverpool.

                 Chaplain of the Grocers' Company; 1795-96, Rector of Braddon,
                 Northants (Van Mildert's cousin); 1796-1820, Rector of St Mary-
                 le-Bow (Grocers' Company); 1804, Boyle Lecturer (refuted infi-
                 delity); 1807-13, Vicar of Farningham, Kent (*Manners-Sutton*); 1812-
                 19, Preacher, Lincoln's Inn (Benchers); 1813, Bampton Lecturer;
                 1813-19, Regius Professor of Divinity, Oxford, Canon of Christ
                 Church and Rector of Ewelme; 1819-26, Bishop of Llandaff; 1820-26,
                 Dean of St Paul's; 1826-36, Bishop of Durham (in all four cases, Lord
                 Liverpool).

Services: Shared a house with *Joshua Watson* (the Phalanx's first H.Q.); edited
                 the works of Daniel Waterland, a high church divine; published his
                 Boyle and Bampton lectures; actually resided in Llandaff (the 'first
                 bishop in many years to do so'); entertained in regal splendour at
                 Auckland Castle; gave Durham Castle and £2,000 a year to found
                 the University of Durham; offered *Hugh Rose* a chair of divinity; the
                 most formidable high churchman on the bench.

WATSON, Ven John James (c. 1768-1839): Rector of Hackney 1799-1839

Father: London wine merchant and contractor (in Hackney).
Family: Grandfather, a small farmer in Cumberland; brother, *Joshua Watson.*
Education: Charterhouse; University College, Oxford (contemporary of Lord
                 Liverpool).
Preferment: *Archbishop Howley* made Watson an archdeacon because he was
                 impressed by his conduct of the Phalanx's business.

                 1799-1839, Rector of Hackney (St John's, Lower Clapton Road),
                 probably presented by a member of the Amhurst family; 1811-39,
                 Rector of Digswell, Herts; 1816, Archdeacon of St Albans (Bishop of
                 London, *William Howley*); 1825-39, Prebend of St Paul's (*Howley*).

Services: One of the triumvirate responsible for the day-to-day direction of the
                 Phalanx, with his brother and *Herbert Norris*; an efficient admini-
                 strator.

WATSON, Joshua (1774-1855): Lay Leader of the Phalanx

Father: London wine merchant and contractor (in Hackney).
Family: Grandfather, a small farmer in Cumberland; brother, *John James
                 Watson*, Rector of Hackney; married the daughter of a London banker
                 (the niece of *Thomas Sikes*); his daughter married *Edward Churton*.

Career: Went into his father's firm (partner, 1792-1814).

Services: 'The virtual leader of the High Church party'; kept open house for
high churchmen in the houses he shared with *William Van Mildert* and
Herbert Norris in Holborn and Hackney; a long-serving official of the
SPCK and SPG; co-founder of the National Society (1811), the
Church Building Society (1817) and the Additional Curates Society
(1837); bought the *British Critic* (with his brother and Norris) in 1811,
to revive it as an organ of the high church party; 1822-37, Member of
the Royal Commission for Church Building; 1828, helped found
King's College, London; 1833, wrote the lay and revised the clerical
addresses to *Archbishop Howley* (proclaiming the signatories' loyalty
to the Church of England).

*WORDSWORTH, Very Rev Christopher, the Elder (1774-1846): Master of Trinity
College, Cambridge, 1820-41*

Father: Attorney in Cockermouth; left his orphaned children little except a
'claim' on Lord Lonsdale (which Lonsdale promptly repudiated).

Family: Brother of the poet; one son, *Christopher Wordsworth the Younger*, Bishop
of Lincoln; another son, Bishop of St Andrew's; grandson, Bishop of
Salisbury.

Education: Hawkshead Grammar School; Trinity College, Cambridge (Tenth
Wrangler, 1798-1802 Fellow).

Preferment: Tutor to *Archbishop Manners-Sutton*'s son and Chaplain to Manners-
Sutton; he owed all his preferment to his employer and his pupil.

1804, Rector of Ashby, Norfolk; 1805, Domestic Chaplain to the
Archbishop of Canterbury; 1806, Rector of Woodchurch, Kent;
1808, Dean of Bocking; 1812, Rector of Monks Eleigh (all these
livings were in *Manners-Sutton*'s gift); 1817, Chaplain to the House of
Commons (*Manners-Sutton*'s son had just become Speaker); 1820-41,
Master of Trinity College, Cambridge (Lord Liverpool, on *Manners-
Sutton*'s recommendation).

Services: Liaison between *Archbishop Manners-Sutton* and the Phalanx;
co-founder of the National Society, 1811; published *Ecclesiastical
Biography*, 1819, eulogising high church heroes; kept the biggest and
richest Oxbridge college in the high church camp (Wordswoth dismissed a tutor, Connal Thirlwall, for broad church leanings and
waited until Peel was in office before resigning, to ensure that his
successor was a Tory).

*WORDSWORTH, Right Rev Christopher, the Younger, (1807-85): Bishop of Lincoln,
1869-85*

Father: *Christopher Wordsworth the Elder*, Master of Trinity College, Cambridge.

Family: Uncle, William Wordsworth; brother, Bishop of St Andrew's; son, Bishop of Salisbury.

Education: Winchester (Scholar); Trinity College, Cambridge (Scholar, Senior Classic, Fellow, Tutor and Lecturer; his list of University Honours was 'almost unique').

Preferment: Wordsworth's patrons were the Tory premiers with whom the old high churchmen cooperated; his preaching impressed Peel.

1836-44, Headmaster of Harrow; 1844, Canon of Westminster (Peel); 1850, Rector of Stanford-in-the-Vale, Berks (Dean and Chapter of Westminster); 1865-9, Archdeacon of Westminster (Bishop of London, Alexander Tait); 1869-85, Bishop of Lincoln (Disraeli).

Services: Author of *Theophilus Anglicanus* (the definitive reiteration of the old high churchmen's theological position) and a monumental commentary on the Bible; a failure as headmaster of Harrow, but a success as a bishop (he stood up to the dissenters and founded a theological college).

The Hackney Phalanx: Some Constituent Groups

The Triumvirate in Hackney

Joshua WATSON (1774-1855): Lay Leader
John James WATSON (*c*. 1768-1839): Rector of Hackney
Henry Handley NORRIS (1771-1850): Rector in Hackney

Relatives of the Triumvirate

Thomas SIKES (*c*. 1766-1839): Vicar of Guilsborough
Edward CHURTON (1800-1874): Archdeacon of Cleveland

London Clergy

Thomas RENNELL (1754-1840): Master of the Temple
George Owen CAMBRIDGE (*c*. 1756-1841): Archdeacon of Middlesex
Joseph Holden POTT (1759-1847): Archdeacon of London
John Hume SPRY (1777-1854): Rector of St Marylebone
George D'OYLY (1778-1846): Rector of Lambeth
Charles James BLOMFIELD (1786-1857): Bishop of London
Richard William JELF (1787-1871): Principal of King's College

Bishop Tomline and his Sons' Tutors

Sir George Pretyman TOMLINE (1750-1827): Bishop of Lincoln and Winchester
Henry Vincent BAYLEY (1777-1849): Archdeacon of Stow
Charles LE BAS (1779-1861): Principal of Haileybury College

Archbishop Manners-Sutton and his Chaplains

Charles MANNERS-SUTTON (1755-1828): Archbishop of Canterbury
George Owen CAMBRIDGE (*c*. 1756-1841): Archdeacon of Middlesex*
William VAN MILDERT (1765-1836): Bishop of Durham†
Christopher WORDSWORTH (1774-1846): Master of Trinity College,
    Cambridge
Richard MANT (1776-1848): Bishop of Down and Connor
George D'OYLY (1778-1840): Rector of Lambeth*

* See London clergy.
† A protégé but never actually a chaplain.

Charles LLOYD (1784-1829): Bishop of Oxford
John LONSDALE (1788-1867): Bishop of Lichfield
Hugh ROSE (1795-1838): Principal of King's College, London

Archbishop Howley and his Chaplains

William HOWLEY (1766-1848): Archbishop of Canterbury
William Rowe LYALL (1788-1857): Dean of Canterbury
Hugh ROSE (1795-1838): Principal of King's College, London
William CHURTON (*c.* 1801-28): Domestic Chaplain (died at twenty-seven)
Benjamin HARRISON (1808-1887): Archdeacon of Maidstone

Other High Church Bishops

Robert GRAY (*c.* 1762-1834): Bishop of Bristol
William CAREY (1769-1846): Bishop of Exeter and St Asaph
Christopher BETHELL (1773-1859): Bishop of Llandaff
James MONK (1784-1856): Bishop of Gloucester
Christopher WORDSWORTH the Younger (1807-1885): Bishop of Lincoln

Notes

Conventions in Quoting

In the interests of legibility, a number of quotations from casually-written original sources have been tidied up without the usual warnings. Spelling and punctuation have been modernised, verbiage has been omitted and phrases have been arranged in more logical sequences, without the forest of brackets and stops this normally entails. If a quotation appears in the text, as distinct from the free-standing quotations at the beginning of chapters or sections, major alterations are mentioned in the relevant footnote. Interpolations are invariably shown in square brackets, and in every case the sense remains unchanged.

Chapter 1
The Church

[1] The standard histories of the Church of England in the nineteenth century are W.N. Molesworth, *History of the Church of England from 1660* (London, 1882); F.W. Cornish, *History of the English Church in the Nineteenth Century* (London, 1910); L.E. Elliott-Binns, *Religion in the Victoria Era* (London, 1936); Owen Chadwick, *The Victorian Church*, 2 vols. (London, 1966-70); and E.R. Norman, *Church and Society in England, 1770-1970* (Oxford, 1976). They should be supplemented by D.M. McClatchey, *Oxfordshire Clergy, 1777-1869* (Oxford, 1960); Owen Chadwick, *Victorian Miniature* (London, 1969); A.D. Gilbert, *Religion in Industrial Society* (London, 1976) and J. Obelkevich, *Religion and Rural Society* (Oxford, 1976).

For the religious militants, see W. Palmer, *A Narrative of Events Connected with the Publication of the Tracts for the Times*, 1st edn. 1843 (London, 1883); R.W. Church, *The Oxford Movement* (London, 1891); Y. Brilioth, *The Anglican Revival: Studies in the Oxford Movement* (London, 1933); G. Faber, *The Oxford Apostles*, (2nd. edn. Harmondsworth, 1954); D.H. Newsome, *The Parting of Friends* (London, 1966); M. Cowling, *Religion and Public Doctrine in Modern England* (Cambridge, 1985); Owen Chadwick, *The Spirit of the Oxford Movement* (Oxford, 1990); E.A. Towle, *John Mason Neale, DD* (London, 1907); J.F. White, *The Cambridge Movement* (Cambridge, 1962); J. Bentley, *Ritualism and Politics in Victorian Britain* (London, 1978); L.E. Ellsworth, *Charles Lowder and the Ritualist Movement* (London, 1982); I. Bradley, *The Call to Seriousness* (London, 1976); D.M. Rosman, *Evangelicals and Culture* (London, 1984).

For the political crisis of the 1820s and the 1830s, see G.F.A. Best, *Temporal Pillars* (London, 1964); K.A. Thompson, *Bureaucracy and Church Reform* (Oxford, 1976); G.I.T. Machin, *Politics and the Churches in Great Britain, 1832-1868* (Oxford, 1977); D.A. Kerr, *Peel,*

Priests and Politics (Oxford, 1982); P. Butler, *Gladstone: Church, State and Tractarianism* (Oxford, 1982); R. Brent, *Liberal Anglican Politics* (Oxford, 1987). For the crisis of faith, see B.M.G. Reardon, *Religious Thought in the Nineteenth Century* (Cambridge, 1966); P.T. Marsh, *The Victorian Church in Decline* (London, 1969); A. Symondson (ed.), *The Victorian Crisis of Faith* (London, 1970); M.A. Crowther, *Church Embattled* (Newton Abbot, 1970); Owen Chadwick, *The Secularisation of the European Mind* (Oxford, 1975). Peter Virgin, *The Church in an Age of Negligence, 1700-1840* (Cambridge, 1988), appeared too late to be used.

[2] The best source (in fact virtually the only published source) on the Hackney Phalanx is the biography of its founder: E. Churton (ed.), *Memoir of Joshua Watson*, 2 vols. (London, 1881). P.B. Nockles' Oxford D.Phil Thesis, 'Continuity and Change in Anglican High Churchmanship in Britain, 1792-1850' (1982) is to be published by Oxford University Press. There are two useful papers by Nockles ('The Oxford Movement: Historical Background, 1780-1833') and R.H. Fuller ('The Classical High Church Reaction to the Tractarians') in *Tradition Renewed*, ed. G. Rowell (London, 1986). The mass of papers now available at Lambeth – the Howley, Blomfield, Watson and Wordsworth collections, to name but four – makes a reappraisal of the old high churchmen long overdue. See E.G.W. Bill, *Catalogue of Manuscripts in Lambeth Palace Library*, 3 vols. (Oxford, 1972-83).

Chapter 2
The Dean

[1] The basic sources for Lyall are his entry in the *Dictionary of National Biography* (hereafter *DNB*); his obituary in *The Gentleman's Magazine* (1857), pp. 491-2; the 'Editor's Notice' by George Pearson in the third edition of Lyall's *Propaedia Prophetica* (London, 1885); the list of Lyall's publications in the British Museum *General Catalogue of Printed Books*, vol. 147, col. 88; Churton, *Watson, op. cit.* I, pp. 237, 249, 284, 316; II, pp. 31, 221, 227-8, 233-4; H. Pigot, *Hadleigh* (n.p. 1859), pp. 222-6; J.M. Cooper, *The Lives of the Deans of Canterbury* (Canterbury, 1900), pp. 220-4; Best, *Temporal Pillars, op. cit.* pp. 164-5, 281 note 2, 316.

[2] Churton, *Watson, op. cit.* II, p. 234.

[3] W.R. Lyall, 'Philosophical Essays: by Dugald Stewart', *Quarterly Review*, VI (1811), pp. 1-37; 'Elements of the Philosophy of the Human Mind: by Dugald Stewart', *ibid.*, XII (1814-15), pp. 281-317. George Pearson claimed that Hegel, in his *History of Philosophy*, 'founded almost his whole appreciation of the genius and impact of Bacon upon [Lyall's article], referred to in nearly every page': Pearson, 'Editor's Notice', *op. cit.* p. v. Stewart's entry in the *DNB* makes very modest claims for him.

[4] G.E. Davis, *The Democratic Intellect* (Edinburgh, 1961); G. Donaldson (ed.), *Four Centuries: Edinburgh University Life* (Edinburgh, 1983).

[5] A. Sullivan (ed.), *British Literary Magazines: The Romantic Age, 1789-1836* (London, 1983), pp. 259-67) (the *Quarterly*) and pp. 139-44 (the *Edinburgh Review*).

[6] Lyall, 'Philosophical Essays', *op. cit.*, pp. 32-6.

[7] *Ibid.*, p. 37.

[8] W.R. Lyall, 'State of Parties in Greece on Conclusion of Peloponnesian Wars' and 'The Age of Agesilaus' in *The Encyclopaedia Metropolitana: History of Greece, Macedonia and Syria*, ed. E. Smedley (London, 1848); *Propaedia Prophetica* (London, 1840; 2nd. edn. 1854; 3rd. edn. 1885).

[9] The 'Editor's Notice' which introduced the third edition was definitely on the defensive.

[10] W.R. Lyall, *The Nature and True Value of Church Property Examined* (London, 1831), *passim*.

[11] W.R. Lyall, *Sentiments of the Clergy on the Question of Church Reform* (London, 1833), pp. 22-3.

[12] Lyall, *Church Property, op. cit.*, pp. 20-1, 33.

[13] R.J. Wallins, 'The British Critic' in *British Literary Magazines*, ed. Sullivan, *op. cit.* pp. 57-62; S. Bennett, 'Catholic Emancipation, the *Quarterly Review*, and Britain's Constitutional Revolution', *Victorian Studies*, 12 (1969), pp. 283-304.

[14] See Blomfield's entry in the *DNB*; Alfred Blomfield (ed.), *Memoir of Charles James Blomfield*, 2 vols. (London, 1863); the references to Blomfield in Churton, *Watson, op. cit.* and Best, *Temporal Pillars, op. cit.*

[15] Pigot, *Hadleigh, op. cit.*, pp. 222-6; W.A.B. Jones, *Hadleigh Through the Ages* (Ipswich, 1977), pp. 115-28; Pearson, 'Editor's Notice', *op. cit.*, p. vi.

[16] R.J.E. Boggis, *A History of St Augustine's College, Canterbury* (Canterbury, 1907), *passim*.

[17] W.R. Lyall, *Some Remarks on the Judgment Pronounced by Dr Lushington* (London, 1842); Lyall, *Church Property, op. cit.*, pp. 8-9; W.R. Lyall, *A Charge Delivered to the Clergy of the Archdeaconry of Colchester* (London, 1837); D.C. Coleman, *Courtaulds* (Oxford, 1964), pp. 218-23; W.F. Quin, *A History of Braintreee and Bocking* (Lavenham, 1981), pp. 118-19.

[18] Lyall, *Sentiments of the Clergy, op. cit.*, p. 18.

[19] Lyall, *Church Property, op. cit.*, p. 10.

[20] *Ibid.*, p. 34.

[21] See the entries for Newman, Le Bas and Rose in the *DNB*. For Lyall's role in the Hadleigh Conference, see the letters of Lyall, Rose, Froude and Newman in *The Letters and Diaries of John Henry Newman*, ed. I. Ker and T. Gornall, vols. III-IV (Oxford, 1979-80), III, pp. 112-13, 120; IV, pp. 13, 17, 27, 37. For Rose generally, see J.W. Burgon, *Lives of Twelve Good Men*, 2 vols. (3rd. edn. London, 1889), I, pp. 116-283; Cowling, *Religion and Public Doctrine, op. cit.*, pp. 6-8; Churton, *Watson, op. cit.*, especially I, pp. 259-60, and II, pp. 7-10, 63-5. For the Ecclesiologists, see White, *Cambridge Movement, op. cit.* W.H. Lyall's letters to J.M. Neale are in the Neale Papers at Lambeth, MSS 2677.

[22] Lyall's negotiations with Newman can be followed in *Letters and Diaries of John Henry Newman, op. cit.*, II, pp. 321-3 and III, pp. 103-5, 112-13, 120. Fuller, 'Classical High Church Reaction', *op. cit.* and Nockles, 'Anglican High Churchmanship', *op. cit.*, set Lyall's disengagement in context. For the Camden Society split, see White, *Cambridge Movement, op. cit.* and Towle, *Neale, op. cit.*

[23] Bishop Blomfield to Archdeacon Lyall, 21 November 1833, in Blomfield (ed.), *Blomfield, op. cit.*, pp. 190-2.

[24] Lyall, *Sentiments of the Clergy, op. cit.*, pp. 9-11; *Charge to the Clergy of Colchester, op. cit. passim*; *Church Property, op. cit.*, pp. 34-6.

[25] George Lyall's entry in the *DNB* adds very little to his obituary in *The Gentleman's Magazine*, 1853, pp. 418-19; W.R Lyall obituary, *op. cit.*

[26] Thomas Darling to W.R. Lyall, n.d. but *c.* July 1848, Lyall Papers (Darling and A.J. Beresford Hope got up a subscription to insert stained glass in the south aisle of the choir to commemorate the restoration of the cathedral by the chapter out of their own revenue); Benjamin Harrison, *Charity Never Failing: A Sermon Preached on the Occasion of the Death of William Rowe Lyall, D.D.* (London, 1857), pp. 12-13; Boggis, *St Augustine's, op. cit.*, pp. 55 ff; Henry Bailey, *Twenty-five Years at St Augustine's College, Canterbury* (Canterbury, 1873), p. 40; M. Sparks, 'The Recovery and Excavation of the St Augustine's Abbey Site, 1844-1947', *Archaeologia Cantiana*, C (1984), pp. 327, 330; Paul Thompson, *William Butterfield*, London, 1971).

[27] 'Report of the Episcopal and Capitular Revenues Commission', *Parliamentary Papers*, XX (1850); Best, *Temporal Pillars, op. cit.*, pp. 369-80. There are letters to George Lyall from Peel, Gladstone, Wellesley, Ellenbrough and Auckland among the Lyall Papers – all dating from the period 1838-42.

Chapter 3
Patrons

[1] Howley's entry in the *DNB*; his entry in *A Dictionary of Church History*, ed. S.L. Ollard, G. Crosse and M.F. Bond (3rd. edn. London, 1948); his obituary in *The Gentleman's Magazine*, 1848, pp. 426-8; Best, *Temporal Pillars, op. cit.*, pp. 225-7, 329-30, 345-7; and a large number of scattered references, including those in Churton, *Watson, op. cit.* Howley's papers are listed in Bill, *Lambeth Palace Library, op. cit. Crockford's Clerical Directory* (35th. edn. 1903) contains a list of the Archbishop of Canterbury's patronage at that date. Sadly, the 'Return showing the Preferment held by every Archbishop, Bishop, Dean . . .', *Parliamentary Papers*, 1851, XLII, omits Canterbury.

[2] C.S. Parker (ed.), *Sir Robert Peel*, 3 vols. (London, 1899), I, pp. 41-60, 269-84, 437-47; III, pp. 413-30; Sir Robert Peel, *Memoirs of Sir Robert Peel*, 2 vols. (London, 1857), II, pp. 69-90; E. Brynn, *The Church of Ireland in the Age of Catholic Emancipation* (London, 1982), pp. 72-87, 310-16; Norman Gash, *Mr Secretary Peel* (London, 1961), especially, pp. 13-14, 17, 114-26, 141-2, 296, 564-5, 636; Norman Gash, *Sir Robert Peel* (2nd. edn. London, 1986), especially pp. xxiv-xxvi, 40, 96-100, 103-4, 188-9, 229-31, 382-3; P.J. Welch, 'Blomfield and Peel: A Study in Cooperation between Church and State, 1841-1846', *Journal of Ecclesiastical History*, XII (1961); R. Shipley, 'Problems of Irish Patronage under the Chief Secretaryship of Sir Robert Peel, 1812-1818', *Historical Journal*, X (1967), pp. 41-56; Laurence Peel to George Lyall, 26 July 1841, Lyall Papers. Gladstone made his tutor at Christ Church (Augustus Saunders) Dean of Peterborough.

[3] Churton, *Watson, op. cit.*; entries for Lyall, Blomfield, Monk and Le Bas in the *DNB*; Blomfield (ed.), *Blomfield, op. cit.*; Welsh, 'Blomfield and Peel', *op. cit.*; W.E. Gladstone, *The Gladstone Diaries*, ed. M.R.D. Foot, I (Oxford, 1968), p. 222; R. Shannon, *Gladstone* (London, 1982); Butler, *Gladstone, op. cit.*; D.W.E. Bohlman, 'The Queen, Mr Gladstone and Church Patronage', *Victorian Studies*, 3 (1959-60), pp. 349-60; John Morley, *Life of Gladstone*, 3 vols. (London, 1903), II, pp. 430-33.

Chapter 4
Clients

[1] Lt-Col. G. Robertson lent me the copy of the Lyall family tree on which this analysis is based.

[2] George Lyall, William Lyall, Alfred Lyall and George Darling all have entries in the *DNB*. Dr Darling discussed the career choices of his sons in several letters in the Darling Papers (e.g. George Darling to his brother Thomas, 9 July 1833).

[3] For the returns to careers in the Church, the City, the ICS, medicine and law, see J.C. Hudson, *The Parents' Handbook* (London, 1842); H.B. Thomson, *The Choice of a Profession* (London, 1857); F. Davenant, *What Shall My Son Be? Hints to Parents on the Choice of a Profession or Trade* (London, 1870); W.J. Reader, *Professional Men* (London, 1966); J.A. Banks, *Prosperity and Parenthood* (London, 1954); Alan Haig, *The Victorian Clergy* (London, 1984); B. Heeney, *A Different Kind of Gentleman* (Hamden, Connecticut, 1976); W.D. Rubinstein, *Men of Property* (London, 1981); B. Spangenberg, *British Bureaucracy in India* (New Delhi, 1976); M.J. Peterson, *The Medical Profession in Mid-Victorian London* (Berkeley, California, 1978); I. Loudon, *Medical Care and the General Practitioner, 1750-1850* (Oxford, 1986); D. Duman, *The English and Colonial Bars in the Nineteenth Century* (London, 1983). Sir Henry Holland gives a few details of his income in his *Recollections of Past Life* (2nd. edn. London, 1872), p. 56.

[4] W.R. Lyall to his nephew, Thomas Darling, 29 February 1836, Lyall Papers (the source of the quotation); Thomas Darling to his father, Dr George Darling, dated 'Wednesday' and clearly written shortly after he went up to St John's ('I have got capital

rooms, they could hardly be better'), Darling Papers; Sir Alfred Lyall to his sister, Sibylla Holland, quoted in Sir Mortimer Durand, *Life of the Rt Hon Sir Alfred Comyn Lyall* (London, 1913), p. 56; Alfred Lyall's entry in the *DNB*.

[5] The performance and parishes of Lyall's clients are discussed in Chapter 6.

[6] See Table 4.

[7] *Ibid.*

[8] See the references in note 3. Several letters in the Lyall Papers discuss the prospects of a legal career. A small sample: John Edwardes Lyall to his cousin, John Pearson, 1 April 1837 ('People say the law is not a good profession for a man idly disposed, but it seems to me the one of all others, for the chances are ten to one against your having anything to do'); Harry Lyall to his elder brother (Sir) Alfred, 24 December 1868 ('A Mr Young who is a friend of Frank's says there will be an opening as one of his clerks is very old and *ought* to die soon'); Mary Drummond Lyall to her son (Sir) Alfred, 4 February 1869 ('Edith has just engaged herself to a young Irish barrister (with) his way to make'); (Sir) Alfred Lyall to his sister, Mary Rivaz, 5 October 1887 ('I suppose a solicitor is still by profession slightly below the high social level at home').

[9] George Lyall and George Darling's entries in *DNB*; 'Lyall of Headley' in Burke's *Landed Gentry* (1952 edn.); George Darling, *An Essay on Medical Economy* (London, 1814); J. Richardson, *Keats and his Circle* (London, 1980), pp. 36-7; B.R. Haydon, *Autobiography*, ed. E. Blunden, (London, 1927), pp. 306, 403, 405; B.R. Haydon, *The Diary of Benjamin Robert Haydon*, ed. W.B. Pope, 5 vols. (Cambridge, Massachusetts, 1960-3), references in the index; George Darling's letters in the Darling Papers (there are hundreds of references to his career and his sons); Thomas Darling's letter to his brother John describing his travels in France in 1857, also in the Darling Papers. George Pearson makes some vivid appearances in Mary Sibylla Holland, *The Letters of Mary Sibylla Holland*, ed. Bernard Holland (3rd. edn. London, 1907), pp. 120, 156.

[10] The patronage of the East India Company is discussed in J.M. Bourne, *Patronage and Society in Nineteenth Century England* (London, 1986), pp. 55-6, 88. Bourne's Ph.D. thesis goes into more detail: 'The Civil and Military Patronage of the East India Company, 1784-1858' (University of Leicester, 1977). Chairman George appears on pp. 39-40 and the 'Scotch connection' on pp. 176-82. For J.E. Lyall's brief career in India before his sudden death, see his obituary in *The Gentleman's Magazine*, 1845, pp. 82-3, and his entry in T.H. Ward (ed.), *Men of the Reign* (London, 1885; reprint 1968). For the echo of his death twenty years later, see (Sir) Alfred Lyall to his brother (Sir) James, 3 November 1865, Lyall Papers. There are constant references to Walter Lyall (one of two Black Sheep brothers) in the Holland and Lyall Papers.

[11] (Sir) Alfred Lyall to his mother Mary, quoted in Durand, *Alfred Comyn Lyall, op. cit.*, p. 81. Cf. Catherine Peter to her brother (Sir) Alfred Lyall, from Cavendish Rectory, 20 June *c*. 1879, Lyall Papers:

> I wish you could see how full the garden is of lovely great roses – heaps and heaps of them. It is warm fine weather and the house is sweet with the scent of the hay and of the garden flowers. We are hay-making. All the maids turn out in the afternoon and we have tea in the pleasant fields – three great parties – ourselves, the maids and the schoolmistress and a number of people of that rank who inevitably drop in on these occasions ('just to see how Mr Peter's hay is getting on'). A swarm of children turn up too, who have to be regaled with cakes, buns and milk under the girls' supervision – these really form Evelina's *corps d'armée* and have great romps under her leadership till the sun goes down and dews fall and it is nearly bed time.

Evelina was Sir Alfred's daughter, left at Cavendish while he served in India. The extract has been abbreviated and the punctuation has been modernised. On the uncertainty of promotion and Sir Alfred's determination not to let his eldest son go out to India, see (Sir) Alfred Lyall to his sisters Catherine Peter (3 April 1875 and 2 January 1877) and Barbara Lyall (16 and 27 May 1878), Lyall Papers.

[12] (Sir) Alfred Lyall to his sister Sibylla Holland, quoted in Durand, *Alfred Comyn Lyall, op. cit.*, p. 57. Cf. (Sir) Alfred Lyall to his brother (Sir) James, 29 July 1878, Lyall Papers.

[13] (Sir) James Lyall to his sister Catherine Peter, 31 July 1874, Lyall Papers.

[14] (Sir) Alfred Lyall to his sister Catherine Peter, 31 July 1874, Lyall Papers. Cf. Sir Alfred Lyall to his brother (Sir) James, 23 February 1882, Lyall Papers.

[15] Sir Codrington Carrington, William Peter, Sir Henry Holland and Viscount Knutsford all have entries in the *DNB*. John Belli, the father-in-law of Sir Codrington and Archbishop Howley, makes a brief appearance in C.E. Buckland, *Dictionary of Indian Biography* (London, 1906). For the antecedents of 'the fathers', see 'Carrington of Great Missenden' in Burke's *Landed Gentry* (1898 edn.); 'Peter of Chyverton' in *ibid.* (1921 edn.); 'Viscount Knutsford' in Burke's *Peerage and Baronetage* (1980 edn.); Holland, *Recollections, op. cit.*; Bernard Holland, *The Lancashire Hollands* (London, 1917).

[16] Dean Lyall married the daughter of Dr Joseph Brandreth (1748-1815); her brother was Dr Joseph Pilkington Brandreth (1781-1858): see 'Watson-Gandy-Brandreth of Buckland Newton' in Burke's *Landed Gentry* (1972 edn.). Lyall met his wife through her brother, Thomas Shaw Brandreth, a friend of Lyall's at Trinity and possibly at Eton also: see Brandreth's entry in the *DNB*. The Rev. Alfred Lyall married the daughter of James Tschudi Broadwood (1772-1851), the son of the founder of Broadwoods, the piano-makers; see 'Broadwood of Lyne' in Burke's *Landed Gentry* (1952 edn.).

[17] (Sir) Alfred Lyall to his sister Catherine Peter, 26 February 1865, Holland Papers. The Lyalls were constantly discussing the tactics and strategy of marriage in their letters: for references, see Chapter 8, note 1.

[18] Sibylla Holland to her husband Francis, 18 July 1885, in B. Holland (ed.), *Mary Sibylla Holland, op. cit.*, p. 106.

[19] R.L. Arrowsmith, *Charterhouse Register, 1769-1872* (London, 1974); W.D. Parish, *List of Carthusians, 1800 to 1879* (Lewes, 1879); Table 6.

[20] Table 4; Peter's entry in J.A. Venn (ed.), *Alumni Cantabrigienses*, 6 vols. (Cambridge, 1940-54); W.E. Gladstone, *The Gladstone Diaries*, ed. H.C.G. Matthew (Oxford, 1982), VIII, p. 23; Sibylla Holland to her sister Catherine Peter, 11 April, 1873, in B. Holland (ed.), *Mary Sibylla Holland, op. cit.*, p. 22; 'Buxton, Baronet', in Burke's *Peerage and Baronetage* (1980 edn.).

Chapter 5
Canterbury

[1] Table 4. The Anglo-Indian Lyalls who lived in Canterbury were Sir Alfred Lyall, Sir James Lyall and George Rivaz (who married Mary Lyall).

[2] Table 4.

[3] Peter Nockles' research will enormously increase our knowledge of the clergy of Canterbury in the nineteenth century.

[4] Thomas Darling to his brother John, 31 December 1847, Darling Papers.

[5] Extracts (in a new sequence) from three of Sibylla Holland's letters: two to her sister Catherine Peter, March 1861 and 20 April 1861, and one to her brother (Sir) James Lyall, 25 September 1884, in B. Holland (ed.), *Mary Sibylla Holland, op. cit.*, pp. 5-6, 9.

[6] Mary Drummond Lyall to her son (Sir) Alfred Lyall, 1 April 1864, Lyall Papers.

[7] Sibylla Holland to her brother (Sir) James Lyall, 20 May 1883, in Bernard Holland (ed.), *Additional Letters of Mary Sibylla Holland* (Edinburgh, 1899), p. 11. The third generation, the grandchildren, were equally attached to Harbledown and Godmersham. Bernard Holland settled at Harbledown Lodge and had his Lyall cousins to stay: Evelina Miller to her father (Sir) Alfred Lyall, 1 April 1903, Miller Papers.

[8] Thomas Darling to his brother John, 31 December 1847, Darling Papers.

[9] Sibylla Holland to her son Bernard, 17 March 1885, in B. Holland (ed.), *Mary Sibylla Holland, op. cit.*, p. 99.

10   *Eadem* to *idem*, 25 August 1887, in *ibid.*, p. 156.
11   Thomas Darling to his brother John, 31 December 1847, Darling Papers.
12   Dr George Darling to his son Thomas, 9 September 1844, Darling Papers.
13   (Sir) Alfred Lyall to his sister Sibylla Holland, 26 February 1856, quoted in Durand, *Alfred Comyn Lyall, op. cit.*, pp. 32-3. Cf. Bernard Holland, 'Preface' to *Mary Sibylla Holland, op. cit.*, pp. xii-xiii.
14   Sibylla Holland to her sister Catherine Peter, February 1861, in B. Holland (ed.), *Mary Sibylla Holland, op. cit.*, pp. 4-5 (the source of the quotation); Sibylla Holland to her brother (Sir) James Lyall, 20 May 1883, in B. Holland (ed.), *Additional Letters, op. cit.*, p. 20.
15   Thomas Darling to his uncle William Rowe Lyall, *c.* July 1848, Lyall Papers; W.L. Bowles, *The Patronage of the English Bishops* (Bristol, 1836), pp. 33-8; John Newman, *The Buildings of England: North-East and East Kent* (Harmondsworth, 1969), pp. 118, 166.
16   Bernard Holland, in B. Holland (ed.), *Mary Sibylla Holland, op. cit.*, p. 80.
17   Sibylla Holland to her son Bernard, 5 December 1888, in *ibid.*, pp. 199-200.
18   Sibylla Holland to her sister Catherine Peter, May 1861, in *ibid.*, p. 8.
19   Sibylla Holland to her son Bernard, 26 June 1891, in *ibid.*, pp. 305-6.
20   *Eadem* to *idem*, 7 November 1890, in *ibid.*, p. 283.
21   Sibylla Holland to 'E.M.', 3 December 1890, in *ibid.*, pp. 286-7.
22   Sibylla Holland's Journal, 18 December 1888, in *ibid.*, p. 204.
23   Sibylla Holland to her son Bernard, 17 December 1887 and 5 December 1888, in *ibid.*, pp. 160, 199.
24   Sibylla Holland's Journal, 18 December 1888, *loc. cit.*
25   Sibylla Holland to her sister Catherine Peter, May 1861, in *ibid.*, p. 9.
26   Sibylla Holland's Journal, 17 December 1887, in *ibid.*, p. 164; Sibylla Holland to Mrs Charles Buxton, 1883, in *ibid.*, p. 91; (Sir) Alfred Lyall to his sister Sibylla Holland, 9 March 1867, Holland Papers. For the evangelicals' fear of the cathedral's ambience, see E.M. Forster, *Marianne Thornton, 1797-1887* (London, 1956), p. 204. There were moments of light relief in the middle of so much reverence, such as the confirmation service which went disastrously wrong:

> The people came in masses to hear the [new] archbishop preach. We thought we would go in good time [but when we got to the north transept] a crowd of people [were] pushing, struggling, and jostling together [trying to get into the choir]. The little archdeacon [moved] about among [them], saying in his clear voice, 'Now good people, sit down, sit down, there are forty seats or more provided for you, if you would but sit down.' 'There ain't no seats', was the rude rejoinder, and they pushed forward so, I thought the little archdeacon would have been crushed. Papa, very tall, stern and commanding, [tried] to make way for the candidates who followed his procession, looking rather alarmed [and] saying, 'Stand back, you *must* stand back, it is no use, you cannot get into the choir'. The vergers and beadles, scarlet with heat and anger, stood helpless by the gates.

Sibylla Holland to her daughter Agnes, 8 June 1883?, Lyall Papers. The new archbishop was E.W. Benson; the little archdeacon was probably Benjamin Harrison. The extract is abbreviated.
27   Bernard Holland, 'Preface', in *Mary Sibylla Holland, op. cit.*, p. xii; Sibylla Holland to her sister Catherine Peter, 9 July 1889, in B. Holland (ed.), *Additional Letters, op. cit.*, pp. 41-2.

Chapter 6
Performance

1   Table 4.
2   Lyall's entry in the *DNB*; Godmersham Parish Register, Canterbury Cathedral Library; T. Tatton-Brown, 'The Parish Church of St Laurence, Godmersham', *Archaeologia Cantiana*, CVI (1988), pp. 45-81; Harbledown Vestry Book, 23 April 1867, and

Harbledown Parish Registers, vol. III (I owe these references to the Rev J.S. Tunbridge); Durand, *Alfred Comyn Lyall, op. cit.*, pp. 4-7; Bernard Holland, 'Preface' to *Mary Sibylla Holland, op. cit.*, p. xi.

   [3] Alfred Lyall, *Agonistes, or Philosophical Strictures* (London, 1856), pp. 45, 53-4.

   [4] *Review of the Principles of Necessary and Contingent Truth* was published in London in 1830.

   [5] *Agonistes, op. cit.*, pp. 150-1.

   [6] *Ibid.*, pp. 125-39.

   [7] 'Preface' to *The Annual Register* for 1822, pp. iii-viii.

   [8] *Agonistes, op. cit.*, pp. 114-16.

   [9] Asa Briggs, 'The Annual Register, 1758-1958', *The Annual Register for 1958*, pp. xix-xxxi.

   [10] Alfred Lyall, *Rambles in Madeira and Portugal*, 2 vols. (London, 1827), I, pp. 4-5, 19-21, 14, 95, 23-4, 75-7, 123-4, 16, 27, 58 (page numbers are given in the order in which the references occur).

   [11] *Ibid.*, I, pp. 22-3; cf. pp. 108, 29-30.

   [12] Table 3; Francis Holland's entry in *Who Was Who*; Francis Holland's obituary in *The Times*, 28 January 1907; Sir Henry Holland's entry in the *DNB*; Sir Henry Holland, *Recollections, op. cit.*; B. Holland (ed.), *Mary Sibylla Holland, op. cit.*; Holland, *Lancashire Hollands, op. cit.*, pp. 302-3; 'Viscount Knutsford' and 'Buxton Baronet' in Burke's *Peerage and Baronetage* (1980 edn.); A. Wawn, 'Introduction', to *The Iceland Journal of Sir Henry Holland*, Hakluyt Society, 2nd. series, 168 (London, 1987). Sydney Holland (Francis's nephew) remembered his grandfather, Sir Henry, as

> a short man with a very clever face, a large choker and a swallow-tail coat. He used to come, every Sunday without fail, to call on my father and would stand with his back to the fire talking. He left in half an hour, to the minute. Indeed, his whole life was mapped out hour by hour, and he used to urge me never to be idle for a minute. He invariably asked me a question in Greek which I was expected to understand and answer in the same language. As the question was always the same I mastered it in time and could answer without hesitation, which pleased him though it made me rather suspicious about his memory. He was always hoping that I would 'try to be a success in life' [and saying that he had never known a third generation succeed]. He meant kindly, but it was decidedly damping for a schoolboy with bad reports for his last term's work still undelivered to his parents.

Sydney Holland, Lord Knutsford, *In Black and White* (London, 1926), pp. 12-13 (the extracts have been arranged in a new order). In the fourteenth century the Hollands broke into the front rank of the nobility as clients of the House of Lancaster and husbands of rich heiresses. Their peerages included the earldom of Kent and the dukedoms of Exeter and Surrey. They fell as abruptly as they rose, back into the ranks of the petty landowners and professional men. The Victorian Hollands were conscious of the contrast between their family's illustrious past and their own modest circumstances.

   [13] *Times* obituary, *loc. cit.*; B.F.L. Clarke, *The Building of the Eighteenth-Century Church* (London, 1963) p. 190.

   [14] *Times* obituary, *loc. cit.*

   [15] F.J. Holland, *Celibacy of the Clargy: A Sermon Preached at the Festival of the Sons of the Clergy* (London, 1873). For the righteous Raj, see F.J. Holland, 'The Victory of Faith' in *Westminster Abbey Sermons for the Working Classes*, Second Series (London, 1859).

   [16] *Times* obituary, *loc. cit.*; Best, *Temporal Pillars, op. cit.*, pp. 120-3; E.H. Pearce, *The Sons of the Clergy, 1655-1904* (London, 1904); Mary Sibylla Holland to Bernard Holland, 4 May 1875, in B. Holland (ed.), *Additional Letters, op., cit.*, p. 8; Mary Drummond Lyall to her son (Sir) Alfred, 29 October, 1868, 12 November 1868, 24 February 1876, Lyall Papers.

   [17] *Times* obituary, *loc. cit.*; Nikolaus Pevsner, *The Buildings of England; London except the Cities of London and Westminster* (Harmondsworth, 1969), p. 334.

   [18] Darling's entries in *The Charterhouse Register, op. cit.*, and *Alumni Cantabrigienses, op. cit.*;

W.H. Brown, *Charterhouse Past and Present* (Godalming, 1879), pp. 147-58; A.H. Tod, *Charterhouse* (London, 1900), pp. 16-17; E.M. Jameson, *Charterhouse* (London, 1937), chapter II; T. Baker, *History of the College of St John the Evangelist, Cambridge*, ed. J.E.B. Mayor, 2 parts (Cambridge, 1869), II, pp. 1094-9; Edward Miller, *Portrait of a College* (Cambridge, 1961), p. 73.

[19] M.C. Bickerstaff, *A Sketch of . . . Robert Bickerstaff, D.D.* (London, 1887), pp. 61-2; see also K. Chesney, *The Victorian Underworld* (Harmondsworth, 1972), pp. 122-34.

[20] Bickerstaff, *Robert Bickerstaff, op. cit.*, pp. 57-77; Charles Booth, *Life and Labour of the People of London*, Third Series, *Religious Influences*, 7 vols. (London, 1902), II, pp. 178-80; C.S. Jones, *Outcast London* (Oxford, 1971); T.H. Shepherd and J. Elmes, *Metropolitan Improvements* (1st. edn. 1829; new edn. London, 1968); *Annual Report of St Giles' Ragged School* (London, 1845); G. Buchanan, *St Giles' in 1857* (to *1865*), (London, 1858-65); *St Andrew's Holborn and St Giles' in the Fields* (London, 1860); G. Halton, *Thirty Years in St Giles'*, (London, 1890); *The Story of St Giles' in the Fields* (London, 1952); *Survey of London*, V, *St Giles' in the Fields* (London, 1914).

[21] Thomas Darling to his brother John, 31 December 1847, Darling Papers.

[22] Dr George Darling to his son Thomas, 31 July 1843 and 27 March 1844, Darling Papers.

[23] 'Church Restoration: St Nicholas, Thanington, Kent', *The Ecclesiologist*, 7 (1847), p. 37; Newman, *Kent, op. cit.*, p. 457; S.G. Wilson, *A Short History of Thanington Church* (Thanington, 1936); *The Parish Church of St Nicholas Thanington* (Thanington, 1951); Thomas Darling to his brother John, 31 December 1847, Darling Papers; Paul Thompson, *William Butterfield* (London, 1971), p. 479. Butterfield's office in Bedford Square was only a few minutes' walk from Dr Darling's house in Russell Square. Darling's widow left four marble fireplaces and a brass garniture for an altar (two candlesticks and a cross) designed by Butterfield: Mary Mildred Darling's will, Darling Papers.

[24] H.W. Clarke, *The City Churches* (London, 1898), pp. 396-409; Booth, *Life and Labour, op. cit.*, III, pp. 5-6; *The Religious Life of London*, ed. R. Mudie-Smith (London, 1904), p. 125; David Lloyd, 'The Character of the City', in *Save the City*, ed. D. Lloyd (London, 1976), pp. 1-14; T.F. Bumpus, *Ancient London Churches* (new edn. London, n.d.), 'Preface' and pp. 11-14; Sir John Summerson, *Georgian London* (London, 1945), pp. 36ff, 276; Chadwick, *Victorian Church, op. cit.*, II, pp. 218-19.

[25] Booth, *Life and Labour, op. cit.*, III, pp. 52, 23-5, 46-51; Chadwick, *Victorian Church, op. cit.*, II, pp. 308-27; Anthony Trollope, *Clergymen of the Church of England* (Leicester, 1974; originally published in 1866), pp. 66-77; Ellsworth, *Charles Lowder, op. cit..*

[26] For the Rev Edgar Hoskins, rector of St Martin's Ludgate from 1881, see his entries in Crockford's *Clerical Directory* and G. Hennessey, *Novum Repertorium Ecclesiasticum Parochiale Londinense* (London, 1898), pp. viii, 258, 410, CXXXIV.

[27] See note 33 for references to Wren churches in the City and their demolition.

[28] Thomas Darling, 'Circular to Members of the Vestry of St Michael's Paternoster Royal and St Martin Vintry', 13 June 1856, Darling Papers; 'Building Intelligence – Churches and Chapels: London', *Building News*, 10 August 1866, p. 537; Thomas Darling, Letter to the Editor, 8 August 1867, *The Ecclesiologist*, 28 (1867), p. 315; Nikolaus Pevsner, *The Buildings of England: London – The Cities of London and Westminster* (3rd. edn. Harmondsworth, 1973), p. 174; White, *Cambridge Movement, op. cit.*, pp. 2, 67-72, 156-77; Thompson, *Butterfield, op. cit.*, pp. 37, 44; Vestry Minutes, St Michael's Paternoster Royal, Guildhall Library.

[29] Booth, *Life and Labour, op. cit.*, III, pp. 1, 14 (extracts arranged in a new order).

[30] Thomas Darling, 'Pastoral Letter', 12 November 1849, Darling Papers; Darling's obituaries in *The Record*, 25 August 1893, p. 815 and *The City Press*, 23 August 1893; Thomas Darling, *Hymns from the Mountains* (London, 1857); Thomas Darling, *Hymns for the Church of England* (3rd. edn. London, 1857; at least eleven editions were published); Chadwick, *Victorian Church, op. cit.*, II, pp. 397-9. Darling's correspondence with the authors of the

hymns he edited survives among the Darling Papers.

[31] Mary Drummond Lyall to her son (Sir) Alfred *c.* 1881, Lyall Papers; Lyall's entries in Crockford's and Hennessey, *Novum Repertorium, op. cit.*

[32] John Edwardes Lyall to his mother Margaret, *c.* 1842, Lyall Papers.

[33] W.H. Lyall (ed.), *St Dionis Backchurch in the City of London* (London, 1878), pp. 29-30 (the source of the quotation). Lyall's correspondence with John Mason Neale is listed in Bill, *Lambeth Palace Library, op. cit.,* MSS. 2341-3118; (Sir) Alfred Lyall to his sister Catherine Peter, 20 February 1865, Holland Papers ('Has William Lyall gone over to Rome or not?'); Mary Drummond Lyall to her son (Sir) Alfred, n.d. Lyall Papers; Ellsworth, *Lowder, op. cit.,* pp. 50, 63-4, 146; A.R. Winnett, *A History of St Dionis Backchurch and St Dionis, Parson's Green* (London, 1935). For ritualism, see Bentley, *Ritualism and Politics, op. cit.,* and Marsh, *Church in Decline, op. cit.* For the demolition of City churches, see Peter Burman, 'City Churches', in *Save the City, op. cit.,* pp. 139-44; Hermione Hobhouse, *Lost London* (London, 1970), pp. 57-63; G. Cobb, *London City Churches* (new edn. London, 1977), pp. 123-5; W. Niven, *London City Churches Demolished Since 1800 or Now Threatened* (London, 1887). For illustrations, plans and descriptions of St Dionis Backchurch and St Michael Paternoster Royal, see G. Clarke, *Architectura Ecclesiastica Londini* (London, 1819); G. Godwin and John Britten, *The Churches of London,* 2 vols. (London, 1838-9); J. Clayton, *The Parochial Churches of Sir Christopher Wren,* 3 parts (London, 1848-9); A. Mackmurdo, *Wren's City Churches* (London, 1883); G.H. Birch, *London Churches of the Seventeenth and Eighteenth Centuries* (London, 1896); T.F. Bumpus, *Ancient London Churches* (London, n.d.); Royal Commission on the Historical Monuments of England, *London,* IV, *The City* (London, 1929); B.F.L. Clark, *Parish Churches of London* (London, 1966).

[34] Peter's entry in *Crockford's*; (Sir) Alfred Lyall to his sister Sibylla Holland, 25 March 1866, Holland Papers; Table 4.

[35] Peter's entry in Venn, *Alumni Cantabrigienses, op. cit.*; R.G. Peter, *A Manual of Prayer for Students* (Cambridge, 1859); R.G. Peter, *Non-Communicant Vestries and Churchwardens: A Letter to the Bishop of Ely* (Cambridge, 1860); R.G. Peter, *A Letter to Churchmen and to Dissenters* (Cambridge, 1870).

[36] Iris L. O. Morgan, *Memoirs of Henry Arthur Morgan, Master of Jesus 1885-1902* (London, 1927), p. 125 (the source of the quotation); Barbara Lyall to her brother (Sir) Alfred, 11 August 187?, Lyall Papers; Mary Drummond Lyall to her son (Sir) Alfred, 18 and 25 July 1869?, Lyall Papers.

[37] Morgan, *Morgan, op. cit.,* pp. 127-8.

[38] W.F. Quin, *History of Braintree and Bocking* (Lavenham, 1981), pp. 100-11; D.C. Coleman, *Courtaulds* (Oxford, 1969), pp. 210-11.

[39] Coleman, *Courtaulds, op. cit.,* pp. 223 note 2 (the source of the quotation), 244ff; Quin, *Braintree, op. cit.,* pp. 224-30; E.J. Evans, *The Contentious Tithe* (London, 1976), chapter 6.

[40] Quin, *Braintree, op. cit.,* pp. 118-19; Coleman, *Courtaulds, op. cit.,* pp. 205, 218-23.

[41] Ann Hoffman, *Bocking Deanery* (London, 1976), pp. 110ff; Coleman, *Courtaulds, op. cit.,* p. 214.

[42] Hoffman, *Bocking Deanery, op. cit.,* pp. 114-15; Robert Long, *The History of St Peter's, Bocking* (n.p. 1981); Carrington's obituary in *The Times,* 3 January 1906.

[43] Hoffman, *Bocking Deanery, op. cit.,* p. 117.

[44] *Ibid.*

[45] E. Wiltshire, *Reminiscences* (1903, publication details unknown, the source of the quotation); Sibylla Holland to her daughter Agnes, 8 June 1883?, Lyall Papers; D.I. Hill, *Six Preachers of Canterbury Cathedral* (Canterbury, 1972), p. 102; Table 3.

[46] Sibylla Holland to her son Bernard, 20 November 1884 (the source of the quotation), 17 March 1885 and 25 August 1887; and Sibylla Holland to her daughter Lucy, 28 January 1880; all in B. Holland (ed.), *Mary Sibylla Holland, op. cit.,* pp. 62-3, 98-9, 156; Sir Alfred Lyall to his sister Sibylla Holland, 14 April 1888, Holland Papers.

[47] Barbara Lyall to her brother (Sir) Alfred Lyall, 3 March 1869?, Lyall Papers (the

source of the quotation); G. Pearson, 'Editor's Notice' in Lyall, *Propaedia Prophetica, op. cit.*

[48] Sibylla Holland to her son Bernard, 2 February 1886, in B. Holland (ed.), *Mary Sibylla Holland, op. cit.*, p. 120.

[49] Pearson's entries in *The Charterhouse Register, op. cit., Alumni Oxonienses, op. cit.*, and *Crockford*'s.

Chapter 7
The End of the Connection

[1] See the references to the impact of the Tractarians on the old high churchmen in Churton, *Watson, op. cit.*; Nockles, 'Anglican High Churchmanship', *op. cit.*; Fuller, 'Classical High Church Reaction', *op. cit.* Lyall's separation from the Tractarians was discussed in Chapter 2. For Manners-Sutton's appointment, see his entry in the *DNB*. For Crown patronage after 1837, see Bohlman, 'Church Patronage', *op. cit.* and Chadwick, *Victorian Church, op. cit.*, I, pp. 226-31.

[2] John Bird Sumner (1780-1862), Archibald Campbell Tait (1811-82) and Henry Alford (1810-71) in the *DNB*; Boggis, *St Augustine's College, op. cit.*, pp. 42-3; Marsh, *Church in Decline, op. cit.*; Bentley, *Ritualism and Politics, op. cit.*

[3] Benjamin Harrison (1808-87) in the *DNB*; Forster, *Marianne Thornton, op. cit.*, pp. 151-2, 204; Nockles, 'Anglican High Churchmanship', *op. cit.*, pp. 485-6. Sibylla Holland said that Harrison's widow burnt the majority of his correspondence (including packets of letters from Gladstone, Manning and Pusey) to save herself the trouble of seeing it sorted out: a few papers survive in the Bodleian. Sibylla Holland to her son Bernard, 1 June 1888, in B. Holland (ed.), *Mary Sibylla Holland, op. cit.*, p. 180.

[4] Haig, *Victorian Clergy, op. cit.*, pp. 289ff; Heeney, *Different Kind of Gentleman, op. cit.*, pp. 111ff; J.F. Stephen, 'The Church as a Profession', *Cornhill Magazine*, IX (1864), pp. 750-60; H.C. Beeching, 'The Poverty of the Clergy', *Cornhill Magazine*, new series, III (1897), pp. 15-28.

[5] Carrington spent money on his church but economised on his curates: Hoffman, *Bocking Deanery, op. cit.*, pp. 114-18. Thomson, *Choice of a Profession, op. cit.*, p. 76; Davenant, *My Son, op. cit.*, p. 20.

[6] F.M.L. Thompson, *English Landed Society in the Nineteenth Century* (London, 1963), chapters X-XI.

[7] McClatchey, *Oxfordshire Clergy, op. cit.*; Obelkevich, *Religion and Rural Society, op. cit.*; Gilbert, *Religion and Society, op. cit.*; Haig, *Victorian Church, op. cit.*, II, pp. 157ff; N. Scotland, *Methodism and the Revolt of the Fields* (London, 1986).

[8] For the clergy as social workers see G. Kitson Clark, *Churchmen and the Condition of England, 1832-1888* (London, 1975); and for the bishops' attitudes to social problems, see R.M. Soloway, *Prelates and People* (London, 1969).

[9] Stephen, 'Church as a Profession', *op. cit.*

[10] Haig, *Victorian Clergy, op. cit.*

[11] Beeching, 'Poverty of the Clergy', *op. cit.*

[12] L.P. Wilkinson, *A Century of King's, 1873-1972* (Cambridge, 1980), pp. 46, 62.

[13] Sibylla Holland to her sister Catherine Peter, June 1875, in B. Holland (ed.), *Mary Sibylla Holland, op. cit.*, p. 27.

[14] Barbara Lyall to her brother (Sir) Alfred Lyall, 12 February 187?, Lyall Papers (the source of the quotation). Although Mildred Darling's father was a layman, 'a wealthy solicitor', he still engaged in religious controversies. He published two pamphlets containing his correspondence with his unfortunate adversaries: William Ford, *The Grant of £1800 made to the National School of Highgate* (London, 1853), and *St Mary's Brookfield: The Right of Schoolchildren of the Lower Classes to Attend Public Worship in Churches* (London, 1876).

[15] Bernard Holland in *Mary Sibylla Lyall, op. cit.*, pp. 78-9.

[16] Sibylla Holland to Mrs Sheppard, 27 May 1889, in *ibid.*, pp. 217-18.

[17] Sibylla Holland to her husband Francis, 4 June 1890, and Sibylla Holland to 'E.M.', 3 December 1890, in *ibid.*, pp. 265-6.

[18] Jane Darling to her brother Thomas, 22 August 1837, Darling Papers.

[19] Sibylla Holland to her son Bernard, 31 August and November 1885, in B. Holland (ed.), *Mary Sibylla Holland, op. cit.*, pp. 115, 128; Mildred Darling's Diaries, recording her holidays in the Italian lakes, are in the Darling Papers; Evelyn Martinengo Cesaresco (née Carrington) became a noted historian of the *risorgimento* – see her entry in the British Museum *General Catalogue of Printed Books*.

[20] Barbara Lyall (Sibylla's sister) to Sir Mountstuart Grant Duff, 12 December 1883, Lyall Papers. Cf. Sibylla Holland to her daughter Agnes, 7 September 1885, and her husband Francis, October 1885, in B. Holland (ed.), *Mary Sibylla Holland, op. cit.* pp. 108, 112.

[21] Sibylla Holland to her husband Francis, 12 November 1889, in *ibid.*, p. 244. Cf. J. Pemble, *The Mediterranean Passion*, (Oxford, 1987), pp. 196-210.

[22] Sibylla Holland to 'E.M.', 1 October 1885, in B. Holland (ed.), *Mary Sibylla Holland, op. cit.*, p. 111. Cf. Mildred Darling's Diaries for Easter 1896, Darling Papers.

[23] Malcolm Lyall Darling to his mother Mildred, 24 January 1896 and 24 January 1897, Darling Papers; Sibylla Holland to 'E.M.', 1 October 1885, *loc. cit.*; Sir Alfred Lyall to his sister Sibylla Holland, 22 April 1889, Holland Papers; Pemble, *Mediterranean Passion, op. cit.*, p. 212:

> Nothing in the Mediterranean was so enticing, nor yet so repulsive, as the religion of papal Rome. Year after year British Protestants flocked to the Easter and Christmas ceremonies in St Peter's, the Sistine Chapel, and St John Lateran; and year after year it was obvious that it would have been better for their own peace of mind, and for the national reputation for *sang-froid* and graciousness, if they had stayed away.

[24] Sibylla Holland to Agnes Bolton, 10 April 1870, in B. Holland (ed.), *Mary Sibylla Holland, op. cit.*, p. 273. The 'vast mixed multitude' was actually in Bruges, but cf. the mass in Genoa which Sybilla witnessed: Sibylla Holland to her husband Francis, 5 October 1885, in *ibid.*, p. 114. Mildred Darling's diaries list the Catholic services she attended and her conversations with Catholic priests. Pemble's *Mediterranean Passion* contains some brilliant pages (128-41) on Protestant reactions to popular Catholicism.

[25] Sibylla Holland to her son Bernard, 20 April 1880, in B. Holland (ed.), *Mary Sibylla Holland, op. cit.*, p. 65. Cf. Barbara Lyall to her brother (Sir) Alfred Lyall, 11 June 1872, Lyall Papers, on the incidence of divorce and religious indifference in Saxony.

[26] Sibylla Holland's Journal, 9 April 1889, in B. Holland (ed.), *Mary Sibylla Holland, op. cit.*, p. 212.

[27] A composite quotation: Sibylla Holland to her sister, Catherine Peter, 11 October 1869 and 20 May 1871, in *ibid.*, pp. 15-17.

[28] A composite quotation: Sibylla Holland to Mrs Deacon, 22 May 1876, and Sibylla Holland to W.H. Bolton, 25 August 1886, in *ibid.*, pp. 40, 189.

[29] Sibylla Holland to her son Bernard, 2 February 1886, and her sister Catherine Peter, 23 August 1886, in *ibid.*, pp. 124-6.

[30] Mildred Darling to her son Malcolm, 9 December 1893, Darling Papers.

[31] A composite quotation: Sir Alfred Lyall to his sister Barbara, 8 September 1889 (the source of the quotation) and 29 November 1889, Lyall Papers. Bernard Holland discussed his mother's conversion (and her reluctance to offend her friends or relations) in *Mary Sibylla Holland, op. cit.*, pp. 78ff. Francis Holland's memorandum on his wife's conversion is among the Benson Papers at Lambeth: *Index to the Letters and Papers of Edward White Benson* (London, 1980), p. 107. Sir Alfred objected to Sibylla's 'absolute (I will not say abject) submission to the Catholic Church's somewhat arrogant assumption of supreme spiritual

knowledge'.

[32] Mildred Darling Diaries, 6 June 1899, 21 and 23 October 1900, Darling Papers.

[33] Bernard Holland stressed the importance of Hales Place in his mother's conversion. She was present when Miss Hales died and arranged her funeral with the Jesuits, who gave her a 'grand send-off'. See also Sibylla Holland to her daughter Agnes, 11 June 1883, Lyall Papers.

[34] Sir Alfred Comyn Lyall (1835-1911) in the *DNB*; Sir Courtney Ilbert, 'Sir Alfred Lyall', *Proceedings of the British Academy*, V (1911-12), pp. 525-9; P. Woodruff, *The Men Who Ruled India: The Guardians* (London, 1954), pp. 64, 74; Durand, *Alfred Comyn Lyall, op. cit.*, pp. 103, 135, 173, 186-7, 363; Sir Alfred Lyall, *Asiatic Studies*, 2 vols. (London, 1899), II, chapter III. Sir Alfred said, in a letter to his sister Mary Rivaz, 26 November 1882?, Lyall Papers: 'Going to church is like charging an enemy's position – everything depends upon who leads: I find that as I don't go, the household becomes lukewarm'.

[35] Durand, *Alfred Comyn Lyall, op. cit.*, pp. 92, 165, 181-5; Eric Stokes, 'Administrators and Historical Writing', in *Historical Writings on the People of India*, ed. C.H. Phillips (London, 1962), pp. 313ff; Lyall, *Asiatic Studies, op. cit.*, I, chapters I, VI, VII, IX; Sir Alfred Lyall, 'The Government of India', *Edinburgh Review*, CLIX (1884), pp. 1-4; Sir Alfred Lyall, 'Brahmanism', in *Great Religions of the World*, ed. H.A. Giles *et al.* (London, 1901), pp. 81-106; Sir Alfred Lyall, *The Rise of the British Dominion in India* (London, 1893), *passim*.

[36] Lord Ripon, viceroy, to J.K. Cross, Under-Secretary of State for India, 6 February 1883, quoted in E.C.T. Chew, 'Alfred Comyn Lyall: A Study of the Anglo-Indian Official Mind', (Ph.D. Thesis, University of Cambridge, 1969), p. 116; cf. Lord Lytton's opinion, Durand, *Alfred Comyn Lyall, op. cit.*, p. 213.

[37] (Sir) Alfred Lyall to his sisters Barbara (1864) and Sibylla (1874) in Durand, *Alfred Comyn Lyall, op. cit.*, pp. 109, 174.

[38] A composite quotation taken from two of (Sir) Alfred Lyall's letters to his mother, both written in 1865, in *ibid.*, pp. 123, 126-7. For his mother's reproaches, see Mary Drummond Lyall to (Sir) Alfred, 27 February 1865, Lyall Papers:

I do not think your way of speaking or writing on subjects connected with religion creditable to you. Without committing yourself – without saying plainly what you yourself hold to be true – you continue to throw ridicule over the subject and to excite something like contempt for those who feel more seriously. This does much harm to ignorant unsettled weak people. I saw, by accident, your last article – Burgon v. Stanley – and it is exactly an instance of what I mean . . . To take away God from the universe is like taking the Sun out of the Solar system.

[39] Sibylla Holland to her son Bernard, 20 February 1881, in B. Holland (ed.), *Mary Sibylla Holland, op. cit.*, p. 191.

[40] *Eadem*, 20 February 1881, in *ibid.*, pp. 44-5.

[41] Durand, *Alfred Comyn Lyall, op. cit.*, p. 479; Bernard Holland, 'Alfred Lyall', *Quarterly Review*, 437 (1913), pp. 202-3.

[42] Bernard Holland's entries in *Who Was Who* and the British Museum *General Catalogue of Printed Books*; M.L. Darling, discarded preface to *Apprentice to Power* (London, 1966), Darling Papers. The origins of Darling's agnosticism are discussed in greater detail in my *Anglo-Indian Attitudes* (provisional title; forthcoming). Sir Alfred's scepticism had a similar effect on his own children: Evelina Miller to her father 9 June and 23 November 1903, Miller Papers: 'You bewilder me with all the finely painted difficulties of Christianity'.

[43] Sibylla Holland to her son Bernard, 20 February 1877, in B. Holland (ed.), *Mary Sibylla Holland*, pp. 44-5.

[44] Mildred Darling to her son Malcolm, 4 June 1912, Darling Papers.

[45] Malcolm Darling to his mother Mildred, 18 January 1911, Darling Papers.

Chapter 8
Hackney

[1] A large number of letters in the Lyall Papers discuss the tactics and strategy of marriage. See, for instance, John Edwardes Lyall to his mother Margaret, *c.* 1842; Mary Drummond Lyall to her son (Sir) Alfred, 4 February 1869, 18 September 1873, 20, 27 and 31 November 1874; Barbara Lyall to her brother (Sir) Alfred, 26 January 1869 and 22 April 187?; (Sir) Alfred Lyall to his sister Mary Rivaz, 1 and 11 December 1887. Cf. (Sir) James Lyall and Harry Lyall to their cousin Bertha Broadwood, 30 December 1873 and 7 June 1892, Broadwood Papers.

[2] David Wainwright, *Broadwood by Appointment* (London, 1892); Burke's *Landed Gentry* (1952 edn.); Burke's *Peerage and Baronetage* (1980 edn.); John Broadwood's entry in the *DNB; Alumni Cantabrigienses, op. cit.; Alumni Oxonienses, op. cit.*; Cyril Ehrlich, *The Piano: A Social History* (London, 1976), pp. 16-29, 35-7, 144-6.

[3] Table 8.

Chapter 9
Patronage

[1] The key work on clerical patronage is M.J.D. Roberts, 'Private Patronage and the Church of England, 1800-1900', *Journal of Ecclesiastical History*, 32 (1981), pp. 199-223. See also Bohlman, 'Church Patronage', *op. cit.*: Chadwick, *Victorian Church, op. cit.*, I, pp. 226-31; Best, *Temporal Pillars, op. cit.*, Appendix VI; Heeney, *Different Kind of Gentleman, op. cit.*, pp. 111ff. Haig, *Victorian Clergy, op. cit.*, neglects patronage; A. Tindale Hart and Edward Carpenter, *The Nineteenth-Century Country Parson* (Shrewsbury, 1954) ignore it altogether. Bourne's path-breaking *Patronage and Society, op. cit.*, is the best introduction to the social implications of patronage.

[2] Even competition-wallahs lamented the decline of *esprit de corps* when the directors' patronage was abolished and the Indian civil service was thrown open to competitive examination. See 'Papers relating to the Selection and Training of Candidates for the Indian Civil Service', *Parliamentary Papers*, XV (1876), especially the opinions of H.H. Risley, Robert Smeaton and T.H. Thornton.

[3] For sample statements of the belief that clerical careers were open to the talents, see W.R. Lyall, *Church Property, op. cit.*, pp. 20-1, and Thomson, *Choice of a Profession, op. cit.*, p. 70. Thomson's sales depended on his plausibility.

[4] For details of the panic over recruitment to the ICS, see C.J. Dewey, 'The Education of a Ruling Caste: the Indian Civil Service in the Era of Competitive Examination', *English Historical Review*, LXXXVIII (1973), pp. 262-85; J. Roach, *Public Examinations in England, 1850-1900* (Cambridge, 1971), pp. 191-200; and Reader, *Professional Man, op. cit.*, pp. 87ff.

[5] This was one of the arguments employed against the abolition of the directors' right to nominate civilians.

Bibliography

The bibliography is restricted to sources cited in footnotes or used for the tables. References to the Darling and Lyall Papers do not distinguish between the different locations in which separate caches are currently held, because they are likely to change.

MANUSCRIPTS

Darling Papers

Papers of Dr George Darling (1782-1862), the Rev Thomas Darling (1816-93) and Sir Malcolm Darling (1880-1969)

General Sir Kenneth Darling, Chesterton, Oxfordshire; Miss Sarah Darling, Hullavington, Wiltshire; Centre for South Asian Studies, University of Cambridge

Holland Papers

Papers of (Mary) Sibylla Holland (1836-91), Bernard Henry Holland (1856-1926)

Mrs Ann Holland, Balcombe, Sussex

Lyall Papers

Papers of George Lyall I (1779-1853), Mary Drummond Lyall (1809-78), John Edwardes Lyall (1811-45), Sir Alfred Comyn Lyall (1835-1911), Sir James Broadwood Lyall (1838-1916), Catherine Peter (1839-1908), Barbara Webb (1845-97)

Mr J.C. Lyall, Perranwell, Truro, Cornwall; Miss Jennifer Lyall, Lockeridge, Wiltshire; India Office Library, 197 Blackfriars Road

Miller Papers

Papers of Sir John Ontario Miller (1857-1943) and Lady (Evelina) Miller (b. 1868)

Lt-Col Godfrey Robertson, Ablington, Gloucestershire

Parish Records

Godmersham (Cathedral Library, Canterbury); Harbledown (Rev J.S. Tunbridge, Harbledown); St Michael's Paternoster Royal (Guildhall Library, London)

Wills

Very Rev Henry Carrington (1906), Dr George Darling (1862), John Darling (1858), Mary Mildred Darling (1912), Rev Thomas Darling (1893), Rev Francis Holland (1907), Sir Henry Holland (1873), Viscount Knutsford (1914), Rev Alfred Lyall (1865), Sir Alfred Lyall (1911), Catherine Lyall (1864), George Lyall I (1853), George Lyall II (1880), Henry Lyall (1915), Sir James Lyall (1916), John Lyall (1805), Mary Broadwood Lyall (1878), Walter Lyall (1903), Rev William Hearle Lyall (1900), Rev George Pearson (1891), William Pearson (1874), Rev William Pearson (1867), Rev Robert Peter (1910)

All at Somerset House, except for John Lyall and George Lyall I (Public Record Office) and Dr George Darling and Mary Mildred Darling (Darling Papers). Searches at the Public Record Office have failed to unearth Archbishop Howley's will or Dean Lyall's.

Dean Lyall's Papers

Sadly, the great bulk of Dean Lyall's papers seem to have been destroyed. His personal effects passed through his childless widow to her nephew, Admiral Sir Thomas Brandreth, and two beautiful miniatures of the dean and his wife are presently in the possession of Sir Thomas's granddaughter-in-law. But none of the members of the Brandreth family have any idea as to what happened to Dean Lyall's papers. The letters which survive are embedded in the collections of the Dean's relatives and collaborators.

Other Collections

There are references in the footnotes to ten collections which contain material directly relevant to the Lyall connection, but not enough material to warrant their systematic exploitation: the *Benson, Blomfield, Howley, Watson and Wordsworth Papers* at Lambeth; the *Newman Papers* at the Birmingham Oratory; the *Harrison Papers* at the Bodleian; the *St Augustine's College Archive* at Canterbury; the *Peel Papers* in the British Museum; and the *Broadwood Papers* in the Surrey Record Office, Kingston upon Thames. See *Index to the Letters and Papers of Edward White Benson* (London, 1980); E.G.W. Bill, *Catalogue of Manuscripts in Lambeth Palace*

Library, 3 vols (Oxford, 1972-83); I. Ker and T. Gornall (eds.), *The Letters and Diaries of John Henry Newman*; C.S. Parker (ed.), *Sir Robert Peel*, 3 vols. (London, 1989); Surrey Record Office, unpublished Catalogue of the Broadwood Papers.

UNPUBLISHED THESES

J.M. Bourne, 'The Civil and Military Patronage of the East India Company, 1784-1858' (Ph.D. Thesis, University of Leicester, 1977); E.C.T. Chew, 'Sir Alfred Comyn Lyall: A Study of the Anglo-Indian Official Mind' (Ph.D.) Thesis, University of Cambridge, 1969); P.B. Nockles, 'Continuity and Change in Anglican High Churchmanship in Britain, 1792-1850' (D.Phil. Thesis, University of Oxford, 1982).

ARTICLES, CHARGES, SERMONS AND BOOKS BY MEMBERS OF THE LYALL CONNECTION

William Rowe Lyall

'Philosophical Essays. By Dugald Stewart', *Quarterly Review*, VI (1811), pp. 1-37.

'Elements of the Philosophy of the Human Mind. By Dugald Stewart', *ibid.*, XII (1814-15), pp. 281-317.

The Nature and True Value of Church Property Examined, in a Charge to the Clergy of the Archdeaconry of Colchester (London, 1831; 2nd. edn. 1832).

Sentiments of the Clergy on the Question of Church Reform Briefly Stated in a Charge to the Clergy of the Archdeaconry of Colchester (London, 1833).

Concio ad Clerum Provinciae Cantuariensis in Aede Paulina Habita (London, 1837).

Propaedia Prophetica (London, 1840; 2nd. edn. 1854; 3rd. edn. 1885).

A Charge Delivered to the Clergy of the Archdeaconry of Maidstone in May 1842, Containing Some Remarks on the Judgment Pronounced by Dr Lushington (London, 1842).

'State of Parties in Greece on Conclusion of Peloponnesian Wars' and 'The Age of Agesilaus' in *The Encyclopaedia Metropolitana: History of Greece, Macedonia and Syria*, ed. E. Smedley (London, 1848).

Lyall edited *The British Critic* in 1816-17, *The Encyclopaedia Metropolitana* in 1820 and *The Theological Library* (with St J. Rose) in 1832-46.

Alfred Lyall

Rambles in Madeira and in Portugal, 1826, 2 vols. (London, 1827).

A Review of the Principles of Necessary and Contingent Truth (London, 1830).

Parts of the 'History of the Christian Church from the Fourth to the Twelfth Century' and the 'History of the Christian Church from the Thirteenth Century to the Present Day' in *The Encyclopaedia Metropolitana*, ed. E. Smedley (London, 1848).

Agonistes, or Philosophical Strictures (London, 1856).

Lyall edited *The Annual Register* in 1822-7 and from 1837.

Henry Carrington

On Marriage with the Sister of a Deceased Wife (London, 1850).
Translations from the Poems of Victor Hugo (London, 1885).
Of the Imitation of Christ: A Metrical Version (London, 1889).
The Siren: A Poem (London, 1898).
Anthology of French Poetry (London, 1900).

Thomas Darling

Hymns from the Mountains (London, 1857).
Hymns for the Church of England (3rd. edn. London, 1857; at least 11 editions were published).
'Letter to the Editor', 8 August 1867, *The Ecclesiologist*, 28 (1867), p. 315.
Darling edited the 'Welsh Church paper', *Llan*.

Francis James Holland

'The Victory of Faith', in *Westminster Abbey Sermons for the Working Classes*, Second Series (London, 1859).
Celibacy of the Clergy: A Sermon Preached at the . . . Festival of the Sons of the Clergy (London, 1873).
The Constraints of Christ: A Sermon (London, 1878).
Essentials in Religion: Being Sermons Delivered in Canterbury Cathedral (London, 1879).
Holland edited his father's papers, *Fragmentary Papers on Science by Sir Henry Holland, Bart* (London, 1875).

William Hearle Lyall

Edited *St Dionis Backchurch in the City of London* (London, 1876).

George Charles Pearson

'Editor's Note' in W.R. Lyall, *Propaedia Prophetica* (3rd. edn. London, 1885).

Robert Godolphin Peter

A Manual of Prayers for Students (Cambridge, 1859).
Non-Communicant Vestries and Churchwardens: A Letter to the . . . Bishop of Ely (Cambridge, 1868).
A Letter to Churchwardens and Dissenters (Cambridge, 1870).

BOOKS BY OR ABOUT DEAN LYALL'S
RELATIVES AND ASSOCIATES

Blomfield, Alfred (ed.), *Memoir of Charles James Blomfield*, 2 vols. (London, 1863).

Burgon, J.W., *Lives of Twelve Good Men*, 2 vols. (London, 1889) (for Hugh James Rose).

Churton, Edward (ed.), *Memoir of Joshua Watson*, 2 vols. (London, 1861).

Darling, George, *An Essay on Medical Economy* (London, 1814).

Darling, John, *Marriage with a Deceased Wife's Sister* (London, 1849).

Darling, John, *Trust Funds under the Trustees Relief Act* (London, 1855).

Durand, Sir Mortimer, *Life of the Rt Hon Sir Alfred Comyn Lyall* (London, 1913).

Ford, William, *The Grant of £1800 made to the National School of Highgate* (London, 1853).

Ford, William, *St Mary's Brookfield: The Right of the Schoolchildren of the Lower Classes to Attend Public Worship in Churches* (London, 1876).

Harrison, Benjamin, *Charity Never Failing: A Sermon Preached . . . on the Occasion of the Death of William Rowe Lyall, D.D.* (London, 1857).

Holland, Bernard, 'Alfred Lyall', *Quarterly Review*, 437 (1913), pp. 202-3.

Holland, Bernard, *The Lancashire Hollands* (London, 1917).

Holland, Mary Sibylla, *Letters of Mary Sibylla Holland*, ed. Bernard Holland (3rd. edn. London, 1907).

Holland, Mary Sibylla, *Additional Letters of Mary Sibylla Holland*, ed. Bernard Holland (Edinburgh, 1899).

Holland, Sir Henry, *Iceland Journal*, ed. A. Wawn, Hakluyt Society, 2nd. series, 168 (London, 1987).

Holland, Sir Henry, *Recollections of Past Life* (2nd. edn. London, 1872).

Ilbert, Sir Courtney, 'Sir Alfred Lyall', *Proceedings of the British Academy*, V (1911-12), pp. 525-9.

Lyall, Sir Alfred, *Asiatic Studies*, 2 vols. (London, 1899).

Lyall, Sir Alfred, 'Brahmanism', in *Great Religions of the World*, ed. H.A. Giles *et al.* (London, 1901).

Lyall, Sir Alfred, 'The Government of India', *Edinburgh Review*, CLIX (1884), pp. 1-41.

Lyall, Sir Alfred, *The Rise of the British Dominion in India* (London, 1893).

Morgan, Iris L.O., *Memoirs of Henry Arthur Morgan, Master of Jesus, 1885-1902* (London, 1927) (for Robert Peter).

Newman, John Henry, *The Letters and Diaries of John Henry Newman*, ed. I. Ker and T. Gornall, vols. I-IV (Oxford, 1979-80).

Towle, E.A., *John Mason Neale, D.D.* (London, 1907).

OBITUARIES

Henry Carrington: *The Times*, 3 January 1906.

Thomas Darling: *The City Press*, 23 August 1893; *The Record*, 25 August 1893.

Francis James Holland: *The Times*, 28 January 1907.

William Howley: *Gentleman's Magazine*, 1848, pp. 426-8.

George Lyall: *Gentleman's Magazine*, 1853, pp. 418-19.

John Edwardes Lyall: *Gentleman's Magazine*, 1845, pp. 82-3.

William Rowe Lyall: *Gentleman's Magazine*, 1857, pp. 491-2.

COLLECTIVE BIOGRAPHIES

Alumni Cantabrigienses, ed. J.A. Venn, Part II, *1752-1900*, 6 vols. (Cambridge, 1940-54).

Alumni Oxonienses, 1715-1886, ed. J. Foster, 2 vols. (Oxford, 1888).

Burke's *Landed Gentry* (1898, 1921, 1952, 1969, 1972 edns.).

Burke's *Peerage and Baronetage* (1980 edn.).

Charterhouse Register, 1769-1872, ed. R.L. Arrowsmith (London, 1974).

The Clergy List (London, 1841-1910).

Crockford's *Clerical Directory* (London, 1858-1910).

Dictionary of Church History, ed. S.L. Ollard, E. Cross and M.F. Bond (3rd. edn. London, 1948).

Dictionary of Indian Biography, ed. C.E. Buckland (London, 1906).

Dictionary of National Biography, ed. L. Stephen *et al.* (London, 1885-).

The Eton Register, 8 vols. (Eton, 1903-32).

Memories of Old Haileybury College, ed. R.L. Danvers *et al.* (London, 1894).

Men of the Reign, ed. T.H. Ward (London, 1885; reprint 1968).

Modern English Biography, ed. F. Boase, 6 vols. (new edn. London, 1965).

Novum Repertorium Ecclesiasticum Parochiale Londinense, ed. G. Hennessey (London, 1898).

Who Was Who, 1897-1915 (London, 1916).

PARLIAMENTARY PAPERS

Papers Relating to the Selection and Training of Candidates for the Indian Civil Service, 1876, XV.

Report of the Episcopal and Capitular Revenues Commission, 1850, XX.

SECONDARY SOURCES

Anonymous, *Annual Report of St Giles' Ragged School* (London, 1845).

Anonymous, 'Building Intelligence – Churches and Chapels in London', *The*

Building News, 16 August 1866, p. 537.

Anonymous, *The Parish Church of St Nicholas' Thanington* (Thanington, 1951).

Anonymous, *St Andrew's Holborn and St Giles' in the Fields* (London, 1860).

Anonymous, *The Story of St Giles' in the Fields Parish Church* (London, 1852).

Bailey, H., *Twenty-Five Years at St Augustine's College* (Canterbury, 1873).

Baker, T., *History of the College of St John the Evangelist, Cambridge*, ed. J.E.B. Mayor, part II (Cambridge, 1869).

Banks, J.A., *Prosperity and Parenthood* (London, 1954).

Beeching, H.C., 'The Poverty of the Clergy', *Cornhill Magazine*, new series, III (1897), pp. 15-28.

Bennett, S., 'Catholic Emancipation, the *Quarterly Review*, and Britain's Constitutional Revolution', *Victorian Studies*, 12 (1969), pp. 283-304.

Bentley, J., *Ritualism and Politics in Victorian Britain* (London, 1978).

Best, G.F.A., *Temporal Pillars* (London, 1964).

Bickerstaff, M.C., *A Sketch of Robert Bickerstaff, D.D.*(London, 1887).

Birch, G.H., *London Churches of the Seventeenth and Eighteenth Centuries* (London, 1896).

Boggis, R.J.E., *A History of St Augustine's College, Canterbury* (Canterbury, 1907).

Bohlman, D.W.E., 'The Queen, Mr Gladstone and Church Patronage', *Victorian Studies*, 3 (1959-60), pp. 349-60.

Booth, Charles, *Life and Labour of the People in London*, Third Series, *Religious Influences*, 7 vols. (London, 1902).

Bourne, J.M., *Patronage and Society in Nineteenth-Century England*, (London, 1986).

Bowles, W.L., *The Patronage of the English Bishops* (Bristol, 1836).

Bradley, I., *The Call to Seriousness* (London, 1976).

Brent, R., *Liberal Anglican Politics* (Oxford, 1987).

Briggs, Asa, 'The Annual Register, 1758-1958', *The Annual Register for 1958*, pp. xix-xxxi.

Brilioth, Y., *The Anglican Revival* (London, 1933).

Brown, D.J., *A History of Weeley Church and Village* (Weeley, 1981).

Brown, W.H., *Charterhouse Past and Present* (Godalming, 1879).

Brynn, E., *The Church of Ireland in the Age of Catholic Emancipation* (London, 1982).

Buchanan, G., *St Giles' in 1857* (to *1865*) (London, 1858-65).

Burman, Peter, 'City Churches', in *Save the City*, ed. D. Lloyd (London, 1976), pp. 139-44.

Butler, P., *Gladstone: Church, State and Tractarianism* (Oxford, 1982).

Chadwick, Owen, *The Secularisation of the European Mind* (Oxford, 1975).

Chadwick, Owen, *The Spirit of the Oxford Movement* (Oxford, 1982).

Chadwick, Owen, *The Victorian Church*, 2 vols. (London, 1966-70).

Chadwick, Owen, *Victorian Miniature* (London, 1960).

Chesney, K., *The Victorian Underworld* (Harmondsworth, 1972).

Church, R.W., *The Oxford Movement, 1834-45* (London 1891).

Clark, G. Kitson, *Churchmen and the Condition of England, 1832-1885* (London, 1975).

Clarke, B.F.L., *The Building of the Eighteenth-Century Church* (London, 1963).

Clarke, B.F.L., *Parish Churches of London* (London, 1966).

Clarke, C., *Architectura Ecclesiastica Londini* (London, 1889).

Clarke, H.W., *The City Churches* (London, 1898).

Clayton, J., *The Parish Churches of Sir Christopher Wren*, 3 parts (London, 1848-9).

Cobb, G., *London City Churches* (new edn. London, 1977).

Coleman, D.C., *Courtaulds* (Oxford, 1969).

Coleman, J.I., *The Church of England in the Mid-Nineteenth Century* (London, 1980).

Cooper, J.M., *The Lives of the Deans of Canterbury* (Canterbury, 1900).

Cornish, F.W., *History of the English Church in the Nineteenth Century*. (London, 1910).

Cory, William, *Extracts from the Letters and Diaries of William Cory*, ed. F.W. Cornish (Oxford, 1897).

Cowling, M., *Religion and Public Doctrine in Modern England* (Cambridge, 1985).

Crowther, M.A., *Church Embattled* (Newton Abbot, 1970).

Davenant, F., *What Shall My Son Be? Hints to Parents on the Choice of a Profession or Trade* (London, 1870).

Davie, G.E., *The Democratic Intellect* (Edinburgh, 1961).

Donaldson, G. (ed.), *Four Centuries: Edinburgh University Life* (Edinburgh, 1983).

Dewey, C.J., 'The Education of a Ruling Caste: The Indian Civil Service in the Era of Competitive Examination', *English Historical Review*, LXXXVIII (1973), pp. 262-85.

Duman, D., *The English and Colonial Bars in the Nineteenth Century* (London, 1983).

Ellsworth, L.E., *Charles Lowder and the Ritualist Movement* (London, 1982).

Ehrlich, Cyril, *The Piano: A Social History* (London, 1976).

Elliot-Binns, L.E., *Religion in the Victorian Era* (London, 1936).

Evans, E.J., *The Contentious Tithe* (London, 1976).

Faber, G., *The Oxford Apostles* (2nd. edn. Harmondsworth, 1954).

Forster, E.M., *Marianne Thornton, 1797-1887* (London, 1956).

Fuller, R.H., 'The Classical High Church Reaction to the Tractarians', in *Tradition Renewed*, ed. G. Rowell (London, 1986), pp. 51-63.

Garret, H.L.E., 'Eccleasiastical History', in *The Victoria History of the Counties of England, London*, vol. I, pp. 339-74 (London, 1909).

Gash, Norman, *Mr Secretary Peel* (London, 1961).

Gash, Norman, *Sir Robert Peel* (2nd edn. London, 1986).

Gatins, W.J., *Victorian Cathedral Music in Theory and Practice* (Cambridge, 1986).

Gilbert, A.D., *Religion and Society in Industrial England* (London, 1976).

Gladstone, W.E., *The Gladstone Diaries*, ed. M.R.D. Foot and H.C.G. Matthew (Oxford, 1968-).

Godwin, G. and John Britten, *The Churches of London*, 2 vols. (London, 1838-9).

Haig, Alan, *The Victorian Clergy* (London, 1984).

Halton, G., *Thirty Years in St Giles'* (London, 1890).

Haydon, B.R., *Autobiography*, ed. E. Blunden (London, 1927).

Haydon, B.R., *The Diaries of Benjamin Robert Haydon*, ed. W.B. Pope, 5 vols. (Cambridge, Massachusetts, 1960-3).

Heeney, B., *A Different Kind of Gentleman* (Hamden, Connecticut, 1976).

Hill, D.I., *Six Preachers of Canterbury Cathedral* (Canterbury, 1982).

Hobhouse, Hermione, *Lost London* (London, 1971).

Hoffman, Ann, *Bocking Deanery* (London, 1976).

Hudson, J.C., *The Parents' Handbook* (London, 1842).

Hutchings, A., *Church Music in the Nineteenth Century* (London, 1967).

Jameson, E.H., *Charterhouse* (London, 1937).

Jones, W.A.B., *Hadleigh through the Ages* (Ipswich, 1977).

Kerr, D.A., *Peel, Priests and Politics* (Oxford, 1982).

Lloyd, David, 'The Character of the City', in *Save the City*, ed. D. Lloyd (London, 1976), pp. 1-14.

Long, Robert, *The History of St Peter's, Bocking* (Bocking, 1981).

Loudon, Irvine, *Medical Care and the General Practitioner, 1750-1850* (Oxford, 1986).

Machin, G.I.T., *Politics and the Churches in Great Britain, 1832 to 1868* (Oxford, 1977).

Mackmurdo, A.H., *Wren's City Churches* (London, 1883).

McClatchey, D., *Oxfordshire Clergy, 1777-1869* (Oxford, 1960).

Maclear, G.F., *St Augustine's, Canterbury* (Canterbury, 1888).

Marsh, P.T., *The Victorian Church in Decline* (London, 1969).

Miller, Edward, *Portrait of a College* (Cambridge, 1961).

Mudie-Smith, R., *The Religious Life of London* (London, 1904).

Molesworth, W.N., *History of the Church of England from 1660* (London, 1882).

Morley, John, *Life of Gladstone*, 3 vols. (London, 1903).

Newman, John, *The Buildings of England: North-East and East Kent* (Harmondsworth, 1969).

Newman, John Henry, *The Letters and Diaries of John Henry Newman*, ed. I. Ker and T. Gornall, vols. III-IV (Oxford, 1979-80).

Newsome, David, *The Parting of Friends* (London, 1966).

Niven, W., *London City Churches Demolished Since 1800* (London, 1887).

Nockles, P.B., 'The Oxford Movement: Historical Background, 1780-1833', in *Tradition Renewed*, ed. G. Rowell (London, 1986), pp. 24-50.

Norman, E.R., *Church and Society in England, 1770-1970* (Oxford, 1976).

Obelkevich, James, *Religion and Rural Society: South Lindsey, 1825-1875* (Oxford, 1976).

Palmer, William, *The Publication of the Tracts for the Times* (new edn. London, 1883).

Parish, W.D., *List of Old Carthusians, 1800 to 1879* (Lewes, 1879).

Parker, C.S. (ed.), *Sir Robert Peel*, 3 vols. (London, 1889).

Pearce, E.H., *Sion College and Library* (Cambridge, 1913).

Pearce, E.H., *The Sons of the Clergy, 1655-1904* (London, 1904).

Peel, Sir Robert, *Memoirs of Sir Robert Peel*, 2 vols. (London, 1857).

Pemble, John, *The Mediterranean Passion* (Oxford, 1987).

Peterson, M.J., *The Medical Profession in Mid-Victorian London* (Berkeley, California, 1978).

Pevsner, Nikolaus, *The Buildings of England: London – The Cities of London and Westminster* (3rd. edn. Harmondsworth, 1973).

Pevsner, Nikolaus, *The Buildings of England: London – Except the Cities of London and Westminster* (Harmondsworth, 1969).

Pigot, H., *Hadleigh* (n.p. 1859).

Quin, W.F., *A History of Braintree and Bocking* (Lavenham, 1981).

Reader, W.J., *Professional Men* (London, 1966).

Richardson, Jane, *Keats and his Circle* (London, 1980).

Roach, John, *Competitive Examinations in England, 1850-1900* (Cambridge, 1971).

Roach, John, 'The University of Cambridge', in *The Victoria History of the Counties of England, Cambridge and the Isle of Ely* (London, 1959), pp. 190-312.

Roberts, M.J.D., 'Private Patronage and the Church of England, 1800-1900', *Journal of Ecclesiastical History*, 32 (1981), pp. 199-223.

Roper, W.J.J.D., *Chronicles of Charterhouse* (London, 1847).

Rosman, D.M., *Evangelicals and Culture* (London, 1984).

Royal Commission on the Historical Monuments of England, *London*, vol. IV, *The City* (London, 1929).

Scotland, N., *Methodism and the Revolt of the Fields* (London, 1986).

Shannon, Richard, *Gladstone* (London, 1982).

Shepherd, T.H. and J. Elmes, *Metropolitan Improvements* (1st. edn. 1829; new edn. London, 1968).

Shipley, R., 'Problems of Irish Patronage under the Chief Secretaryship of Sir Robert Peel, 1812-1818', *Historical Journal*, X (1967), pp. 41-56.

Soloway, R.M., *Prelates and People* (London, 1969).

Spangenberg, Bradford, *British Bureaucracy in India* (New Delhi, 1976).

Sparks, Margaret, 'The Recovery and Excavation of the St Augustine's Abbey Site, 1844-1947', *Archaeologia Cantiana*, C (1984), pp. 35-44.

Stephen, Sir James Fitzjames, 'The Church as a Profession', *Cornhill Magazine*, IX (1864), pp. 750-60.

Stokes, Eric, *The English Utilitarians and India* (Oxford, 1959).

Stokes, Eric, 'Administrators and Historical Writing' in *Historical Writings on the People of India*, ed. C.H. Phillips (London, 1962).

Sullivan, A. (ed.), *British Literary Magazines: The Romantic Age, 1789-1836* (London, 1983).

Survey of London, vol. V, *The Parish of St Giles in the Fields* (London, 1914).

Symondson, A. (ed.), *The Victorian Crisis of Faith* (London, 1970).

Tatton-Brown, T., 'The Parish Church of St Laurence, Godmersham', *Archaeologia Cantiana*, CVI (1988), pp. 45-81.

Thompson, F.M.L., *English Landed Society in the Nineteenth Century* (London, 1963).

Thompson, K.A., *Bureaucracy and Church Reform* (Oxford, 1976).

Thompson, Paul, *William Butterfield* (London, 1971).

Thomson, M.B., *The Choice of a Profession* (London, 1857).

Tindale Hart, A., *The Curate's Lot* (London, 1920).

Tindale Hart, A., and Edward Carpenter, *The Nineteenth-Century Country Parson*, (Shrewsbury, 1954).

Tod, A.H., *Charterhouse* (London, 1900).

Trollope, Anthony, *Clergymen of the Church of England* (Leicester, 1974).

Virgin, Peter, *The Church in an Age of Negligence, 1700-1840* (Cambridge, 1988).

Wainwright, David, *Broadwood by Appointment* (London, 1982).

Welsh, P.J., 'Blomfield and Peel: A Study in Cooperation between Church and State', *Journal of Ecclesiastical History*, XII (1961).

White, J.F., *The Cambridge Movement* (Cambridge, 1962).

Wilkinson, L.P., *A Century of King's, 1873-1972* (Cambridge, 1980).

Wilson, S.G., *A Short History of Thanington Church* (n.p. and n.d. but probably Thanington *c*. 1936).

Winnett, A.R., *A History of St Dionis Backchurch and St Dionis' Parson's Green* (London, 1935).

Woodruff, P., *The Men Who Ruled India: The Guardians* (London, 1954).

Index

Small capitals indicate a member of the Lyall Connection. Dates of birth and death are given (where known) for (1) Dean Lyall's relations; (2) members and allies of the Hackney Phalanx.

KING ALFRED'S COLLEGE
LIBRARY